FAKE

A startling true story of
love in a world of liars, cheats,
narcissists, fantasists
and phonies

Stephanie Wood

VINTAGE BOOKS
Australia

VINTAGE

UK | USA | Canada | Ireland | Australia
India | New Zealand | South Africa | China

Penguin
Random House
Australia

Vintage is part of the Penguin Random House group of companies whose addresses can be found at global.penguinrandomhouse.com.

First published by Vintage, an imprint of Penguin Random House Australia Pty Ltd, 2019

Cover photography/illustrations by Stocksy
Cover design by Adam Laszczuk © Penguin Random House Australia Pty Ltd
Author photograph by Nic Walker
Internal design by Midland Typesetters, Australia
Typeset in 12.5/18 pt Adobe Garamond Pro by Midland Typesetters

Printed and bound in Australia by Griffin Press, an accredited ISO AS/NZS 14001 Environmental Management Systems printer

A catalogue record for this book is available from the National Library of Australia

NATIONAL
LIBRARY
OF AUSTRALIA

ISBN 978 0 14379 220 8

penguin.com.au

MIX
Paper from
responsible sources
FSC® C009448

In memory of my father

CONTENTS

Ourself, behind ourself concealed,
Should startle most;
Assassin, hid in our apartment,
Be horror's least.

From 'One need not be a chamber to be haunted',
Complete Poems, Emily Dickinson, 1891

PROLOGUE

LOOKING FOR A MAN

I'm on the highway a few miles out of town when the noise starts: a scraping, grinding din that jackhammers my heart into my stomach. Behind me, semi-trailers menace and the road shoulder is narrow, but I brake, pull over, and when there's a pause in the traffic, scramble from the driver's seat to investigate what I'm sure must be a mechanical catastrophe. I crouch in the dust beside the front of the car and peer underneath. The damage is obvious. Some form of panel has dropped from the under-carriage and is dragging on the asphalt. The semi-trailers roar past and I decide my only option is to get back on the road and into town.

I wanted to arrive unnoticed. I'm looking for a man, or traces of him, but I don't want to see him. I'd even considered wearing a wig. But my car's discordant chorus is such that I might as well have hired a brass band to trumpet me into this country town on the New South Wales Southern Tablelands. In a dry paddock dotted with rusted farm equipment sheep lift their heads; a boy on a bike in the main street pauses his aimless circling to stare; a bloke in a beanie stands in the driveway of the service station and watches as I scrape and grind to a stop.

He takes a couple of steps towards me and I wind down my window. 'You've got a problem there,' he says. His mud-splattered truck is parked at a petrol bowser. A kelpie stands alert on the back, tied to the truck's bars. I'm flustered: the last noisy miles into town have shaken me and now I'm here, 100 metres from the motel I'm afraid of returning to, and there's no running away from the decision I've made to come back.

'I know, I know,' I say. 'It started on the highway . . . scared the life out of me.' I get out of the car. The wind is icy.

'I'll take a look,' he says. The bloke is young, well built, fetching in his roughness. A hint of flannelette shirt at the collar of his sweater. Open, unlined face and square, stubbled jaw. I can't stop looking at his hands. Powerful, leathery, the dirt running through crevices of heart, head, life and fate lines, a map of honest exertion.

'Oh, would you?' I thank the man and he asks me to drive over to a patch of grass at the service station's edge. There, he lies on his back and thrusts his head under the front of the car.

'Nothing major,' he says, showing his face again. 'Just a splash-guard panel . . . can hold it up with a cable tie . . . always carry some.' He swings himself upright and goes back to his truck, rummages in tool boxes. The kelpie whirls in excitement, its lead jerks it back. The man ignores it, returns with ties and a knife, and in a minute my undercarriage is stitched up.

'Good to go.' I gush thanks. 'No worries,' he says, seemingly uninterested in small talk. I try to make some, as a way of leading into a bigger question. I introduce myself, extract his name. It's Des. He has a farm in this district. Sheep. Merinos. Loves the work. It's Sunday, nearly lunch, and he's heading out to bring some sheep in.

I tell him I'm a journalist and that I've come to town to look for a man. It's a strange, awkward thing to explain, but Des seems to get it. I tell him about the man – that he said he too had a sheep farm here, a few hundred acres. Said he fattened dorpers for the Chinese market on land out this way.

'Dorpers, eh,' Des says. 'Not many of them round here.' I don't tell him that the man scoffed at merinos and said that dorpers – a hardy South African breed that thrive on native grasses and shed their fleece – were where the money was. Des doesn't need to know the details: that I once believed that when the man wasn't in the city making love to me, or raising his two children and protecting them from his crazy ex-wife, he was here. Regenerating his land with native grasses, bringing eroded waterways back to life, building fences, slashing sifton bush, shepherding his dorpers; and then, at night, filthy and bone-tired, drifting off to sleep in a rough shack with a fire blazing and his kelpie at his feet. Dreams in his head of me and the house he had designed, which he would soon build on his land beside the rubble of a 100-year-old stone cottage near a crumbling headstone standing sentry over the diminishing bones of some colonial tragedy.

'Nah, don't know him.' Des studies the photograph I show him, registers the name I mention. 'Sorry. Haven't seen him round here.'

•

3

I'd hate to be misunderstood: I'm looking for a man but without the least romantic intent. It's long over. These days, more than a year since we parted, I think of him as a specimen. Today I'm on a field trip to study his habitat. But I'm jittery; I do not want an encounter with this creature. Once, in his smiling eyes I saw good and gentle things. I held him tight and hoped for so much. Now I know that the smile was a simulation, the eyes black holes. I know to keep my distance.

My undercarriage restored, I drive out of town. I want to find the land and the shack. If I can find them, I will get closer to the truth. The property was the first thing the man told me about the day we met, his foundational story: the land was his purpose, the shack a cocoon in the aftermath of a bruising divorce, his work here an alibi for his absences. In emails, he wrote of this place as he might a lover, my rival for his affection: 'I am off to my part of the country . . . the itch of not being there is getting to me.' He described in evocative detail the challenges and joys of his farm: the heavy rain that had brought trees down on fencing he would now be kept busy replacing, the lush grass that had given his stock the runs 'in a biblical-tide-like catastrophe', how he would need to bring them in for drenching. 'Oh, the joy of that, as more than a thousand of the shitty things push up against me in the race.' On the afternoons he left Sydney to drive to the farm, he would text me photographs – his Land Rover Defender's bonnet cresting a hill, a golden sunset dropping into the earth. 'Nearly home.'

By the time the man brought me to see the land and shack, months into our time together, I had surrendered and did not think I would ever need to find my own way again. In the cab of his Defender ute, his red kelpie squirmed at my feet and I let my head rest back, soaked up sharp-blue sky, gum-tree blur, white cockatoos rising, sweet magpie song. Such dreamy content: this man beside me, this country, these paddocks, that little creek, that box gum with the undulations in its trunk like the plump rolls of a baby's belly. I felt I was folding into him, folding into the landscape. But I wasn't paying attention to the road.

Now, I am trying to find my own way: I try to feel the route he took to the shack. I recall a hairpin turn out of town over a stone railway bridge, a straight stretch through the bush for some kilometres, then a Y in the road. Here now, here is a Y; I take the right arm onto a narrower, pock-marked road and it feels correct. At some point along here we went through a gate on the right, then climbed a winding track up a hill. Here is a gate now and, beyond it, a hill. This feels right. I get out, open the gate, return to the car, drive through the gate, get out, close the gate, return to the car, take the dirt track up the hill, tyres slithering, my little car unhappy with this work. It's a dead end. I return to the road and drive on, and open and close other gates and take other rough tracks up other hills. I find an Angora goat stud and conservation management zones and a building site, but I cannot find the track with the shack at the end of it and my unease is growing; I don't believe the man will be here, but what if he is? The light is fading. I check, more than once, that my car's doors are locked. I pass a little old cemetery. I come upon a sign pointing up a side road on the right. A sign on the gate across the road says 'Sheep grazing: please drive with care'. Now I know the way. Gate, track, dirt, hill, rut, dust, cattle grid, jolt, bend, bump.

And there it is, the enchanted abode: a squat, square brick and corrugated iron shack with a chimney tacked to the side and a bloom of rust. A scrubby hill rises behind it; a wire fence encloses it, separating the rough structure from both the track I'm stopped on and a neighbouring property and its alpacas, sheds and bullet-peppered sign ('NO TRESPASSING: Violators will be shot. Survivors will be shot again'). I survey the scene from my car. It is all as I remember but for an unfamiliar white ute parked beside the shack. Someone is there but I feel sure it's not him. As before, I will not be going inside.

By the time the man finally brought me here, he was reminiscing. By then he had, he said, sold this land and shack and a new owner had taken possession; the man had a new, grander passion in his sights – he was negotiating to buy a substantial property closer to Sydney. He idled the Defender in about the same spot I'm paused now with my engine running. He looked at the shack and talked of his sadness at leaving this place, 'where the landscape is familiar, and the people know me'.

Now I have the map coordinates I need to do a land title search. As I drive away, a cloud of dust rises behind my car and I flick on front and back windscreen wipers. In my rear-vision mirror the shack recedes, framed by a smudged arc of filth left by the wiper. Before me, the late-afternoon sky glows pink, a rose-breasted cockatoo swoops low and kangaroos startle and bound away across paddocks. But the rosy fantasy is gone. I can see everything clearly now: the shack behind me is pathetic, the land around it harsh and degraded.

A thought flashes into my head: I stop the car, pull out my phone and find a photo of the shack the man sent me during the early days of our relationship. 'Abode', he typed. I zoom in and notice something I missed before: the wire fence is in the foreground of the photo. He must have taken it from the track where I stopped moments before. He did not send me shots of the shack from any other angle, or of its interior. Could he have invented his ownership of it and the land? Perhaps he was never more than a sightseer in this place, never slept in the shack, never fenced or drenched or jostled here with a thousand shitty sheep.

•

I hoped to slip in quietly. I thought I might order a shandy, hide in a corner and plan how I could continue my research, ask the locals some questions, without appearing like a romantic halfwit. But at this little hotel in a hamlet a short drive from the shack, the low-ceilinged room is intimate, the Sunday-afternoon session poorly attended and I'm an instant curiosity. When I open the door, heads turn, mouths gape. I scan for the most sympathetic face: a tiny older woman behind the bar. I order a drink, she asks where I've come from. I murmur an explanation – if I'd bought the Brooklyn Bridge I could not feel more foolish.

'Everybody, meet Stephanie,' the woman broadcasts to the half-dozen or so drinkers. 'She's looking for a man.' I'm reminded again of the fact that I won't be able to reach any understanding of this episode of my private life without revealing myself publicly to one degree or another.

I introduce myself to the drinkers. They've clearly been at it for a few hours. Flushed faces, a mist of bonhomie settled upon them. I reach for my phone, pull up a photo of the man, pass it around. People peer at it, shake their heads; one bloke, bottom drooping over his barstool like a Salvador Dalí clock, thinks he might have seen the man before.

'Know that face, darl?' he asks a woman passing behind him on the way to the bathroom. No, she doesn't. I drop the man's name; no one knows it. In the man's story, his property was at one point in a Southern Tablelands triangle of cheer in which the other vertices were the country town, with its motel, pub and cafe, and this hamlet and its tiny hotel. In another century, bullock carts and carriages and horses tied to hitching posts idled outside a flourishing public house; in this century, the hotel is a scrappy hold-out in the face of rural exodus. The man introduced the hotel to me early in his story: in a text message to explain his online dating profile photo he wrote that he'd 'scrubbed up' to go there for a drink and a steak. In the photo he wore a checked shirt, battered Akubra and a sullen expression that I chose to interpret as brooding. The man in the photo was lean. When I met him a year or so after the photo had been taken, his physiology had set a course towards dissipation: some drooping in the jowls, a swelling belly tucked in behind shirt and trousers, and strapped in by a plaited leather belt – a costume for the role of a countryman. 'My goodness, I was hands-on then,' he wrote. He vowed he'd drop 15 kilograms.

'Curiosity killed the cat, you know,' says a woman with messy short hair. She's in jeans and work shirt, and stands with her backside to a wood-burning stove. The bar laughs as one. 'How long ago since you seen this fella? I reckon he's leading you on.' On my phone, I pull up a photo of the shack. She looks at it, shakes her head, passes the phone on.

'Reckon he led her on, well and truly,' says a bloke with an unloved beard, hooting with laughter, all cockiness and broken capillaries, the room's ringmaster. 'Most likely took a photograph of someone else's house.' The drinkers cackle with him. I grit my teeth, attempt a smile and roll my eyes towards the ceiling. It's too low for the man, this room too tight. He would have been trapped here, forced to account for himself; these people would have seen through him immediately.

I tell them where the shack is.

'The final frontier,' says the ringmaster.

'When I was a kid, I used to go rabbiting up there,' says the man with the bottom.

'Top little spot,' says the ringmaster. He has a mate with some land up that way. 'They call them "blockies".' Subdivisions of a few acres, roo-shooting on weekends, cartons of beer, bawdy jokes. I think of the shack, the property next door with the alpacas, and another on the other side of the road flying an Australian flag, its front gate adorned with bleached sheep's skulls. Farmers grazing sheep on a few hundred acres don't have blockies as next-door neighbours.

I think of the man's hands – soft and pale and clean. Once, I asked him how a farmer's hands could be so fine. 'I wear gloves,' he said straight back at me, pointing out his sun-spotted fair skin. A few days later he reintroduced the subject. 'I've been thinking about why my hands are so soft,' he said. 'It's the lanolin in the sheep's fleece.'

'But you said you wear gloves when you work?'

'You can't wear gloves when you're working with sheep.'

9

I think of Des's rough hands. I think of the man's swerving, colliding, fantastical stories, the decisions we make about the information that is placed before us and our capacity for self-delusion.

I've given the hotel's regulars enough free entertainment for one day. It will be dark outside now, the road back to the country town is unfamiliar and the day's challenges are not over: I still have to check into the motel. The ringmaster scribbles down his blockie mate's phone number and hands it to me. 'He'll know if your bloke ever had that shack.' He shakes his head; he's softer now. 'There are a lot of clowns out there who treat women really, really badly.'

'Lots of roos on that road,' the man with the bottom warns as I move towards the exit.

'Got a bull bar?' asks the ringmaster. A hatchback, I say, and he shakes his head again. He offers advice: go slow, use your high beam, don't try and dodge a roo because you'll end up hitting a tree. Better off hitting the roo. He repeats his advice: 'Do not swerve for the kangaroo. Mow the fucker straight to the ground. Do not swerve, do not swerve.'

•

Of all the fiendish tricks in the man's spectacular performance, I think the motel room was his finest. Only a master illusionist could have made that miserable place appear ripe with romantic possibility. He told me it was his retreat when frigid winter nights wore him down. He described a place of warmth and humour. He had a nickname for the motel owner's wife, and said she sometimes washed his clothes. He transformed a shabby country motel into another magical cocoon and spun out my entry to it for months.

Finally, at the end of the day he drove me into the countryside to see the shack, he unlocked the door on his favourite room at the motel and led me inside. He told me I was the first woman he'd ever taken there. It was a gold star, an elephant stamp – I'd excelled and he was admitting me to one of his special places. By then, I was in thrall to the story he had woven and the character he was playing.

I think about the man's storytelling abilities as I drive back through the inky country evening, dying light dropping into the horizon, stunned moths hurling themselves at my headlights, ghostly eucalypts looming from the roadside. So vivid were the hues of his self-portrait that I internalised it; so contagious was his reality that when he told me he was on his property working the land I could smell the sheep shit and feel the sun on my skin. Now the first lights of town appear ahead and I open my window to let the air rush in, chilled, wood-smoke-scented. My stomach is churning; I am minutes from the motel.

When I was there with him, I saw romance and ironic humour in its great Australian ugliness, in its cheap Tom Roberts pioneer prints inside and scattered blue-painted, metal peacock garden ornaments outside. It was, I thought, our private joke, weighted with meaning. It would be a year before I learnt how far apart our thoughts had been; that the man had made love to at least two other women here – one while he and I were together – and he'd told them they too were the first he had taken there.

And now here I am again. In the motel's reception, I ignore the tourist brochures, pick up my room key, and tell the woman behind the counter that I won't need a jug of milk for the morning. I won't be staying that long. I don't need to show her a photograph of the man's face: I suspect he so regularly wove his dreams here that she might well recognise him as she might a travelling salesman. I let myself into the room, throw my bag down on a palm-frond-patterned bedspread, feel suddenly unsteady. A rush of physical memory strikes: the sense of the ball I curled into after it was all over, the swollen eyes through which I looked at a bewildering new world, the desolation that washed over me. There is no romance in this place. The facts come into focus: lilac walls, thin sheets, bedspread's palm fronds casting suspicious shadows, paper-strip-wrapped toilet (hygienically cleaned and sealed) in a brown-tiled bathroom. I splash water on my face and, when I catch sight of it in the mirror, I realise I am deathly white.

At the local pub, I order a meal. An awkward young barman sells me a bottle of red. I take a table under a framed photo of a bunch of blokes – 'Carp Shoot-Out, 2005'. Another shows the 1996 Rugby League Football Club – promising, strapping young men. On football finals nights, the man said he was often here. He called it 'the festival of the boot', a daggy expression that made me cringe even when I thought I was in love with him. He came here for 'chat and cheer', he said. I can see now that it's unlikely he chatted. He would have stood apart, sized up the room.

The pub's quiet tonight. An old man in a stetson sits hunched and alone at the public bar and flicks his eyes across the screens above – the trots, the dogs, the races in Singapore. Three middle-aged men (stubble, extended middles, flannelette) stand around a table near the door. Their voices dip, then rise and I hear stray words – 'land', 'sales', 'prices', 'sausage roll'. My fish and chips lands with a limp salad and a squeeze-pack of tartare sauce. A balding middle-aged man with a blank, ruddy face, rheumy eyes and a big beard sits with a blonde, ponytailed woman at the next table. Their beer glasses are frosty, their eyes lifted and fixed on another screen showing *The Block*: 'Up next, the boys' wallpaper debacle goes from bad to worse.' They don't talk.

I can't imagine it now, but in the morning I will muster the energy required to make final inquiries about the man's story before returning to the city. At the local cafe I will have eggs for breakfast and show the owner a photo of the man. Yes, she will say, he was an occasional customer. He told her he had a farm in a different district, 50 kilometres away; she thought he was always too clean and lingered too long to be a busy farmer. I will stop by the agricultural supplies store and speak to the owner. He will not recognise the man's face or name but he will invite me into his office and spread a detailed fire map out on his desk. He knows all the property owners in the area I explored. He does not believe the man is now, nor has ever been, one of them, he will tell me. 'He went that far, eh?' he will say when I tell him of the man's stories about dorpers and native grasses. 'You don't fatten sheep on native grasses; farmers don't plant native grasses.' Besides, he will say, 'Not many dorpers round here.' I will tell him about the man's lanolin-softened hands and he will cock an eyebrow. Dorpers don't have much lanolin on them, he will say. Then I will sit in my car before leaving town and call the ringmaster's friend, the blockie, and discover he actually owns the property with the alpacas next to the shack. I will describe the man, and the blockie's response will be all I need to be sure, finally, that the man's foundational story was a fabrication. Or a delusion. 'This character was telling porky pies if he said he owned it, because he never lived next door.'

But tonight, I have no more questions in me, just an over-whelming tiredness. I return to the motel room. I put the key in the lock of my door, push it open and am hit with a cold front. I try the heater but it shudders so violently and blows out such foul dust that I abandon it. I fumble for the electric-blanket switch and lie shivering until the bed is hot and think of the warmth I'd had last time I slept here, the warmth I thought I'd finally found.

•

Among many psychological phenomena I now know about, one of the most curious is the ego defence mechanism 'projection'. Or, as it appeared in Freud's letters to a collaborator, *projektion*. It's a complicated concept, a splitting of the self, a blame-shifting tactic. Should you possess qualities, motivations, thoughts, desires or behaviours that threaten you, or which are intolerable to have as your own, or which you can't handle emotionally, you might deny and exile those characteristics by splitting away a part of yourself and attributing those characteristics to others. *Projektion* is a common behaviour of those with a weak sense of self, of the personality disordered, of narcissists.

Through the night, as I toss from one side of the vile motel bed to another, I think about *projektion* and the stories the man now tells himself and others about me. He has conjured up a new character for me – as a wicked woman, conniving, deceitful, delusional.

This is what he says and thinks about me: I was fired from my job. I'm obsessed with wealth. I'm blackmailing him. I siphoned money from my mother's bank account to buy my apartment. I have a criminal history. I have periods of mania followed by despair. If I don't take my medication, my behaviour is unpredictable. He says that I studied YouTube videos to learn how to give blow-jobs and that I'm a lesbian.

The first time I heard of what he was saying about me, my stomach twisted. Now I just laugh. It is all fake news. But for one germ of truth. Despair. That is true. In the safety of an embrace I once confided to him that I take medication for depression. 'I thought that might be the case,' he said, drawing me closer, tucking the information away to weaponise later.

I know now that there is in the world a silent epidemic: emotional abuse perpetrated by an army of liars, cheats, grifters, charlatans, con artists, narcissists, fantasists, flim-flam men and phonies. A disproportionate number lurk on dating websites and apps, feeding grounds for those with low instincts and impulses. Once, in an idle moment, the man observed, 'There are so many lonely women online.' A profusion of easy prey.

•

I come to the edge of awareness, realise where I am. The motel. He is here with me but only in spectral form, alongside questions crowding in on me like hungry ghosts. They follow me, leering, grotesque, from bed to glacial shower, dun-coloured curtain twitching at my legs, a mean little disc of disinfectant-scented soap in a packet. The water is hot, but only a trickle. It cannot wash away anything, least of all the trauma I have endured at his hands. How did he come to be? What seethes below that innocuous surface? What was in me that made me so vulnerable to his wiles? *How could that have happened to me?*

This trip has given me fragments only, field notes. Still, the less I have found of him here, the more I have understood. As I throw on clothes, words he wrote in a message he sent me after everything was finished tick through my head. He told me I was on to him early. As I loved him, he was sizing me up.

Dressed, I scan the room for anything I've forgotten, shivering with the cold. But it's all I feel. I don't feel sad, or wistful, or regretful, or angry. I just want to get warm, get out of this pitiful room and go home. I load my car, hope my undercarriage holds until the city, and pull out of the motel driveway. On the highway again I accelerate until I'm hovering just above the limit. I don't look in the rear-vision mirror.

1

AN INTRODUCTION TO ROMANCE

I'm running late, stuck in a cab in city traffic with a Lebanese driver who is telling me how tragic it is that he can't get a cheap meal over the border in Syria anymore. He, the man, I'll call him Joe, is early to the bar, warming himself by 'a roaring candle and feeling like a total wallflower'. His text message lands as the taxi driver is lamenting past pleasures – $150 for 10 people with arak! 'Hey, want a wine?' Joe asks in another text and then, in surprise, announces that one of his best friends has just walked in.

When I rush into the bar, there are two sets of eyes on me: Joe has an obvious unfair advantage from the outset and my first impressions are flustered and muddled as I shake his hand, sit down, turn to acknowledge his friend across the bar grinning at us.

I struggle now to get a fix on Joe, on his face, as he was that low-lit night in the early days of winter 2014, as he was at any point we were together. I try to form an image of his face in my head and I see a plain man with a placid, genial expression, but the contours are blurred, and the more I try to focus the image the more it recedes from view. I remember I had a notion he was short; I remember being distracted by that belly, pushing against a crumpled shirt's buttons, and by his broken top tooth. I remember thinking I should not judge by appearances, that we all are imperfect. And I remember thinking that, like so many men, he had a lot to say about himself.

I listen to his chatter, and to keep things moving along for a polite amount of time I switch to journalist mode, ask questions. About his children: a girl and a boy I'll call Charlotte and James – she just a teenager, her brother a few years younger; Joe shares custody with his ex-wife, Mary. About his work: he is a retired architect who for a time worked for a private equity firm; now he dabbles in property deals but he'd never go back to an office – the Savile Row suits are all packed away, he says – and he has a small sheep farm on the Southern Tablelands. About his land: he is working to regenerate it, and the shack on it – not much more than a shed really – will soon be supplanted by a house he has designed. About his meat and livestock – sheep; dorpers, specifically.

He tells me about the small harbourside home he built himself years ago in the suburb where he grew up; he retained it after the divorce and his little yacht is moored below it. He tells me about the gully near the house, which he planted with hundreds of trees and turned into a rainforest. He tells me about his late grandfather, a businessman who founded a major company and whose name is familiar to me. Every so often he pulls a photo up on his phone to illustrate a point; here, for example, is his young red kelpie, and he embarks on an odd story in which the kelpie disappears, he's frantic and he eventually finds a collective of constables fussing over the puppy in a police lock-up, where they've put her for safekeeping.

Joe has interesting things to say, his life seems rich and intriguing, yet I'm not finding him riveting company. Something about his conversation, his manner of talking, is strange, shallow even; there is a sense perhaps that he has rehearsed for this moment, or that he is relaying information by rote. And when he finally asks me about myself and I talk about my work as a journalist at Fairfax Media's *Good Weekend* magazine, he appears only vaguely interested. He does, however, show some curiosity when I add that I was once a food writer and restaurant reviewer. He drops the name of a food celebrity and asks me if I know the man and his wife, and when I say that I briefly met the couple years before, he embarks on another story. Something about a function he'd attended with an ex-girlfriend during which the food celebrity's wife, Susan, a member of their group, confronted him. 'Get away from me, Joe,' she told him, and he demonstrates how, as she spoke, the woman made stop signs with her hands. He seems amused by the memory.

'What on earth was that about?' I ask.

'I have no idea.'

'Perhaps she was drunk?'

'Perhaps,' he says, and shrugs and smiles.

He asks me another question: 'You must be well connected?' It's breathtakingly gauche. 'Oh lord, no – no, no, not at all,' I say, and I think then that he must be a social climber, an opportunist, and it's time to go home. My discomfort must be evident because now, for the first time, although I don't know it,

Joe demonstrates his special skills: the retreat, the manoeuvring and regrouping, the new formation. He would be uncomfortable if I were well connected, he says. He hates publicity. Why, even when he had his business he refused to allow the practice's work to be published in architectural magazines. He hates his photograph being taken. He was furious when his ex-wife turned their wedding reception into a fandango and notified the social pages. He stays away from social media. 'I'm very private,' he says.

The exchange has thrown me off-centre, although it will be more than a year before I understand why. I tell Joe I must go, I have a deadline tomorrow. He says something about a babysitter. I offer to split the bill with him but he declines. I wait at a distance while he pays and as we walk out on to the street he tells another story. Something about the barman overcharging him, or his card not working . . . I can't remember. I wave down a taxi and we shake hands again. As it pulls away I look back. Joe is diminishing behind me. He's looking down at his phone. He fades from view. He's gone from my mind almost immediately.

I UNDERSTAND NOW WHY HIS FACE evades my mind's eye. There was never just one. If I'd paid more attention, I would have seen the swift shifts that might have served as powerful diagnostic tools. Now, photographs of him offer dazzling hindsight. The basics are fixed – his thick dark wavy hair, grey-sprinkled, and the hawkish nose – but from one photo to the next he is recast. Here's one of him smiling, plain-placid. In the next there's an arched brow and a wry, knowing look. Another shows a flicker of disdain, a micro-second of superiority caught in pixels. Some reveal a coldness, others a ruddy ugliness, there one moment, gone by the next photograph. One or two, the ones I returned to again and again when we were together, show him as terribly handsome. But it is not just the expression that changes between photographs; it is as though he is a different person in each.

Some months after that night at the bar, I had a dinner party to introduce Joe to a group of my friends. Afterwards, a writer friend said she'd seen something swashbuckling in him and at the same time a Heathcliff quality, the brooding I saw in his dating profile photo. Another friend, a sensitive artist, saw something else. Much later, she described a vignette: she watched him watch me as I moved between kitchen and table and poured wine and laughed and got tipsy. She didn't like the way he did that, she said. There was something unpleasant about it, something calculating.

•

When Joe emails me soon after our first date and suggests we catch up again, I accept. The moment I've done so, I'm filled with doubt. What is there left to say? In a cab on the way to meet him, I phone a friend and assail her with my misgivings about him. And about something else – that the modest wrap dress I've chosen clings to curves I wish weren't there.

I descend steep stairs into a basement bar. Joe is waiting for me at a table at the bottom of the stairs. He is watching me. Lying in my bed in weeks to come, he will tell me that he thought at that moment *what a woman!* and I will be overcome by the flattery. Now, I am sucking in my abdomen and preparing an opening line and a smile. All the while, flitting at the edge of my consciousness is the awareness of how bored I have been, how lonely; how I have shut down romantic inclination and physical desire for so long. I am aware, too, that I am carrying baggage down the stairs – a muddle of insecurity, indoctrination and imagery.

MY PARENTS STORED THE PROJECTOR and the neat yellow boxes of slides in a cupboard in our family room. If I wheedled enough, my father would pull them out and I would watch, enthralled, as their Kodachrome-hued love story unfolded.

Click, and a shaft of light spears the first image on to the wall: my mother on a Lord Howe Island beach, a flying boat on the water behind her. She has a lei around her neck and her polka-dotted dress is full-skirted and cinched at her little waist, a mash-up of Dior's New Look and *Blue Hawaii*.

Click, and here she is tanned and shapely on Coolangatta sand. I wish she'd kept the swimsuit: a striped, strapless one-piece with a bow under the bust, a vintage wonder. (I'm glad she got rid of the man reclining in bathing trunks behind her; he wasn't my father.)

Click, and my little brother has rubbed his eyes and grizzled and gone to bed, but I stay to see my mother svelte in a black polo neck with another unidentified man in a Klosters ski resort restaurant.

Click, and now she's on a footpath; behind her, a gentleman in what looks like a bowler hat moves towards the camera. My mother is slender; her hair is neatly waved and just about touches the wide collar of a boxy, tweedy suit jacket. (The night before, to preserve her perm, she would have pinned up her hair with crossed bobby pins in flat little rolls she calls 'kiss curls'.) Her skirt reaches her knee. There are white gloves on her hands, a square handbag at the crook of her elbow, sheer stockings on her legs and high heels on her feet. She has a shy-satisfied smile on her face. It is 1964, London. She is twenty-eight, elegant and beautiful, and visiting the West End on a day off from her work as a supply teacher.

As the images click through, my mother provides a commentary and I can never hear the stories too many times: about her dingy flat in Knightsbridge; 'taking off', just like that, for 'the Continent'; a camel-hair sweater from Harrods; cheap seats for Puccini and Verdi at Covent Garden (look, her opera glasses are on a shelf in my study); a trip to the USSR (her guide book is there, too: faded fabric cover, translated from the Russian and offering reassurance that all restaurants have a large selection of hors d'oeuvres, main dishes, Russian vodka, Soviet champagne and Georgian dry wines); decorous parties with smart young men and a record player spinning 'The Girl from Ipanema' and 'I Want to Hold Your Hand'.

Click. And now here's my father. Another young Australian traveller, once an Anglican Church altar boy, by then a teacher with political aspirations. A handsome man. Neatly cut black hair, a straight nose and strong jawline, the most vivid blue eyes. We follow his travels: his ship from Sydney to Southampton via Colombo, Bombay, Aden and the Suez Canal, where passengers go ashore to visit Cairo and my father is photographed in a suit and tie on the back of a camel in front of the Great Pyramid of

Giza. In the Alps he crouches beside a snowman and grins up at a friend whose hair adds half a foot to her height and takes her hours each morning to do. In Atlantic City, he's on the way to observe the 1964 Democratic National Convention, neatly dressed, grey trousers, long-sleeved shirt, tie, knapsack.

I don't recall any images of my mother and father together in London. But I don't need a slide thrown up on a wall to bring to mind the scenes my mother has described, nor to hear the soundtrack she determined was theirs: 'Moon River', two drifters, off to see the world. They met at a party in Clapham. He drove her home. She took off for the Continent. He wrote her a letter. She wrote back. He was deterred by what he read as a cool tone. She went to the Soviet Union. Months later they bumped into each other in Regent Street and he went back to her flat for a party. In the weeks and months that followed: close dancing, canoodling in a 1950s Ford Prefect in Pall Mall, love letters.

Click. And now we come to a wedding. How radiant my mother is – striking bone structure, hair swept up, veil cascading from hairpiece, a princess-line dress with lace bodice and silk chiffon skirt to the floor. This is 1965. Nine months after this picture is taken, I arrive, an accident. My mother acknowledges now that she might not always have chosen her words so well; that perhaps reminding her daughter through her childhood and teenage years that she married because she loved my father, not because she wanted children, and that she'd hoped for more time with her new husband before she was washing nappies, might have contributed to some of the uncertainty I have felt about myself.

But my mother has always felt her thoughts better out than in. Lectures, especially about love, were her speciality. You'll know, she told me time and again, when you're in love. 'She's not in love with him,' she might observe of someone's relationship she judged to be equivocal. 'I never had any doubt about your father.' Or, scoffing about someone else's evidently inferior union, 'She said she couldn't make up her mind about him; if she can't make up her mind, she's not in love with him.' You know when you're in love. My mother would come to wear the kaftans of the 1970s but would continue to pass on the mythology of another, more moralistic, starry-eyed era, divorced from the new era, an unwitting accomplice to the increasingly dominant media/advertising/fashion complex and its relentless message that what matters in life is men, beautifying yourself for men, wooing men, finding a man.

My mother has other strong opinions that she likes to share: she is not a superficial woman but dressing well is a matter of grave importance. 'If you let me dress you, you'll have men following you,' she has consistently told me. She wants me to wear pastel tones. I like black. In fabric shops across the country she has grabbed bolts of fabric and pulled me close as I've made for the exit. She's draped the fabric, apricot-flowered, pink-hued, blue-patterned, yellow-speckled, across my shoulder and turned her head this way and that and studied me. Yes, no; that colour's lovely on you, that colour doesn't work with your skin; yes, no, hmmm, maybe. After I added some kilos in my late twenties, the pressure intensified. 'You had a lovely figure,' she would say accusingly. 'I watched men look at you in the street.' In my mother's eyes, and increasingly my own, I had become an incorrectly sized woman who wore the wrong colours and could not possibly hope to attract a man.

My mother and I argue now about the weight and influence of the story about love she told: she is surprised when I tell her how powerfully it found its way into my psyche, a romantic osmosis. Her memory is of insisting I focus on study, build a career, travel the world, and of telling me it was 'better to be without a man than be with the wrong one'. Yes, I remember those messages, but the love story – so hallowed, so rich, so finely grained – had the greater impact. You will know *the one* when he arrives for your fairytale. Mr Right, *the one*, the prince to your princess. This is what the world should look like. And when it doesn't?

We all carry a weight. Which of us encounters another human without a sack of history, memory, story, mythology, experience, impression, belief, delusion slung over our shoulder, burdening us to one degree or another? How can any man or woman know the tumult the other brings to the table? How can a man sitting in a bar know what the woman approaching him contains? How is the woman approaching that man meant to know that she should turn around and run?

SO THERE WAS JOE. What did he look like? Friendly, I think, happy to see me. How did I feel? Curious, nervy, eager to impress. What was the conversation? Fluttery and shallow at the outset, before we started to find common ground – a shared liking for nature, politics, words. He told me that a broadcaster was looking at a script he'd written for a comedy about office cleaners. He said that sometimes he went to the ballet on his own. I told him I liked gardening. He said that, next time, he'd bring me some sheep shit. Something I said gave him an opening to another wacky story: when he was a schoolboy, he let a duck loose in the art gallery where his mother was a volunteer and chaos ensued. And I don't doubt any of it – why would I? I just laugh and he seems to twinkle before me.

We delve into personal history. Joe reveals that his parents divorced when he was a child; he adores his mother but has had almost nothing to do with his father for years. He has a sister who lives overseas and two brothers in Sydney, about whom he is dismissive. Perhaps then I talked about my late father and his political career, the cancer, his death in 2010. Or my mother, elderly, living alone in Queensland, and a constant worry to me.

I ask tentatively about his marriage. He tells me that Mary had mental-health issues related to her thyroid. She was on and off her medication. Once, he says, he had a bad fall from a ladder; she contributed to the fall, he thinks. Bumped the ladder, pushed it? Then she left him for two days in agony and unable to move. I indicate astonishment as he tells the story. Much later, I will stroke a strange protrusion in his collar bone, evidence of an injury.

Next discussion point: his children. He is close to his daughter, he says. She is more like him than her mother; she loves animals and nature. The moment she is old enough, he knows she will tell a court that she wants to live full-time with him. She smuggles frogs into the house, enraging her mother, with whom she has terrible arguments. Sometimes she will run away and arrive at his place, begging to stay with him. When he has the children everything is perfect: cuddles in his bed, summer evenings splashing in the harbour below the house, bacon and eggs on the barbecue for breakfast, cakes and biscuits that he bakes himself for their school lunch boxes.

I look at him now in this dim basement bar and find he is assuming a more pleasing form. He goes to get more drinks and I see that he is actually tall, over six feet. When he returns to the table I note his erect posture; he's a little stiff, but there is about him something distinguished. I admire the landscape of his face: the creases around his green eyes when he smiles, and the furrows between his brows. I decide I like the plumpness around his middle and the solidity in his forearms. I sense in him a gentleness, a kindness, a stability. He seems uncomplicated, a little old-fashioned, the sort of man who manages life's problems with courage and decency and without rancour.

•

There is a misunderstanding. In a text message Joe asks if I would like to have a meal with him, to, as he puts it, duel cutlery. A telephone conversation is still a step too far for either of us, so we discuss the venue in emails. When we agree on a restaurant, I ask him if he wants to make the booking; his reply arrives and I recoil. He suggests I book – he's interested to see how we get treated if it's under my name and they recognise me.

Later, I try to unpack the reasons for my reaction – another hint that perhaps he's a climber, an opportunist; a suggestion that his intentions are more cynical than affectionate? – but now I slam my fingers on to my keyboard and fling an annoyed response at him. He has, I write, completely misunderstood who I am; I hate being recognised by ingratiating restaurateurs or chefs or waiters, and anyway these days it hardly happens, so he will be disappointed if that's what he's interested in. I hit 'send' and think, without regret, that I'll not be hearing from him again.

HERE, AS IF I NEEDED IT, is more evidence of the badlands of twenty-first-century online dating; a shadowy swamp where horrors lurk, the looming freak, the submerged monster. I have waded into it during the past few years, had brushes with creatures I'd prefer to forget, retreated. In again – perhaps there's buried treasure there – then out, empty-handed. I've seen others stay longer, brave souls, squelch through to reach the other side, haul themselves on to solid ground and then, bathed in rays of sunshine, hold out their triumphant discoveries for all to see. Look: a friend has pulled up a cuddly, bearded animator who has a passion for American-style barbecue and who one day will make a fine father to the little girl they will have. Another, a friend of a friend, believes the swamp to be a numbers game, and persists until she finds a wonderful, loving bachelor.

I am caught uncomfortably in a historic middle point between the new normal – online connection – and an antediluvian world in which first contact was likely a smile, or a drink, or a pash in a corner, followed by either a scribbled phone number or a hot mess of a cab ride home. Not that I did that myself – the hot mess of a cab ride, I mean. Not with strangers, anyway. I was too shy, too uncertain, a wallflower in the shadow of prettier, more self-possessed friends. I needed time to rummage for courage, to make an impression. I needed situations that were fixed and ongoing to find the simpatico.

Such as that which presented itself to me in my first week at university, orientation week at a Brisbane co-ed residential college, a gladiatorial experience in which seventeen-year-old 'fresher' female naïfs were pounced upon by older male students, while their male counterparts were forced to complete humiliating endurance contests. (The mandated running races fuelled by dog food and beer and strewn with vomit, the shouting and jeering, all of which had the fallacious intention of sorting the men from the boys and which instituted a college hierarchy of swaggering jocks and likely forever wounded the gentle boys who mistakenly thought they had come to the city to study.) 'Show us your tits!' the mob cried, when, on the first day of O-week, I took my turn to introduce myself to a braying room of drunken older students. It would be the second shocking experience of my first day as a university student, coming as it did soon after my first meal in the college dining room, a prawn curry.

But I found the simpatico. He was wearing a toga. He was lanky and funny, and two years older. A day or two after I'd not shown my tits to anyone, he introduced himself to me as my new 'big brother' and I was lost in that instant. I wanted to cling to his draped bedsheet forever. The college's Presbyterian elders could not have thought through how their mentorship program might work after the college started to admit women in the 1970s. My 'big brother', who was in his third year of journalism, would become my first boyfriend, guaranteeing that I would take very little notice of my first-year arts/journalism studies and a lackadaisical approach to the remaining years of my degree.

On our first date we went for pizza and red wine at a restaurant near college. What a wondrous thing that first kiss was, planted after dinner as we sat on my single bed. Even now, decades on, my mother will still loudly air her regret that she didn't send me to the women's residential college up the road, dubbed 'the fridge on the hill', which required male visitors to sign in to women's rooms and, most definitely, to sign out. I regret nothing. Not the bongs shared with my boyfriend's friends in one college bedroom or another, redolent with that strange sweet-musty-stuffy scent of stale pot and incense and unwashed clothes and young men's sweat, as turntables spun music I'd never heard before – the Violent Femmes, Siouxsie Sioux, Grace Jones. Not the night I trailed after him and his best mate as, with torches and watering cans, they tended their marijuana plants concealed in the rough alongside a par four at the local golf course. Not the night, some months after he and I had started to go out, when we snuck away from a college ball and returned to his room. I'm not sure what I expected of the first time, but how could I have ever imagined that the next morning, feeling lost, I would drive my father's old brown Valiant to the station, cry for a bit, then catch a train to my casual job at the Royal Queensland Show, the Ekka, where I was required to spear sharp sticks into Dagwood dogs/Pluto pups that were deep fried and served dripping with tomato sauce.

Of course the feeling of letdown passed. Less than a year before, I'd hovered awkwardly on the edge of a circle of schoolmates, wary of a handful of venomous bullies who taunted for pleasure, focused on schoolwork and books because I had little else to focus on. Now I was flying. Living away from home, the proud owner of a boyfriend (*a boyfriend!*), dizzy with love.

I didn't see things then as they really were: that the mad fucking in one or other single bed and the highs from joints and the nights we swayed as one at gigs had a looming end point. I was in a dream, finding a refuge and self-esteem I'd never had before, and I was helpless in the grip of it all.

The boyfriend was momentous. Not because he or we were especially interesting (what relationship between a seventeen-year-old and a nineteen-year-old ever is?). Not because he was the first. He was momentous because he was the first one I hoped might be *the one*. And because he was the first who left me, and left me feeling I might die of pain.

He was gentle in the dismantling. About eight months after we had met, he came to see me in my college room and told me how much he'd enjoyed our time together. End-of-year exams were over – his timing was considerate – and now he would be graduating and looking for a job. When my parents arrived at college to take me home for the year, I was distraught.

'You didn't do anything stupid, did you?' my mother asked as she helped me pack. I shouldn't have answered, or I should have said 'no'. I hadn't done anything stupid at all. But, heaving with sobs, I neither dissembled nor got my answer right.

'Yes,' I said.

It was a grim two-hour trip home. My father drove in silence. I wept in the back. In the front seat my mother communicated her thoughts with vigour and emotion. My missing virginity was a catastrophe. I should have saved myself for the right man. I should have exercised restraint. I should have waited so it was 'special'. She hadn't wanted me to have regrets. I should have listened to her. '*I* listened to my mother,' she said. '*I* took *my* mother's advice.' My mother isn't a religious woman, but she venerates chasteness before marriage with as much zeal as a pimpled teenager about to take a purity pledge. My mother was a virgin when she married and so was my father and so I should have remained.

I was reasonably certain I hadn't ruined myself, but I'd clearly dealt a heavy blow to my mother's sense of self. She realised her impotence as an influence and she didn't like it. In the months that followed, as my broken heart healed, she returned to the subject frequently and randomly with obsessional intensity. 'I hope you took precautions,' she said one day, as I tossed a pack of tampons into her supermarket trolley. It was clear to what she was referring.

I was wild that the subject was again up for discussion. 'Yes! I was on the pill!'

'I thought you only did it once!' I cannot recall how I handled this strange misunderstanding; it's unlikely I was sympathetic to my mother's outpouring of dismay as she interpreted the meaning of this appalling new information – that the sex had been ongoing. But I could not quiet her, and for months her views about the year's events drowned out my own reflections.

My mother still says that she only wanted the best for me. She protests when I tease her by saying there is only one degree of separation between her influence and that of Queen Victoria. My mother is the daughter of a woman born in 1896, the year the tiny queen became Britain's longest-serving monarch. Grandma counted Communist Party members as friends. 'She was way ahead of her time,' my mother says, but, given my own mother's conservatism, in some matters I suspect Grandma was more closely aligned with the sort of Victorian values expressed by *Downton Abbey*'s dowager countess. 'In my day, a lady was incapable of feeling physical attraction until she'd been instructed to do so by her mama,' Dame Maggie Smith's character sniffs in one episode. My mother recently told me of a conversation she'd had with her mother, perhaps in the mid-1950s, about a young unmarried woman Mum knew who'd fallen pregnant. Mum expressed some prim judgement about the woman. My grandmother scolded her. 'Don't ever condemn a girl for becoming pregnant,' she said. 'It's the good girls who get pregnant; the others know how to avoid it.'

I was one of the 'others': I avoided it then and continued to avoid it for the next two decades, as I dithered over disappointing men and kept hoping the right one, *the one*, might come along. And now I live in a world where most of my contemporaries have children, my neighbourhood is full of gay men walking out with small, well-groomed dogs, and a single heterosexual man of any description, never mind one who is interesting and decent, is as rare as a northern white rhino. Statistics and anecdote support the argument that there is a demographic black hole. 'It's a buyer's market,' a heterosexual male friend in his mid-forties, Leo, tells me over lunch one day as he checks his phone for messages from his new thirty-year-old girlfriend, one of a parade of much younger women he has talked about over the years. Meanwhile, women's magazines and the ignorant admonish single women who complain about the dearth of decent single men. 'You're too picky for your own good,' they say. 'Don't be so judgemental.'

It wears you down, being judgemental. And I have been on my own for too long. When Joe found my profile on a dating site

I had only recently resurrected it after several years of inactivity. So it is that I go out with him again.

A few days after my annoyed email, he replies, offering a back-tracking apology. I can't remember how he explained himself, the artful dodger, but it was enough to convince me that I'd misinterpreted his words. Some weeks after our first date, we have our first meal together.

He's early again, I'm late. A text message arrives as I fret in the back seat of another traffic-jammed cab. He asks if I'd like a Dalrymple pinot. A man who seems to know something about pinot noir. It's a winning opening. He follows that text with another. He is, he says, playing 'incompatible couples'. There's something about that line that appeals; my mind hits pause on an image of him curious about the interactions around him, insightful and wise.

When finally I sit down opposite him, he is flushed and jolly. He's been out for a long lunch, he says. I start to relax with him, and to wonder where we go from here. It seems promising that after dinner he suggests we move to the hotel bar. But rather than a lounge, he steers me towards a high bar table and moves to one side of it, away from me. I'm puzzled. Have I mistaken his interest? I must have because after a couple of drinks he says he must go. He escorts me to a cab and says goodnight. On the way home I think about him for a few minutes before my thoughts wander to other matters. But as I unlock my front door just after midnight, another text lands: 'Is there a word for that moment when you want to kiss someone goodnight, but you don't, and hurry away from the awkwardness instead.' He wants to kiss me.

•

It's impossible to concentrate on a movie when a man who has said he wants to kiss you is sitting beside you in the darkness. Joe has chosen an Irish film about a priest, a whodunnit. It's interminable. Every so often I turn my head slightly to gauge his disposition. He seems to have awareness only for the unfolding black comedy. I inch closer, brush my sleeve against his, stretch a little so my hand falls on his armrest. He doesn't move. I endure 102 minutes of desolate vistas and tormented souls. I think the priest is murdered at the end. I can't be sure though. I've lost my brain.

Afterwards, Joe asks if I want to eat and I'm thankful; if nothing else, I need a drink. The theatre is near the Opera House and we stroll to a restaurant by the water. I don't remember the conversation but I know that for every word I uttered there were many more in my head remaining unsaid, a psychic quickstep. *What's he thinking, what does he want, what do I want, what if, will he, should I, will I?* But on this night, with this intoxicating brew – moonlight, man, wine, harbour – boldness takes hold. I lean across the table and kiss him. Later he will tell me that he had a mouthful of lettuce at the time, but I don't notice it. The kiss is slow, long, substantial, and, when we pause for breath, I can see the lights sparkling on the Harbour Bridge.

I want more. I've always been greedy like that.

IF ONLY GOOD KISSES WERE A measure of the man. But I have some evidence that the quality of the kiss is in inverse proportion to the quality of the man. Eric was a good kisser. He worked at the local newspaper where I had my first job as a cadet journalist, and waged a determined campaign to convince me to go out with him. Eventually I did, but he was verbally vicious and it was a miserable time. Then, after a year or so, he left me. I was shattered again. Now, with a clear view backwards, and the elucidation of the American writer Vivian Gornick, I can see what happened. 'To sleep with a man was to start drowning in need,' Gornick wrote in her memoir *Fierce Attachments*. My craving for intimacy and affection had enslaved me to the point that when Eric visited me unexpectedly late one night some weeks after he had announced it was over, bringing warmth and apologies, I held him close. I was later told by a friend that when he left my bed in the early hours of the morning he returned, triumphant, to his mates. They were drinking somewhere. A cruel game had unfolded. Eric had apparently wagered I would sleep with him if he visited me that night. I had consented, yes, but what sort of consent was it? An unwitting consent, ignorant of his agenda. I think of it now and all over again I am awash with hot shame.

There were other kisses, good, bad and indifferent. Good, bad and indifferent men. One I even thought might be the one. But I was so young and silly: I spent my twenties in a ridiculous entanglement – ridiculous for both its duration and the attached drama, with this man, Ben, another journalist. We talked about the future but the relationship ended, and badly. I shared other kisses: with a minor television actor whose cologne made me swoon; with a chef who dipped strawberries in French champagne and dropped them into my mouth; and with an avant-garde entrepreneur, whose clumsy and overwrought kissing technique always made me think of sea cucumbers, and whose behaviour gave lie to my theory that bad kissers might be good men.

I moved again, to Hong Kong and a job as an editor at the *Asian Wall Street Journal*, and dated a man I knew from the start would never be *the one*. I met him at a beach party. He hovered and, from a distance, I was fascinated. We spoke only briefly but after the party, in an atypically daring fashion, I rang the host and asked for the man's phone number. He fell asleep on our first date – at a symphony orchestra concert for which I had tickets. I can't remember what his kisses were like. But he was an intriguing creature, tall and well built with jet black hair that reached below his shoulder blades. He wore small spectacles and flowing yogic robes. He was a Chinese dissident poet who, the year before, had been locked up in a mainland detention centre for a fortnight, charged with illegally publishing a literary journal, then exiled from his homeland.

In broken English he talked of his friendship with the Nobel Prize winner Wole Soyinka. I bought Seamus Heaney's translation of the Anglo-Saxon epic *Beowulf* to impress him, but couldn't get past page two. I may have read some of his own poetry, I don't recall, but I do recall a shopping trip with him to the markets near my apartment. He walked ahead of me, talking on his phone in urgent Mandarin and every so often turning to look at me and point: once to a food item he wanted (a piece of pink-tipped young ginger, a bundle of *gai lan*, a pile of sticky-sloppy rice noodles), then to my wallet. He arrived one day at my office and demanded to use a photocopier; embarrassed, I bundled him out as he protested. In the hushed and chilled Wong Nai Chung public library I waited while he prowled, leaning over people's shoulders to see if they had the Chinese newspapers he wanted. In my kitchen he cooked feverishly, leaving a great mess and producing a murky soup which he ate at intervals over the next couple of days. Then he departed, leaving behind his hairs in the shower – long, dark, rough, as though from a horse's mane – and the sour smell of vinegar and preserved fermented vegetables.

Some weeks later, he invited me to meet him in Taipei for a weekend. It wasn't until I reached the writers' colony where he was staying that I realised I would not be his focus. He would be busy at a book fair, he announced. I would need to amuse myself. For two days I went sight-seeing on my own. Then I got angry. The day before I was due to fly back to Hong Kong, I told him I wanted to share a meal with him, that I would pay for it, and he should give me his time and not argue.

I chose the wrong restaurant. A colleague had recommended a spot in a laneway: no frills, he said, formica tables, paper napkins, plastic cups, but the lobster (with ginger and garlic) was the best he'd ever eaten. The dissident poet offered some language assistance in finding the right bus route but by the time we'd found the lane, the restaurant and a table, he was showing signs of surliness. A few minutes later he stood up and without saying anything walked out to the street. I assumed he had gone to find a bathroom but he did not return. I ate my lobster dinner in wretched solitude. He reappeared as I was paying the bill and, as we walked to the bus stop, scolded me.

'Lobster,' he muttered. I looked at him, at the set square jaw and the scowl behind the spectacles.

'What is your problem?'

'Spending money on lobster!' His tone was laced with disgust.

'What would you have me spend my money on?' I was angry, but embarrassed too that I had offended him.

'You could publish poetry books.'

The following morning when I emerged from the shower I learnt about the poetry book he had already published. There were piles of books on the floor next to my bags which I'd packed the night before and which he was now emptying.

'Take these to a bookshop in Kowloon,' he said, as he replaced my clothes with his books. 'I will give you the address.'

How many occasions are there when we do not do what we should do, or say what we should say? I took over the packing, fitting about thirty books written in Chinese into my bags. We walked in silence to the airport bus stop. Some hours later, after I'd passed unimpeded through Hong Kong customs, it struck me: he'd had an ulterior motive in inviting me to join him in Taipei. I had been a dissident-poetry mule and the customs officers might well have taken issue with my subversive baggage. I ignored the poet's calls over the next few weeks. The books stacked in my spare room gathered dust. The Kowloon bookshop called repeatedly to demand I deliver the books. I refused. Eventually, someone came to pick them up.

TOO MANY TIMES I HAVE BEEN MEEK when I should have roared. Too many times I have made decisions based on instinct, on the desire for adventure, or a fairytale and a prince, or for connection. Rational thinking and cool calculation have rarely been deployed, and they are absent again, more than a decade after that weekend in Taipei, when I lean across a table in the shadow of the Opera House and kiss Joe. There is then, as there usually is at these moments, a shift in the tenor of things. An understanding has been reached that there is a level of mutual interest and we shall proceed on that basis.

I make it clear to Joe that I would like to continue with the kissing, but he is decorous. He pays the bill, escorts me to a taxi and waves me off, a habit I decide must be broken soon. And it seems it might be. A text message pings as the cab's easy-listening radio romances me home. It is after midnight. He wants me to go away with him the following weekend. And, he writes, 'one other thing before I pass out, you are ridiculously attractive and a damn fine kisser'.

2

THE OTHER WOMAN

On the night of my first kiss with Joe in the shadow of the Opera House on a Saturday in winter 2014, his other girl-friend was hosting a slumber party for her youngest daughter's fifteenth birthday. This woman thought the man she'd been dating for more than a year was at his place with his children, recovering from the party he'd hosted that afternoon for his son's seventh birthday. He had sent her photographs of his son and a bunch of boys gathered around a battleground-themed cake, their faces smeared with camouflage paint, remarking that he'd gone 'a tad over the top' with the lolly bags.

Joe's other girlfriend – I'll call her Kirstie – is a forthright, beautiful woman with a voice that rasps low like a film noir dame's. In mid-2013 Joe found her profile on the same dating website on which he would later find mine. Soon after reaching out to her, he suggested they meet. After she'd fallen in love with him, she would tell him how weird he was during their first date, how he wouldn't look her in the eye.

By the time Kirstie met Joe, she was fed up with weird men. After her divorce, she'd hoped to re-partner with someone intelligent, strong, secure, but the men she was meeting online were flakes. They had problems with alcohol, or their children, or they had PTSD for one reason or another, or within a few dates they were suggesting pooling finances. For a while she dated a senior public servant and he seemed decent enough – until she chose to wear a purple dress with a plunging neckline for a night out with him. The man told her that when he saw her in that purple dress, he knew at once she would be perfect for the dinner parties he went to at the home of another couple. The next thing she knew his phone was ringing and he was passing it to her. The dinner party hostess was at the end of the line. 'Now, Kirstie,' the woman said, 'we women have had such bad sex for so long, you really should keep an open mind and come and enjoy this.' After the call ended, the senior public servant told Kirstie that the hostess wore an apron but no underwear when guests arrived for these dinner parties. He told her he'd look after her, whatever happened for dessert.

Kirstie refused to see him again. Her friends' eyeballs nearly fell out of their heads when she told them the story. This wasn't the way things were meant to be; dinner parties weren't meant to end in group sex. How could she be in this position at her age, muddling around in this ugly world of online dating? She grieved for her marriage, for her old life, the life she'd been raised to expect would be hers forever.

Her parents' relationship, despite the challenges thrown in its path, was the way things were meant to be – sturdy enough, till death do us part. The nice neighbourhood, the life that ran like clockwork. Her mother's sticky lessons about how to keep a man: make sure you look your best when he gets home from a hard day's work, she advised, and she'd be in the bathroom at half past five doing her lipstick, dinner on the table for Kirstie's father by six.

Kirstie started rehearsals for this life in her Catholic high school. Richard was the first, a lovely boy who was two years older and an excellent soccer player. He was dark and muscular and had shaggy hair to his shoulders and they loved each other like crazy, but she made him wait until she'd nearly finished school because she didn't want to lose her reputation. In the meantime she sought out information about matters on which her mother remained silent. Kirstie's high-school biology textbook, *The Web of Life*, was helpful. She read the chapter about human reproduction and paid particular attention to the parts about the female cycle. When she'd reached a clear understanding of things, she copied the pages and, when the nuns weren't looking, handed them out to every girl in her class. 'Don't have sex around these days,' she said. Then, some time later, she taught them about orgasms. She thought, *wow, what in the hell!* when she finally slept with Richard. She couldn't ask her mother about what her body had done to her so she consulted *Cleo* magazine. Harold Robbins' *The Carpetbaggers*, lifted from her father's bedside table, shed more light on the matter. Again, this was a matter for discussion with her school friends as they sat in the quadrangle, screeching with laughter, their skirts hitched high and their newly shaved legs stretched out to soak up the sun.

They were together for three years, Kirstie and Richard. In the early days he hitchhiked the 20 kilometres between their houses. Later, he bought an old Holden. On Friday nights he'd pick her up and they'd get Kentucky Fried Chicken, drive to the oval around the corner from her parent's place, and lie on a rug clutching each other all night. 'We were so in love,' Kirstie says. Sometimes she'll look at the old photos; she especially likes the one of the two of them on a beach, sitting close on a red li-lo, her slim in a bikini, half-turned towards the camera, him smiling broadly, their backs to the sea and a cloud-flecked horizon. Everyone wanted her to marry Richard. But she was nineteen and took no notice of anyone. When she turned and squinted she could see over the horizon and he wasn't there. By the time she started university – economics, geography – she had wanderlust. Richard was left calling her mother, begging to know what he could do to get Kirstie back.

For Kirstie, however, the world was new and generous and required exploration. Next it gave her Don, a dark and handsome engineering student so tall he had to bend over to kiss her; when he did he tickled her face with his thin moustache. The chemistry was fireworks, but she was restless. Don couldn't keep her attention and nor could university – in the huge lecture theatres she couldn't find her tribe. When she dropped out, her mother ordered her to do a secretarial course. It gave her a shorthand speed of 100 words a minute, and, eventually, high-level executive assistant jobs.

Still, she had her mother's lessons etched in her psyche and society's expectations clamouring for attention; everyone trying to tell her what she should do. Find a man. Build a career.

Get married. Have kids. Find a man. Michael Douglas's Gordon Gekko was laying waste to decency in *Wall Street* as Kirstie started to climb the ladder – she would graduate from taking dictation to a role as managing director of a big public relations agency and a pale blue corner office with a view.

And the world kept giving: to her glamorous, fast-paced life it introduced Geoff, an ambitious senior executive with an incipient double chin who would, in the not-too-distant future, turn to watch her walk down the aisle of a country church. Before the ceremony there was a drama with the veil – someone had forgotten to bring it from the city and her mother, having conniptions, said she'd have to wear a mosquito net because no daughter of hers would get married in a Catholic church without a veil – but a courier delivered it just in time for Kirstie to emerge, fashionably late, from a white vintage Rolls-Royce wearing an off-the-shoulder cream lace gown and carrying a bouquet of cream and blush-pink roses tortured into a V formation designed to highlight her pretty waist. The wrap-around tiara and veil were perfectly in place. She was a princess. Her mother calmed down. Their friends said it was the best wedding they'd ever been to.

The members of Geoff and Kirstie's group were tight, and over time their annual social calendar assumed an easy rhythm – en masse Easter holidays in the same beach town; skiing trips for the girls in winter; new outfits for the races each year in Melbourne; Boxing Day barbecues at Geoff and Kirstie's with their two girls and a bunch of other kids crazy in the pool; dinner parties that would end with AC/DC pounding from the lounge-room stereo. She remembers one night vividly: everyone was dancing and she and Geoff were at the centre of it all and they pashed. Their lives, when all was said and done, were fabulous.

Kirstie thought Geoff was happy. Well, yes, they had their ups and downs. She struggled with his moods. He thought she spent too much money. Kirstie believed she was spending what was required to maintain the lifestyle he expected. Towards the end of the week he'd be asking her what social activities she'd arranged for the weekend. On Friday afternoons she would race off to the deli to spend up and stock up – her girlfriends teased her about it. 'I had to make sure I had Geoff's dips in the fridge.' She says it was his decision to upsize to the big house with the pool.

Kirstie hadn't thought that Geoff meant it when, during their increasingly frequent arguments, he threatened to leave her. Until one day, after another argument about money, she realised he did. 'I am going to get a divorce this time,' he said. Her knees crumpled under her. She fell to the kitchen floor.

She had everything. Then she had nothing. The world that had just kept giving was now taking – initially, her capacity to function and five kilos: the 'divorce diet'. A year after Geoff had moved out, it took two tumours and 25 per cent of her right breast. The chemotherapy stole her beautiful brown hair and her confidence. The lawyers and the acrimonious financial settlement swept away the big house and lifestyle and left her with a little flat. Time robbed her, too: in the years she'd been a stay-at-home mother, the public relations world had changed, her contacts had dissipated, and there were brighter, younger things in the corner offices. She was forced to take lesser roles. She'd knocked off the cancer but her new world was bleak. 'I had my whole life taken away from me.'

She wanted to still fit in with her coupled friends, but the invitations dried up. Oh, we'd invite you, her girlfriends would tell her, but, well, you know, Seb or Craig or Frank, or whichever husband it was, wanted male company. An odd number wouldn't work. 'Yeah,' Kirstie would say, 'I get it.' She had been tossed into a different box, like an out-of-favour child's doll.

Kirstie met other women in the same position and started to think that being a disempowered divorced women was almost a syndrome; sometimes she even felt she was part of a different gender. But she kept herself busy and tried not to let it eat her up, tried not to sound like a whinger – especially when she talked about the Family Court – tried not to fall into the bitterness trap. After all, she knew there were men who felt equally ripped off by their divorce settlements because she was meeting them on dating apps!

And then, from amid that rabble of weird men online whom she had been reduced to investigating, Joe came forward. They exchanged messages on the dating site's platform and discussed whether or not it was wise to swap email addresses. She thought not and he concurred, saying she could be a 'Russian princess' and 'I could be a scammer on day release'.

They messaged back and forth for a little longer, then set a time to meet. On their first date, a coffee catch-up, he told her about his children, and about how he shared custody with his crazy ex-wife, Mary. He told her that he worked in private equity, dabbled in property deals and had a small sheep farm south of the city. He told her about the harbourside home he'd built years earlier for his young family; the little yacht moored below it; and about his late grandfather who was prominent in business.

She wasn't fussed about him – she thought he was a plain man – but he asked her out again and she went and, by the third date, she was starting to see something in him that she liked. *Hallelujah*, she thought. *Here's someone who has a young man's nous in him.* He was assertive, in a good way, and a few dates in, at a piano lounge in the early hours, between mouthfuls of Kahlúa and milk, Joe swung her around and kissed her for the first time.

•

I was in a state. In the early hours of the Sunday morning after Joe and I had kissed, not long after Kirstie had tried to calm her teenage daughter's slumber party, I sent him a text agreeing to go away with him the following weekend. Mid-morning I issued a brazen follow-up: 'My head hurts and I can't stop thinking about you.' He replied to say that I intrigued him, that he thought there was some 'exploration' to be had. I was giddy with the flattery. I took little notice of the photograph he sent to accompany his text message – a solitary candle on a plate surrounded by individually packaged chocolate biscuits and cans of bubble-gum-flavoured soft drink – and another line of text: 'Here is what happens when you forget to bring the birthday cake.' I had a vague memory he'd told me he was having a little celebration on his yacht for his son's birthday that day; I had a fluttering sense that it was odd to forget to bring your child's birthday cake.

In the space of twenty-four hours I had turned into a basket case. I couldn't sit still. I was trembly and fidgety and prickly. My stomach lurched and my throat caught and my skin tingled. It was my old companion, anxiety, but it was more than that. It was *forelsket*, an unscientific Norwegian noun I like a lot. I am feeling *forelsket*; you are immersed in *forelsket*; she is stricken with *forelsket*. It is that euphoric, addictive, obsessive feeling that takes hold when you are falling in love, or think you might be, and there is a shiny new sexual charge and a delusional sense that this person might just be perfect. It is a delirium, the hyper-charged crush, the rose-coloured glasses and the intrusive, vivid daydream. Psychologists sometimes use another term: 'limerence'. There are limerent objects and limerent hope and limerent reactions. Limerence and *forelsket* thrive in the fertile grounds of desire and uncertainty.

In the days leading up to Friday, I am mad with *forelsket*. I feel it when I drive through the city and change down through the gears and accelerate out of a bend. I hear it in the key change of a pop song and sense it in the slow fall of my knife on a board, chopping chilli and garlic for spaghetti. I see it in the bubbles shimmying up the inside of a bottle of soda water beaded with condensation. I am the glittering star of my own fabulous film. I toss my hair back or smile wryly or stretch languorously and sense an audience. It's as though he is watching. I am admired and wanted. I am Bacall in *To Have and Have Not* – 'Anybody got a match?' I ask, and Bogart throws a box at me and I catch it, and I am silk and satin as I light up; I am Elizabeth Taylor with Richard Burton and Katharine Hepburn feverish for Spencer Tracy. I am in a dream.

Joe and I exchange a flurry of text messages. We discuss arrangements for our weekend away: the destination, the supplies we require. I will take music. I will take sourdough and cheese. Joe will provide a leg or a shoulder from his sheep, carrots from a friend's garden. We will both contribute bottles of wine. He will drive north from his farm, I will drive south from the city. We will meet at a cottage he has booked in a valley.

We also discuss kisses. He asks if I remember my first kiss. I tap into my phone: 'Oh I remember it explicitly. I thought the world was going to explode.' That afternoon he messages to say that he's had enough of the city and is off to the farm – I assume he has handed over custody of his children to Mary. The next morning he texts me a picture of a dirt track running through a country landscape. 'Arriving at work this morning,' he captions it. 'Too many days before I see you,' I reply. He tells me that he's slashing sifton bush, a native weed that can grow into a towering, prickly jungle; nature's way of telling us we've fucked up, he says.

On the Wednesday morning, Joe sends me a text asking why Friday seems such a long way away. Later in the day, he paints a picture of his life as a farmer – he stinks of 'diesel, sweat, dog and maggoty fox'. He enhances the image, telling me he's shot a rabbit. On Thursday he texts to say that he needs some comfort and company and he'll be staying at the motel for the night and seeking out 'chat and cheer' at the local pub. He sends me a photograph of the pub, utes and four-wheel drives angle-parked on the street outside it, an ominous dark sky backdrop. And then 'an admission': I was on his mind today; he was wondering what I'm really like. I reply quickly, worried he's having second thoughts: 'I am wondering the same about you. I am hoping not an axe murderer!' His reply pings back within minutes. Am I a Russian princess in disguise? I ask for clarification. He tells me a Russian princess is an Eastern European looking for a husband, looking to be rescued. I don't have the right fingernails for such a role, I reply. And I don't need rescuing from anything.

By Friday, I am completely beside myself. I have studied myself in the mirror. I have shopped for new underthings. I have thought about revealing my body for the first time in too long. My thumb aches from scrolling through his texts trying to read between his lines. I have attempted to get a fix on his face, on the aqueous depths of his green eyes and his shy smile. This feeling, this intoxicating feeling. *Forelsket* has had me in its grip before; its appearances over the years have left behind an internal shadowy slideshow that now throws up images and senses of moments past: the sigh of corks eased from champagne bottles, explosions of bubbles, music crescendos, fishnets and boots, long gazes, brushed skin, dim restaurants, stolen kisses. Drugged with love.

•

When I look back and feel foolish, I know now that I can't be held responsible for the decisions I made – at least not at the beginning of my relationship with Joe. Deep in the pink–grey-vesselled goo of my brain, electrical signals and chemical messengers were surging through the pathways of my dopamine reward system. Now I think of my brain as it was at that time as an overloaded vintage switchboard playing havoc with an ordered office; I think of the 1958 film *Auntie Mame*, of Rosalind Russell as a switchboard operator in the offices of Widdicombe, Gutterman, Applewhite, Bibberman & Black, of the chaos and cacophony, of the buzzing, flashing, plugging, unplugging, tangled cords, mixed lines and babbling voices.

After I have put myself back together again and started to research why my brain betrayed me, I have a Skype conversation with a happily married couple. I am alone, in my study in my apartment. Despite a fuzzy connection, I see that Jacqueline Olds and her husband, Richard Schwartz, married for forty-plus years and the co-authors of three books, are sitting close in their home in Cambridge, Massachusetts. 'When we're in love in that infatuated stage, there's a lot of activity in what is called the brain's dopamine reward system,' Richard says, and, as he waves his hand to make the point, I see his wedding ring flash. Richard and Jacqueline are psychiatrists, couples therapists, associate professors at Harvard Medical School, and consultants at the affiliated McLean psychiatric hospital. Jacqueline is also a consultant at Massachusetts General Hospital.

I ask them if, when they met, it was heady. Was it love at first sight? 'It was for me,' says Richard, a fond glance at his wife. 'It took a little longer to convince Jackie.'

I tell them that I'm as silly as a teenager when I start to fall in love. 'I love that, that's a wonderful quality,' exclaims Jacqueline, who is warm and engaged behind spectacles.

'Well, not really,' I say. 'Not when you end up in the situation that I did.'

Richard and Jacqueline, who have studied the evolution of love, marriage, the collapse of love, and loneliness, lead me on an exploration of a truly, madly, deeply messy place – the brain in the grip of *forelsket* and acting on a primitive biological urge to find a mating partner and reproduce.

As we exchange messages with a new love interest, meet in a bar, scan a face, brush hands, touch lips, that dopamine reward system deep in our brain's ancient limbic structures floods with neurotransmitters and hormones, which create a range of physical and emotional responses. Amid the feverish activity in reward system structures, including the amygdala, the hippocampus, the caudate nucleus and, most significantly, the ventral tegmental area (VTA), levels of the stress hormone cortisol leap: the brain decides that love is a crisis to be managed.

Levels of cortisol are also high in people with generalised anxiety disorder. Levels of the neurotransmitter serotonin, which is higher when we have feelings of wellbeing and less active when we are depressed, are depleted to such an extent that the serotonin levels of someone in the midst of new love are similar to those of someone with obsessive-compulsive disorder. 'Love is actually in its own way a little like a kind of obsession,' says Richard. 'So the kind of repetitive, I-can't-get-it-out-of-my-mind thoughts that you see in OCD, you also see in love.' Meanwhile, the neurotransmitter dopamine, the most important reward chemical, spikes. All of this feverish activity is taking place in the same regions of the brain that are active in a person addicted to cocaine or alcohol. And, as with a substance addiction, we are driven to crave more and more, and to take risks to get what we are craving.

With a dopamine reward system in such a state – stirred up, as Richard says, in 'very wonderful and strange ways' – how could anyone possibly be expected to make sensible decisions? And yet, as Richard and Jacqueline continue their intercontinental explanation of a brain in love, I learn that it's not just the dopamine reward circuits in my brain's flighty limbic system that have gone crazy. That calculating frontal lobe has let me down, too.

'The cortical circuits which help you make good critical judgements are affected by love such that negative information isn't sifted as well as usual. We cannot judge character as well because of this effect,' says Jacqueline. 'When you fall in love there's this sense that maybe your inner loneliness will be relieved, it's this kind of desperate thirst to not be so alone . . . so for a brief period you sort of feel like, *oh my gosh, I'll be relieved of that terrible loneliness.* And it will be almost like back to the parental protection state. So I think that's part of what makes it such an altered state of consciousness.' Jacqueline uses an analogy to describe the early stages of love: it is as though all the equipment keeping a ship on course is out of commission.

But, on a Friday afternoon in late winter 2014, I have no sense that I'm a ship off course and heading towards rocks. I believe I'm about to spend the weekend with a kind and uncomplicated farmer. 'Slight delay,' he texts as I prepare to leave the city. A fence has come down and sheep have roamed, he writes. I'm running late too. I reverse out of my garage, stomach fluttering, and head into end-of-week traffic jams. On the highway the traffic thins, the road opens up before me and I hit play on the mix I've made. Marianne Faithfull joins me in the car. She's singing Noël Coward. She's mad about a boy. She's insane and young again, pained and enchained by a dream. I know how she feels.

•

Friday night. How odd. The intimate items of another. In the bathroom, his sponge bag, toothbrush and toothpaste tube are laid out on the side of the basin, next to a razor. I'm wobbly and linger behind the closed door. I wash my hands. I check my face and my hair in the mirror. I note a candle on the edge of the bath tub and two pairs of complimentary slippers gift-wrapped in clear cellophane. Joe has brought in my bag and left it in the bedroom but I couldn't possibly open it now and move my things into the bathroom. Too soon. I might yet decide to flee. I have taken precautions: I have cash in my wallet ready to hand to him for the accommodation should I want to leave. I have looked at the map and worked out the nearest motel to which I could retreat.

When I emerge from the bathroom he hands me a glass of red and a predicament arises that gives us something to laugh about: he has a leg of his lamb but the cottage does not have an oven. There is a serendipitous solution – a barbecue in the little garden. Firelight will throw kind light on our faces. If conversation stutters, a fire can be gazed into and then a silence becomes a light, easy thing. It is cold outside: we must stand close to stay warm. His kelpie, leashed on the veranda, is not happy. She spins anxiously and whines.

Of dinner, I only remember that we ate it inside at a small table. I do not remember when or what was said to indicate the meal was over, or how we were so suddenly standing in the bedroom and he was putting his lips to mine and gently raising my top. I remember, though, that I had put music on, '*E lucevan le stelle*' from *Tosca* – 'the stars were shining and the earth was scented . . . and I never before loved life so much'. I remember that the light was dusky and it was tender and perfect.

Saturday morning: I don't remember washing our bacon-and-egg-greased plates but if I did it was to busy myself and clatter over the awkwardness that had descended when we resumed upright positions, not to demonstrate I could be a domestic goddess (although that is a retrogressive, eager-to-please instinct I find hard to stifle). After breakfast, Joe sits on the couch and picks up a newspaper. He doesn't talk. I'm not sure there is an invitation on offer for me to sit on the couch beside him. I wonder what I should do. Wobbliness is returning to my limbs and the flutter to my stomach. I wonder if I'm still welcome. I hover and feel unwanted and out of place. It is an old feeling.

IN THE ALBUM OF MY LAST days of high school is a photograph that always stops me. It has faded but the memory bites. A girl in my year had invited twenty or more graduating students, boys and girls, all of us high-achieving and well-behaved, to a sleepover at her parents' home outside town. There was a bonfire and a happy circle gathered around it. I tried to find a place in the circle but it did not open and I hovered on the fringes, wondering what to do. I went inside the house. Other students were draped around the lounge room in a rough circle. I recall laughter. I recall that no one looked up to see me, no one opened up a place for me. I did not push. I have never pushed. It was not a deliberate exclusion; I was simply surplus to requirements. The photograph that bites would be taken the next morning. It is, on the face of things, innocuous: five unsophisticated seventeen-year-old girls in tracksuits, jeans and sweaters. I'm smiling and physically connected to my friends – the girl beside me has her knees drawn up and my arm is hooked around one of them in a pose that indicates comfortable familiarity – but I look at that photo now and feel with piercing clarity the pain of the disconnection that the fair, shy, young version of myself who bruised so easily felt at that moment in time. And I look at that photo and think it was a premonition of the years to come; of all the circles I would feel had no place for me; all the dreams I would have in which I was alone, all the panes of glass that would seem to stand between me and others, all the times I would look for my place and fail to find it and feel lost.

I'M NOT SURE THERE IS A place for me now beside Joe, so I tell him I'm going for a walk. For a moment I talk to his dog on the veranda, but she offers friendship only in a nipping form, so I wander into the garden. I take photographs – blushing cherry blossoms, cobwebs pearled with water droplets and draped over bare winter branches, black and white cows in a damp field – and then poke my nose into an old hut. Suddenly Joe is at my shoulder. I realise that the hut is a mini-museum of pioneer photos and farm equipment: shovels and pitchforks, scythes and saws, an axe. I joke about the axe.

'What was I thinking? I still have no idea who you are,' I say to him. We laugh then together and it is easy again. He leans to kiss me. He leads me back to the cottage.

Saturday afternoon. There was the bed. Now there is the couch and a fire. Joe loves a fire. He has told me that on several occasions. He stuffs kindling in the grate, layers wood, tucks more kindling in. A match, a flame, the fire crackles to life. We sit on the couch touching. *We* sit. *We* touch. We. It is the most wonderful personal pronoun. It is the cruellest personal pronoun. Those whose circumstances are such that they can use it freely don't know the effect it can have on those of us who can't. A 'we' can be a dagger in the belly – 'We are taking three months off to hike around Japan'; 'We decided to move to the country'; 'We ate at that new restaurant last night'. For too long I have been an *I* in a world of *we*.

Much later, I stumble on a TED talk given by Esther Perel. She is a Belgian psychotherapist and, according to *The Times*, 'the world's most wanted sex therapist'. Sexy accent, lip-gloss sheen, compelling presentation. Her talk is titled 'Rethinking Infidelity'. I dig around online and on her website come upon more of her thoughts. 'Never before has the couple been such a central unit in our social organisation,' writes Perel (who has her own 'we' – a husband and two children). 'Never have we expected more from our intimate relationships, and never have we crumbled under the weight of so many expectations.'

Perel's thoughts reflect those of American clinical psychologist Sue Johnson. 'Inevitably we now ask our lovers for the emotional connection and sense of belonging that my grandmother could get from a whole village. Compounding this is the celebration of romantic love fostered by our popular culture,' writes Johnson in her insightful book *Hold Me Tight: Seven Conversations for a Lifetime of Love*. 'Movies as well as television soap operas and dramas saturate us with images of romantic love as the be-all and end-all of relationships, while newspapers, magazines, and TV news avidly report on the never-ending search for romance and love among actors and celebrities.'

My mother started it and now I have succumbed to the saturation. I look for left hands, for wedding rings. A wedding ring can be a dagger in the belly, too; I've never felt a great need for a white-dress extravaganza or even state-sanctioned vows, but a wedding ring speaks to me of commitment, attachment, connection, a 'we'. And who am 'I' if I haven't found a 'we'? I have fallen under the wicked spell of the idea that without a 'we' I cannot be me; that I am lesser, a half not a whole, unworthy, incomplete, unsuccessful. I have not been chosen; I cannot be my best self.

'The humiliations of lovelessness' is how the American literary critic and writer Elizabeth Hardwick described it in her book *Seduction and Betrayal,* writing about women writers and relations between women and men. Jeanette Winterson wrote of the matter in her memoir, *Why Be Happy When You Could Be Normal?* Of her former teacher, the widow Mrs Ratlow, Winterson wrote, 'She adored men, though the lack of one rendered her invisible in her own eyes – the saddest place in the township of invisible places a woman can occupy.'

The dagger twists when I read about relationships that, from the outside at least, seem to be vessels for love of the most exceptional kind. With wet eyes, I read a story in the *Washington Post* about the great love affair of Supreme Court Justice Ruth Bader Ginsburg and her husband, Martin. He cherished her brain. She described him as her 'best friend and biggest booster'. In 2010, he wrote her a note. 'My dearest Ruth,' it said, 'you are the only person I have loved in my life . . . I have admired and loved you almost since the day we first met at Cornell some 56 years ago. What a treat it has been to watch you progress to the very top of the legal world!!' Bader Ginsburg found her husband's note beside their bed after he'd been admitted to hospital in the late stages of cancer. He died ten days later.

'I have had more than a little bit of luck in life, but nothing equals in magnitude my marriage to Martin D. Ginsburg. I do not have words adequate to describe my supersmart, exuberant, ever-loving spouse,' Bader Ginsburg wrote in the *New York Times*.

I would take the pain of loss to have had the love. I would take the pain to have been known. It is something that Canadian writer Mandy Len Catron has talked about since her now famous essay 'To Fall in Love with Anyone, Do This' was published in the *New York Times*'s 'Modern Love' column. Her theme, subsequently expanded upon in a book, and based on the American psychologist Arthur Aron's research, is that two strangers can quickly reach a great level of intimacy – love, even – by asking each other questions: thirty-six specific personal questions designed to expose the participants' vulnerabilities. Questions such as 'When did you last cry in front of another person?'; 'Of all the people in your family, whose death would you find most disturbing? Why?'; 'How do you feel about your relationship with your mother?' A few months after her article was published, Len Catron gave a talk at Chapman University in Orange, California. She told the audience that the thirty-six questions provided a mechanism for getting to know someone quickly, 'which is also a mechanism for being known, and I think this is the thing that most of us really want from love: to be known, to be seen, to be understood'.

Philosopher and author Alain de Botton has thoughts on this matter as well. In his analytical novel *Essays in Love*, he calls it the "'I'-Confirmation': 'Perhaps it is true that we do not really exist until there is someone there to see us existing, we cannot properly speak until there is someone there who can understand what we are saying, in essence, we are not wholly alive until we are

FAKE

loved . . . To feel whole, we need people in the vicinity who know us as well, sometimes better, than we know ourselves. Without love, we lose the ability to possess a proper identity, within love, there is a constant confirmation of our selves.' I am not known. I have longed to be known.

NOW, IN THE COTTAGE, WE – Joe and I – are on the couch talking, asking questions of each other. Not Len Catron's questions, which I will only learn about later, but our own free-form back and forth. More than the exact questions and answers, I recall how I leant into him, my head on his chest; how I could hear his heartbeat, how his arm was around me, how I reached up and ran my hand through his thick hair. He asks me what travel destinations are on my bucket list. 'Japan, over and over,' I say. 'Costa Rica, Alaska, Corfu.' I explain that Gerald Durrell's *My Family and Other Animals* was on the reading list for English when I was in high school. A friend and I were so enthralled by Durrell's depiction of the Greek island that we decided we'd stop buying snacks at the school canteen and instead divert our money to a Corfu fund. The saving was soon enough forgotten, the snacks resumed, but, for me at least, the idea has remained.

'I loved that book,' Joe says. My brain snaps. It is, I'm immediately convinced, an omen, a sign of our compatibility, that we are destined to know each other. Perhaps he said then that he loved the character of Margo, beauty obsessed, trailed by suitors. But, looking back, I can't be sure he said anything about Margo, or anything specific about the book at all. My crazy brain latched on to his line and took off on a dizzying trajectory.

Now, Joe stretches and glances at his phone. He gently disentangles me and sighs and says he must do a little work – emailing related to a major property deal he is working on. As he opens up his laptop and sets himself up at the table, I stay on the couch, humming with happiness, staring into the fire, building dreams on foundations wispier than the smoke rising up the chimney.

Years later, I will learn about the work Joe did on his laptop that Saturday afternoon.

I will learn that on the previous Thursday night as I packed for the weekend and fretted, Joe was drinking vodka martinis with his other girlfriend, Kirstie, at her apartment in the city and talking about plans for their weekend ahead. On the Friday afternoon, around the time I was hitting the highway to drive towards him, feeling quite insane and young again, Joe stood Kirstie up. He texted her to say that he couldn't get to her daughter's school art show that night as planned because there had been a drama with Mary and he had to rescue his children.

I will learn that at 4.18 pm on the Saturday afternoon, as I stared into the fire, he sent an email to Kirstie with the word 'Space' in the subject field. 'Hello you, I dont know how to put this, but I'll do it this way,' he wrote, showing little regard for the apostrophes I had valued in our early correspondence. He told her he wanted to take some time to work out a few things. He was feeling terribly guilty, he wrote, about how he had not been giving his children the attention they needed. He would have called her but he'd lost his phone and wouldn't get a new one until the following day. He was so so sorry to have mucked her around and left her in the lurch.

3

WE MADE LOVE

How quickly 'I' became 'we' and the 'we' seemed immutable. Soon after our weekend in a cottage in a valley, Joe arrived at my apartment and plucked a toothbrush from his shirt pocket. 'I'll leave this here,' he said. I cooked him breakfast the next morning. Later that day he sent me a message that left me swooning. Three short, sharp sentences. I interested him a great deal. I was 'delightfully surprising'. He was exclusively mine.

We made love.

We stayed in and cooked. Joe liked steak: medium to well done. He built burning timber towers in my barbecue and would stand staring into the flames, glass of wine in hand, while in the kitchen I rushed to assemble salads so I could get out to all that warmth as quickly as possible.

We watched television, sitting close on my couch, his kelpie watching us with yellow-eyed disgust from my courtyard.

We. We. We.

We had a pre-theatre meal at the bar of a fine restaurant one night – Sydney rock oysters and a toasted sandwich with five cheeses and black truffles – and when it came time to leave, we looked at each other, leant close, whispered and, instead of picking up our tickets for the theatre, returned to my apartment.

We went away for another weekend, to a little house on a river, accessible only by water. Chickens scratched in the garden's damp cold soil. A magnolia tree flaunted early blooms. I lay on a divan in the boathouse while he cooked us salmon for lunch in the house. I tried to concentrate on a book but my mind roamed. 'Boat shed is rather lovely' I texted him. 'So are you' Joe texted back. Later, I took the tiller on a tinnie and we explored mangroved inlets and oyster-shell-studded shorelines in the shadows of leaning angophoras. His dog stood with her front paws on the foredeck, sniffing the muddy air. I nearly upended us with an amateur's manoeuvre. Joe took control. We laughed. His hair was shaggy and in need of a cut. He'd left his shoes at the house and had rolled up his jeans, a grown-up Huck Finn. When we returned to our little house, he checked his messages and made some comment about how his ex-wife had sacked yet another lawyer in a long line of lawyers and now she couldn't find anyone who would represent her in their custody stoush.

We made love.

We sat on the bare boards of the jetty in moonlight, rugged up against a chill breeze, the river's black waters lapping below us, the sky irresistible. I asked him about the stars. Because when you're silly with *forelsket*, it is in the script that your lover will know about the universe, about planets and solar systems and galaxies; he will know where to direct his lover's eyes when she asks him to show her the Milky Way. Joe pointed to something in the sky. For all I know it could have been space junk. I snuggled into him and told him how clever he was. I was deranged.

We were rueful when it was time to leave the little house on the river. I interrupted our packing to undress him. 'You are so right,' he sighed through my caresses. An hour or so later, when we returned to the boat rental marina where we'd left our cars two days earlier, I slipped a chocolate bar into the pocket of his coat when he wasn't looking. He had a six-hour drive ahead of him – he was off to collect some new rams in western New South Wales.

THE COUNTRY THING: I WANTED EVERY last clod of it, from his R. M. Williams boots to his rough shack and maggoty foxes. I thrilled to the messages he sent from the country, to their pastoral representations of masculinity. When he told me one night he'd be out of phone range stalking the foxes that butchered his lambs, I enhanced the image as I drifted off to sleep. I put him in a Driza-Bone and an Akubra. He grew taller and broader, and every time he put a bullet into a beast it was a clean, quick kill because his compassion was infinite. I wanted to kiss him hard when he sent me a message saying his ego was 'fit to burst', that the stud manager had looked at his numbers and how he was running his stock, was impressed, and would be pushing other owners to follow his lead. I wanted to have been crouching with him when he took the photo of a newborn lamb suckling at its mother's udder; to arrive bearing sandwiches and a thermos of coffee as he took a break from trimming ewes' rotten hooves and straining fences and going deaf slashing. I wanted to be rubbing his shoulders when he examined the quotes for fencing that he said had him gasping for air. When he sent me a photograph of his ute, axle-deep in mud and captioned 'my day', I wanted to get filthy helping him dig it out. I wanted to be curled up with him in his shack on the night he texted to say that he couldn't call me because it was raining so hard that he'd had to put earplugs in.

But when he told me, as he so often did, that he was shutting the farm's gate behind him and heading towards the highway, to the city and my apartment, well . . . that was even more thrilling. I had become as single-minded as an opiate addict in my pursuit of his touch. The days and nights spent in my bed, skin to skin, flesh to flesh, wrapped in his arms, a floating dream state, a glimpse of paradise, safety. One night he emailed to say he was going to drift off to sleep thinking of the next time he could feel me against him. I read it over and over. 'Where did you come from?' I murmured to him soon after. He repeated my words back to me, as if in wonder.

We made love. And the only terror was the passing of the time, the ever-looming moment when he would vanish again.

IN THOSE EARLY DAYS, A ROUTINE of sorts emerged: in the weeks his children were with their mother, Joe and his dog divided their time between his farm and my apartment. His place held unhappy memories, he said; for now, he'd rather be there only when it was his week with the children. Besides, he said, his mother was staying with him until the chemical smell wore off the newly polished floors of her apartment overlooking the Opera House.

He sent me images of his domestic life: a picture of the bush falling into the harbour captioned 'my Tintagel'; his daughter cuddling the dog on a little wooden boat; a picture of the children in a rowboat back-dropped by green water, rocky shoreline, gum trees. One day he's reading the paper while his children are in the creek catching frogs; another and it's so hot that his water-averse dog has paddled out to where his daughter is swimming. Nights after such days are peaceful. He describes sleeping curled up with his children, burnt, tired, and smiling in their sleep. He sends me a picture showing the children's heads and shoulders protruding from crisp white linen. Leaving his children after such days are painful and he runs late to reach me. I want to be there catching frogs and rowing and swimming with the three of them. But I don't want to crowd him or scare him off. We are only three months into our relationship. I don't push to see his farm or his house, or to meet his children. No one likes a pushy woman.

Beyond farm and children, Joe describes a third arm to his life – that of under-the-radar entrepreneur. In partnership with two other men, he talks of working on a substantial property deal for land near Canberra, about meetings with agents and the builder they have contracted to develop it into a housing estate. One day he texts me to say that he's spent a day with solicitors and everyone wants to be 'my mate for life because this business is sooooo successful' and I buy a bottle of champagne to open with him that night, trying not to be irritated by the message's blowhard tone.

He also tells me about work he does for two men he describes as 'the Yanks' – something about silver dealing, or silver mines. At one point they're so impressed with the profit he's helped them make that they want to fly him and his children to Hawaii for a holiday. Another time they want him in LA for a meeting. He puts them off: he has a dodgy ear and doesn't want to fly. One day he tells me that the Yanks are in town and he's meeting them for lunch. He suggests I join them afterwards for drinks but, mid-afternoon, texts to say they've finished earlier than expected and he's heading home to his children.

We have breakfast regularly at a cafe around the corner from my apartment, where the coffee is adequate and the decor brings to mind *The Collector*, John Fowles' disturbing novel in which a butterfly-collecting sociopath holds captive a young girl with whom he is obsessed. In the cafe, vintage naked dolls in various states of decrepitude crowd the shelves and paper cut-outs of butterflies flutter across the walls. One day there, Joe lifts his head from the *Australian Financial Review* and tells me that former treasurer Wayne Swan wants to meet him to discuss his ideas.

'You're kidding!' I say. 'What in particular?'

'Not sure,' he replies, adding that a friend who admires his business acumen is arranging the meeting. It seems extraordinary and the cogs in my brain momentarily clatter. But with all he has told me about his grandfather's business history and his own work, it doesn't seem impossible. He has also told me that occasionally he gives ideas to a Fairfax Media finance/business columnist, although he refuses to say which one – it would be too embarrassing for the columnist, he says. I wonder if he's not far more brilliant and well-connected than he has let on.

OF COURSE, I GOOGLED HIM. But the search gave me no reason to think that what Joe was telling me was anything but the truth. Among the limited information that came up was a link to a family tree on an ancestry website, which included his name and those of his grandparents, parents, siblings and ex-wife, matching what he'd told me. I found a photo of his late grandfather. There could be no doubt about Joe's relationship with the man, a businessman who had founded a major national company; they shared the same extreme nose and dastardly brows. Nor could there be any doubt about Joe's stories of the suburb in which he was raised and had built his house: at one point, he opened his wallet in front of me and I caught sight of his driver's licence and a waterfront address in that neighbourhood. In an archived online newsletter for the suburb's progress association, I found mention of his mother – she had been its secretary. The old newsletter referred to a walking tour of the historic area, which Joe had led.

His social media presence was limited, consistent with the concerns he'd expressed on our first date about privacy; the bio line on a fallow Twitter account listed his interests (the environment, politics, science, agriculture) and two tweets, one asking for advice about converting land to organic pasture. I found only two references to his past life as an architect, but that matched what he'd told me about resisting publicity. It also occurred to me that perhaps he hadn't been a very successful architect. The first reference was a document showing that Joe and his co-director, a man I'll call Peter, had registered a bus shelter design under intellectual property laws. The second pulled me up: a news item from some years before about Peter – he'd been struck off the architect's register for professional misconduct. I asked Joe about the story and he said he'd known for a long time that Peter was a problem. 'I stuck by him for too long.' He seemed exasperated and I retreated from asking more questions.

I had, after all, no reason to doubt the intensity of his feelings for me. One night, pulling me close, he told me he was thinking about things he'd thought were in the past for him. 'Commitment,' he said, was a word on his mind. He'd had a fond vision of me with grey hair, he said. For my birthday he gave me a tiny and unusual silver antique box, finely engraved with a floral design. He guided my hands to open the oblong piece. Inside was a slim pencil. 'For a writer,' he said. Just before Christmas he sent me a message asking about my plans for January. Around the same time, we were at my place one night and I was light-hearted and as happy as anything and who knows what I was doing, and he looked at me. 'You're quite madcap, aren't you?' he said. And I took that as a compliment and wrapped it up and held it close and felt loved and seen. He had identified the humour and silliness that I mostly keep to myself. He was starting to know me. I thought.

•

I have not told the full story. By the end of the year, anxiety attacks were puncturing the bubbles of elation in which I floated when Joe and I were together. He was becoming increasingly unreliable, cancelling plans on multiple occasions. We can debate this now: was it simply a reprise of the anxiety I have suffered sporadically for some years in certain situations, or was it a response to an instinctual sense that something about him was off-key?

Monday 3 November, I'd not seen him for a week – he'd been with his children – and we'd planned dinner. I was longing to see him. 11.50 am: a text message landed that would be the first in a long line over the coming months to send me into a state. The first cancellation. But, as would become the pattern, it didn't start as a cancellation. It started as a problem that might become a bigger problem that might lead to a cancellation. 'Arghhh! Potentially trouble at mill,' he wrote. I stumbled over the odd, old-fashioned phrase. He might, he said, have to head to the farm that afternoon instead of coming to see me. Obviously he'd try to put off going, and he'd let me know as soon as possible. As I would make sure was the case each and every time he let me down in the months ahead, my response was calm. 'OK,' I replied, aiming for a jaunty tone. 'What's happened?' A bore was pumping out mud, Joe said. The water level had dropped and he needed to set it deeper or it would have to be bored out again. But he might be able to find someone else to deal with it. He'd let me know. Within a few hours, he'd messaged to say he had to head to the farm.

Monday 17 November: text messages flying all day – discussions about dinner (steak, my craving for spinach; he'll pick up some from his local organics shop), his dog's misdemeanours in a park (a slain bird), my writer's block, his business meeting (full of difficult people) due to finish around 4.30. And then, at 4.28, a text to say his work has 'gone totally tits up' and he'll be at it through the night.

Thursday 20 to Sunday 23 November: Joe tells me he needs to go to Hobart for a day to be present for a high-level meeting about wind farm technology with a delegation connected to the visit of the Chinese president. In the saga that follows, he texts to say he has overdone it on the farm and has heatstroke but is returning to the city so he can take a crack-of-dawn flight to Hobart the following morning. I check on the location of the Chinese president. He has indeed been in Tasmania dealing with matters connected to wind farm technology. Joe keeps me updated on his day in Hobart with a volley of messages, then, late in the afternoon, sends one to say he's on his way home but feeling even sicker. He won't come to see me when he gets back in case he infects me. The next day he texts to say he's seen a doctor, who has declared that Joe has poisoned himself with sheep drench. As a result, he misses two planned evenings with me and a party at which I was going to introduce him to my friends and colleagues for the first time.

Saturday 6 December: he's huddled in a ball in the shack on his farm clutching his stomach and it doesn't look like he's going to make it back to the city for the weekend we've planned. He sends me a picture of the outdoor 'dunny' in which he's spending an unhappy amount of time. My reply is calm. I offer my sympathies and scratch around for some humour when I'm feeling none. 'That is a monument. It is superb,' I say of the structure, and add that I hope he will keep it forever, even after he's built the new house. He replies to say that one day he will line its walls with old newspapers.

I spend the afternoon in a friend's kitchen trying to help with Christmas baking but my body is fretful, tingling and fluttering with anxiety and I am a useless kitchen aid. I drink too much wine. I want to cry. I want to go home and retreat to my bed.

It is the only thing I feel able to do when my brain makes my body behave in this way. I check my phone repeatedly but it is not until the following morning that Joe texts to say he's still 'completely laid up'. I suggest that if he could manage the drive to the city, my place would be far more comfortable than the shack and I would make a decent nurse. He doesn't reply until the evening, when he says that friends are driving him up the highway, he can barely move his neck, and he has an 8 pm doctor's appointment. A few hours later he messages to say that a bad tooth has given him a jaw infection that has spread to his neck. The doctor has prescribed extreme doses of antibiotics. He feels 'like merde' and is guilty about me and our aborted weekend.

I email a friend. 'I need a night out with you and your calm to convince me that I'm completely and utterly mad and have no reason to be insecure about the farmer . . . I'm trying so hard to be cool about things.' I go to bed before it's dark and stay there, balled up and ruminating until I fall asleep. Late the following morning, somehow, I drag myself out of bed and into the office.

Saturday 20 December: I am barbecuing an extremely large leg of one of Joe's dorpers for an early dinner in my courtyard at which he is to meet my family. It feels like some enormous leap in proceedings. I pile kindling and timber in my barbecue, a fire roars to life, and within minutes the lamb has burst into flames. I text a photograph of the conflagration to Joe, hoping he's on his way to aid my beginner efforts. He replies to tell me that I've let the fire have too much oxygen, and he might be delayed. I slam the lid down. I make salads. I finish the dessert. My mother is staying with me and we discuss the possibility that Joe might not make an appearance. I feel sick. My brother and sister-in-law arrive with my two nieces and my nephew. Joe is not answering his phone. Around 5 pm we start eating without him. I can barely sit in my chair. I am shaking. Joe does not answer his phone.

ON PAPER, IT LOOKS BAD INDEED. My journalism skills deserted me; I was a feeble interviewer. I can see the questions and follow-up questions I might have asked Joe, that I was professionally equipped to ask, but didn't. How can one man untrained in this work set a bore deeper on his own? Tell me more about the work you do that puts you at a meeting in Hobart with a Chinese delegation talking about wind farms? Why, when I google 'can you poison yourself with sheep drench', do I find nothing to suggest you can? If you were so sick, how is it that you could take a photo of your 'dunny' and send it to me? Why didn't you call me to say you wouldn't be able to make it to dinner? (The next day he would text to say, 'God, sorry'. His daughter had had an asthma attack.) There were also questions I might have asked myself. Why didn't I ask him more questions? Why did I allow so much of the conversation to take place through text messages? Why did I so meekly forgive him for all the cancellations?

But there was little possibility of frontal-lobe rationality through this time. And there were other factors I will cite in my defence. Joe *was* the grandson of a notable businessman; he presented as an entrepreneur carrying that legacy forward, an extremely busy man engaged in multiple large-scale projects while simultaneously running a farm and negotiating parenting with a difficult ex-wife. And those cancellations? Not only were they sprinkled amid our dates and encounters, during which I sank deeper and deeper into the joy of 'we' and 'us', and during which he was kind and gentle and loving, but almost every one of them came with plausible explanations, sprinkled with wry humour and rich detail. They were compelling little three-act plays: act one, the situation is revealed; act two, the escalating drama; act three, the cancellation and denouement.

At some point I summoned up the courage to call Joe and tell him about the effect the cancellations were having on me, that I was finding them even more difficult because I hadn't seen anything of his life and everything so far had been on his terms. After that phone call, he texted me. He understood what I was saying, he said. He reminded me it was 'early days'. And he thanked me for being understanding.

I WROTE LISTS. DOING SO MIGHT, I thought, help my brain to calm down. Writing as therapy, if you like; channelling the chaos and cacophony of my head through to my hands on a keyboard and out on to a page where reason might prevail.

'Why he's not lying' was my first list's headline.

- There is no evidence he is.
- He has said he wants to make our relationship work.
- He wants to meet my family.
- He said that he feels he can talk to me about anything and that he could listen to me all night and he loves hearing my brain work.
- He hasn't had time yet to show me his house or his farm and he's being cautious because it's still early days.

- He said it was a dream to have found a woman like me.
- He has had urgent issues to attend to.
- He seems to be a good, decent man with a balanced and even temperament; he has repeatedly talked about honesty and trust.

Perhaps for a few minutes, the list, and the ones that followed, stilled me. But soon enough my brain was grinding again.

The day after Joe failed to show up for dinner, my mother and I flew to her home in Queensland for Christmas. I worked feverishly in her garden in the tropical heat, looked out at the sea and the horizon from her deck through misted eyes, and tried to convince myself that I was prepared for the relationship to end early in the new year; that I was prepared for 'I' again.

•

Soon after I returned to Sydney in January 2015, Joe arrived at my place and pulled a string of black pearls from his pocket. They were loose and unwrapped, strange I thought, but I was too excited to worry about it. I didn't need the pearls, but my need for the message their lustrous charcoal surfaces seemed to emit was acute. And then, sitting beside me on the couch, he told me he wanted to show me his world, to 'break the bubble' that kept his life with his children separate from mine. He was ready for me to meet them, he said. When I told him I was going to the confirmation of my nieces and nephew, he asked if he could join me. 'It's time I meet your people too,' he said. After the ceremony, we had morning tea with my brother and his family.

The children were wide-eyed. 'You looked so natural together,' my sister-in-law said afterwards.

Within days, though, another drama was upon us. Joe was due to drive up from the farm for a weekend with me. A text mid-afternoon Friday. He'd lost his dog. 'Haven't left yet is what I'm saying.' Without hesitation, my brain decided it was the occasion for an anxiety attack. Around 6 pm, as I lay in a ball, tremors and tingles ripping through my body, another text pinged introducing a new scenario. He'd arrived at the vet, it looked as though the dog had been bitten by a snake. Around 9 pm he messaged to say that things were looking okay, but he wouldn't be able to pick her up until the following day. 'Chat?' I asked. My phone remained silent. I emailed a close friend about the situation. Her reply merged sympathy and rebuke: 'Oh dear. Yes, well, I guess you just have to trust him until you can't. He hasn't actually done anything wrong so don't force it upon him by being a weirdo! Give him the benefit of the doubt as if you were a fresh-faced 17-year-old until he does something concrete to prove your trust is not justified. You live too much in your head.'

At 6.30 on Saturday morning, Joe texted again. His phone and internet connections had been hopeless and he'd only just got my message. There followed through the day a patter of texts, a slight shift in direction each time, an accumulation of detail.

8.47 am: the dog was on a drip at the vet's and would be there for a few days. He might as well come up to Sydney, he said.

9.09 am: the vet said his dog should be all right, but he wouldn't be certain until around lunch.

10.56 am: he will arrive at my place 'late afternoon'.

2.46 pm: he was about to leave. 'Let's do dinner.'

2.49 pm: A one-word response to my query about whether he wanted to eat out or in and that I had excellent steak on hand – 'Steak'.

6, 7, 8, 9 pm: nothing. I don't recall trying to call him. I was in too much of a mess.

9.05 pm: he'd had a second opinion from a vet friend, Ross, who thought he could save the kelpie. They were taking her to Ross's clinic in Moss Vale. Joe would leave there the next morning, Sunday, and arrive at my place around 10 am. 'See you for a late breakfast if that's okay?'

9.07 pm: I tried to inject a spirit of support and care into my reply. 'Do what you need to do. I'm here xxx.' I put the pillow back over my head.

On Sunday morning, I googled 'Ross, vet, Moss Vale'. I got a hit and I recognised the surname that came up – Joe had talked about this friend before.

He finally arrived at my place mid-Sunday afternoon. We stood in my lounge room and hugged tightly. We moved to the couch, and I held him and his eyes were damp as he talked about the experience, about how his dog's eyes had been distended and frightened, her body wobbly. He had thought he would lose her.

THERE WERE THREE OF US IN this relationship: Joe, me and Joe's intriguing, unfolding narrative. He talked. I listened and asked questions. Had I written an article about him then, it would have been a puff piece. I would have highlighted his loving nature, his tenderness and evident devotion to his children and his dog, and contrasted those qualities with his busy, daring, big life as an entrepreneur. I would have glossed over the things that were bothering me – the constant cancellations, the contradictions in his stories, his odd sense of humour, the fact he seemed to have little interest in anything I had to say, or offered glib responses. I would not have mentioned that I still had not seen his house.

After his mother returned to her apartment, he told me that he'd packed up the contents of his house into boxes in preparation for a substantial renovation, which would make space for his forthcoming teenagers. He was looking for somewhere to stay for the duration of the work and around that time sent me photographs of potential rental properties. He also talked about the idea of moving on to a large vintage wooden pleasure cruiser he was having renovated, but he was concerned about the impact on his daughter: he thought her friends might tease her if she had such an unusual home. He sent me photographs of his children on the cruiser, the *Blue Goose*. ('Isn't she a beaut?')

I tried to stop worrying. Here, after all, was someone remarkable, a man to whom interesting things seemed to happen; a man who talked enthusiastically about the 'tiny houses' revolution and the small, environmentally friendly home he had designed for his farm, which was being built in a factory, soon to be trucked down the highway in pre-assembled pieces. Perhaps I might help him equip its kitchen when the time came, he suggested. A man who valued the organic, the artisanal and the authentic. And I was impressed by his creativity and initiative: one day he told me that he had missed a call from Cupertino in Silicon Valley. He said he knew what it was about: he had contacted Google with an idea for a new social network he'd dubbed 'Cicada'.

I gave his Cicada story, as unlikely as it now seems, little further thought. At that point, my general state of unease was dominated by two specific, devastating possibilities – that he might be cheating on me, or he might just not be that into me. I did not have the awareness then to know there might be other things I should be concerned about. And meanwhile I tried to focus on what I could see. And what I could see was that our relationship seemed to be entering a bright new stage. In February, Joe took me away for another weekend – this time to Mackerel Beach, a remote beach north of Sydney – and, while we swam naked in late-summer's warm sea, pulled me close and told me for the first time that he loved me, that he loved everything about me.

Later that afternoon, while behind a newspaper I struggled to contain feelings that overwhelmed, Joe sat with pencil and architect's scale ruler and sketched out a plan for a little stone chalet he wanted to build on land he'd bought in the Victorian Alps. I leant over his shoulder and he pointed out features of the house. The plan was exquisitely drawn with notes in fine architectural lettering.

The next morning we went for a walk and Joe pointed out a block of land near the beach that he liked and described the house he would build there: low-slung, verandas and cross-ventilation, set among the trees. After we returned to the city, he told me he'd contacted the owner of the block and made an offer.

As though wanting to lay himself across the land, to stamp himself upon it, property seemed Joe's pre-eminent concern. In March he announced that he wanted to farm on a grander scale: he was investigating a substantial grazing operation in the Southern Highlands. One Saturday morning, the four of us – Joe, me, the dog and the intriguing, unfolding narrative – piled into his ute for a day trip into the country to look over the property. It was hundreds of acres and as we drove through it Joe jumped out to open, then close behind us, one gate after another. He pointed out a rocky rise above a lake – that would be the best position for a new house. I rested my arm across the seat backs and stroked his neck. The dog squirmed at my feet. A large black snake slithered across the road in front of us.

On the way back to the city we pulled into a cafe at a winery off the highway. Joe lowered his voice and told me that sitting across the room was a man he knew, a former lawyer called Howard Hilton, who'd served jail time for corruption in the late 1980s – in an attempt to get his clients out of jail early, Hilton had bribed the infamous Rex 'Buckets' Jackson, the New South Wales prisons minister in Premier Neville Wran's Labor government. Joe told me that Howard loved fishing. If he bought the property we'd just visited, he'd invite Hilton to fish in his lake. For now, though, he wouldn't interrupt him: Hilton was reading, and besides, since he'd come out of jail, he preferred to keep to himself. I finished my coffee and went to find the bathroom, leaving Joe at the table flicking through his phone. A few minutes later when I returned to the cafe, Joe had vanished.

MONEY. SUCH AN AWKWARD TOPIC. One day I mentioned to Joe that my mother had helped me fund my apartment purchase. Tentatively, I asked him whether his family had ever given him assistance. His answer was emphatic, derisive, and I shrank a little, sensing some scorn for the likes of me. No, he said, from the day he'd hit university he'd never sought, nor received, financial help from his family.

It was the only direct question I ever asked him about his financial circumstances, but from things he said I assembled a version of events that made sense. An elderly neighbour who was fond of him had sold him harbourside land at a good price before the property boom. With a developer associate, he had subdivided it, keeping a block for himself. His grandfather laboured alongside him to help him build a modest house of his own design. He'd played around in the stock market since he was young, and after he set up his architectural practice in the late 1980s, property development became a key part of his business. At some point he'd closed the practice and, in his Savile Row suits, moved to work for the private equity firm he'd mentioned on our first date.

I recall now that Joe talked about a period of financial stress after his divorce, during which he had nowhere to live but the shack. 'At one time, I had absolutely no money,' he said. I think I assumed that with his investment expertise he had easily returned to affluence. He said Mary was greedy and he had established a trust fund for his children to protect their interests; he said all his money and assets were in it and the only things in his name were a few sheep.

He talked about options agreements he and his partners had over tracts of land and tried to explain to me how options worked, but I'm no property or finance journalist – numbers terrify me – and my attention wandered. I was also careful not to ask too many questions. I didn't want him to think I was prying. But from what he told me, it seemed that in the months we'd been together, things had moved forward on the deal he'd been negotiating related to the land near Canberra and his wealth had increased. He started to talk about another even bigger deal in progress relating to a large parcel of land on the south coast. He said most of it would be subdivided for a housing development, but he'd retain a small and stunning block on a headland over-looking the sea.

He seemed to let me into this information slowly, shyly, modestly, as though he was starting to trust me and wanted me to know more about his affairs.

And then came the day, on our way to the butterfly cafe, he said something to me so quietly I could barely hear him. 'I have a disgusting amount of money,' he said, almost sheepishly. He sounded almost embarrassed by the fact.

I am not immune to the mystique of money. I have no desire for designer handbags or multiple mansions, but freedom from worrying about my future as a journalist in a declining media industry, a little house by the sea, a farm in the country, a horse, perhaps, a vegetable garden and fruit trees . . . with a man I love . . . Yes, of course, please, when can I start? I adopted a posture of nonchalance. And with absolute truthfulness I replied, 'I'm not interested in your money, I'm interested in you.'

Besides, Joe himself didn't seem to have much interest in his money, or at least in appearances. His clothes were sometimes scruffy and his ute was battered. He told me he had a new Defender on order – it would soon roll off the West Midlands production line from the second-last batch that would ever be made – but, in any case, the old one was a collector's item and he'd turned down offers for it. I interpreted his loyalty to it as a preference for the understated, a sign of an endearing eccentricity. And it made me laugh. One day we drove through the centre of the city in the ute, a bale of hay and his near-hysterical kelpie in its tray.

One day I told him that his strong values were one of the reasons I loved him. And I liked how he spread out his generosity. On Halloween night he texted to say he had been trick or treating with his children and had given out mini bottles of Moët & Chandon to frazzled housewives. On Melbourne Cup day at the pub in the country town near his property he had won the sweep and put the proceeds on the bar for all. He tipped taxi drivers, and when I commented on his generosity, he said something about the raw deal cabbies get. Eventually, he brought me a bag of sheep shit and dug it into my garden.

Our weekends away were never lavish, but he paid for them. He paid for restaurant and cafe meals and taxis, extracting bills from neat folds of cash he kept tucked in his phone case. This made me uncomfortable, so I also paid for restaurants and cafes and taxis. And when that didn't feel like enough, and I feared it might look as though I was taking advantage of him, I returned to my kitchen over and over and cooked for him. I hand-washed a sweater he was wearing to death. I fed his dog. I became a kowtowing caricature; the besotted woman Doris Day overhears on the party line in *Pillow Talk*, who wheedles Rock Hudson's playboy composer to let her visit him.

'I'll come over and cook for you, yes?' the sultry, accented girlfriend asks.

'Well, if you like,' he says.

'Thank you, darling,' she says.

4

A MANSION IN THE COUNTRY

On a plane together, side by side, flying towards a holiday. This is a solid thing. We hold hands and I nuzzle Joe's face with mine. He kisses my forehead and then exclaims, 'I have something for you!' He reaches into his pocket and extracts a small envelope. I scrunch my face in puzzlement. What is this? The envelope holds a little plastic packet. Three opals, oval, large, medium, small. 'I thought you might be able to do something with them,' he says.

In an amateurish fashion, I make jewellery. I go to class and wear down my fingerprints with the work of sawing, filing, sanding and soldering silver. The thrill of the soldering: silver-wire end to silver-wire end, the flame that caresses the silver, the tiny wedge of solder that explodes into a hot red bubble before the two pieces become one. I have set a tough aquamarine cabochon the colour of a spring sky in a ring. Opals, though, are another thing entirely. They are soft, they scratch easily. Opals need to be treated gently.

I shower Joe with thanks, kiss him again. He is vague about the stones' source; perhaps he said something about someone giving them to him in gratitude for services rendered. I don't recall. I didn't dwell on it. I am giddy with excitement. It's late April and ahead of us are five days in Tasmania. I have been only once before but Joe has been visiting the state for years. Once, he hiked on his own in the wild south for weeks; he was in such a remote area that at the end of it he had to be picked up by helicopter. He came close to buying a major grazing operation in the state's north-east – until Mary broke her promise to him. Before they married, she told him she would support his dream of farming, but she changed her mind.

Each time he is here, Joe visits MONA, David Walsh's modern art museum, and on our first day in Hobart we plan to take the ferry there. But even before we board there is an issue. He can't withdraw cash from the ATM. It's a bank account he still shares with Mary, he says; she has obviously drained it. He tells me he'll work it out and disappears at intervals to make calls. My excitement is extinguished. I try to shove the wretched bodily sensations of anxiety away. I tell myself that it's just a hiccup he's explained satisfactorily; that issues with an ATM and a bank account do not signify anything sinister.

At MONA he is nonchalant. I practise deep breathing and snap photographs of a wall covered with women's vulvas cast in clay. The piece is called 'Cunts . . . and other conversations'. I take a shot of Joe inside an installation that resembles a lift well, lit only around its base. The photograph shows a silhouette of his legs, trousers bagging around his ankles, his hands outstretched beside him, his back against the wall. His face is in darkness.

Later, back in the city, an ATM spits out cash for him and the stress runs out of my body. I inhale wine over dinner. 'You thought I wasn't going to be able to get any money out, didn't you?' he asks, and now, years on, I am certain he was trying to get a reading on my thoughts.

We drive south. We take the car ferry to Bruny Island, from where we are chauffeured in a speedboat to a second, smaller private island. I am to write a travel article about what I find in this heavenly place: a bedroom in a boathouse on a jetty around which pristine Southern Ocean waters flow; a simple house high on a hill slicked with grey and white paint and decorated in a Scandinavian manner; in the fridge, enormous wild oysters and a southern rock lobster pulled from nearby waters hours earlier, slow-motion legs grasping at life; outside, stags and black-faced sheep, chickens and guinea fowl. The silence is acute. The air is piercing in its clarity, a nudge to some primordial memory.

We take a couple of hours to circumnavigate the island, examining the scattered bones of long-dead sheep and deer, and fossils embedded in cliff faces. We crouch at rock pools alive with anemones, sea snails, pinky palm-sized crabs and drifting emerald seaweeds. We throw our clothes off and plunge crazily into the frigid water, and in seconds are clambering back on to the jetty, laughing and gasping and grabbing each other for warmth. We make love. We cocoon ourselves in the boathouse and watch the water shift through a spectrum of blue-greens over jutting oyster-shelled rocks, kelp forests and deeper water. The sky dims, the grey-tinged clouds blur into an apricot sunset, the crests of the mainland's mountains fall into blackness. We make love. We feast in the house near a blazing stove by candlelight – the wildly voluptuous oysters, the crustacean barbecued with garlic and lemon and butter, wine in vintage crystal, cheese. We return to the boathouse and sleep with the doors open, autumn's chill air on our cheeks, cypress branches crackling in the fire pit outside, the sound of moving water. Joe whispers to me, 'I wish I'd met you twenty years ago.' We are so close in our nakedness I feel we have become one and the world is all before us.

Back on the mainland, we take a road trip. Joe has a meeting in Launceston with a man who has flown in from overseas to look at investment opportunities. Over dinner at an expensive restaurant, I listen as Joe shares with the investor his thoughts on agriculture, export markets and farm finance. I am relieved when the man seems to run out of questions; he signals for the bill and puts out his credit card. Afterwards, as we walk back to our hotel, Joe says he was glad to have me with him. I tell him my sense is that it would be a poor idea to do business with the investor.

In the morning I remember that we have not booked accommodation for our last night in Hobart. While Joe drives I phone a number of hotels, but they are all booked out. Finally I ring the city's priciest hotel; it has a room but it won't be cheap. I hold my hand over the receiver and ask Joe what he thinks. He tells me to book it.

An hour or so later we pull into the hotel driveway. While Joe goes inside to reception, I wait for a parking valet. One appears at my window and tells me the car park is full and we'll have to find a spot on the street. A minute or so later Joe returns from reception; his face has changed – it is cold and angry. I convey the parking information to him and his face darkens further. He tells me to get out of the car. 'Watch this,' he says and stalks across the lobby. I follow at a distance. Joe dumps the car keys on the reception desk and returns to where I'm standing. 'Sorted,' he says. In the lift up to our room, he is silent and glowering, and when I ask him what is wrong he says something about a receptionist's rudeness. I realise I'm feeling a little bit frightened of him. I have not met this man before.

In our suite I stay in the bedroom while he sits in the lounge. The air seems charged with his fury. I have a booking at a hot Hobart restaurant and wonder now what is to become of that. I shower and when I return to the bedroom Joe pulls me towards him and apologises for his mood. 'Let's go out for a drink,' he says. It is the man I know again. Still, when he vanishes into the bathroom, I worry over what has happened. Perhaps it is my fault. Perhaps he thinks the hotel was an unnecessary extravagance. I decide I will pay for drinks and dinner.

Hours later, after I've pulled the bill for the meal towards me and signed the credit-card slip, Joe kisses me. 'I knew you would pay for dinner,' he says.

Once in the past, I asked Joe why he didn't have a credit card and he told me he hated banks and refused to pay credit card fees. Now I realise that if he was able to withdraw only a limited amount of cash at the beginning of our trip, by the time we reached the hotel in Hobart he'd have been running low. So the issue at reception likely related to how he would pay for the room. I still have no idea how he did.

In the early hours of the morning, I'm woken suddenly and roughly. Joe, thrashing and muttering in a nightmare, has hit me in the face.

•

My mother comes to stay with me again and Joe takes us out to dinner. Afterwards, we stop by his ute to pick up a bag of his lamb – a leg, some shanks – from a cold box strapped to the vehicle's tray. The parcel he hands me seems heavy enough to contain a whole sheep. I pretend to slump under the weight of it and he reminds me about the size of dorpers. The next day, I demand my mother's thoughts about him. 'He seems very nice. He's interesting to talk to,' she says. 'But fancy going out for dinner wearing a shirt as crushed as that.'

Not long after this, I meet his children. I am overwhelmed with relief that the meeting is finally taking place, but also terrified. They are shy. Over a suburban Thai meal I do my best. James keeps his head low over his fried rice and is a lost conversational cause. I tell Charlotte that I love her hair: it is long and curly and ever so pretty. She blushes. I ask her about school, and her love for animals, and she murmurs replies. At some stage James says he feels sick and Joe goes with him to the bathroom. I'm conversationally desperate and clumsy now. I ask Charlotte if it's hard to remember to pack everything she needs when she moves between her mother's and father's homes. 'Sometimes,' she says, and blushes again. Father and son have returned to the table during this exchange and Joe now says that they'd better go, the boy is not well. We've barely touched dinner. On the footpath outside the restaurant, we part quickly, but before we do, Joe leans towards me and kisses me on the lips.

In the weeks ahead, he will suggest other child-friendly events and I will dutifully note them in my diary: Sunday night pizza in my neighbourhood on their way home from a weekend at the farm (cancelled); an art gallery outing with Charlotte (cancelled);

and, finally, an invitation to dinner at his house with them. He's had issues with the builder engaged to renovate the house, he says, and the project is at a standstill; when he has custody of the children, they are still living in it.

On the day of the occasion I have been anticipating for so long I am nervous and fidgety. To fill in the hours, I go for a drive. Perhaps I have an instinct for the dramatic, but I end up at that sprawling city of the dead, Rookwood. I've long wanted to find the graves of my mother's great-grandparents, Amelia and Henry. A melancholy Victorian portrait of Amelia hung in my grandparents' home; it haunted me when I was a child. From all I've heard on the family grapevine, hers was another great love story. My mother has a copy of a letter Amelia wrote in 1870: 'Harry is very good and kind to me.' She was twenty-nine then, gravely ill with tuberculosis. She was dead within three years, leaving a distraught Henry and six small children. Decades later, in jewellery class, I made a locket and embedded a miniature of the portrait in the silver. I wear the sorrow of Amelia's story against my skin, my private *memento mori*.

But I can't find the graves. Time has treated the small section where they are recorded to have been buried poorly. The plots have subsided, wind-sheared sandstone headstones lie in pieces amid weeds, and only stray words are legible in the epitaphs carved on those still standing.

I am resigning myself to disappointment when Joe calls. More disappointment. Charlotte is unwell after an asthma attack. We'll need to postpone the milestone dinner. The cemetery suddenly overwhelms me; the wind seems to have picked up and the sky darkened. As I return to my car, I tell myself that this is the price of a relationship with a man who has children; that, when I know them better, I will be by Joe's side when there are problems. I try to console myself with the thought of the Thai meal. Raggedy as it was, it felt like a move towards a greater connection between his life and mine, and in the days ahead I will be reassured when Joe talks to his children from my place. 'Hello, Daddy,' is the little voice I hear coming from his phone one night. Another time he says to someone on the phone he's 'at Stephanie's'. When he gets off the phone I ask who he was talking to. Charlotte, he says. I have an interview with a major footballer who has written a children's book and I give Joe an autographed copy of the book for James. A review copy of a book about animals lands on my desk and I give it to Joe for Charlotte. He tells me they are thrilled with the books and have started to read the articles I write. He texts me one day to say he's been fielding 'exactly one bazillion questions' about me from the children on the way to school. I decide he's getting his budding teenager and her little brother used to the idea of me.

But still I have not seen his house. I worry that perhaps the real reason he hasn't shown it to me is because he's not convinced of his feelings for me, and that if I push him too hard he might pull away. I have another worry: I believe I'm dealing with an extremely delicate situation – a bruised man and his two damaged children – and that I need to tread very carefully if there is a hope of our relationship working. Nevertheless, filled with trepidation, I tell him it's a deal-breaker. 'Yes,' Joe replies calmly. 'I understand.'

ONE EVENING WHEN WE MEET IN the city Joe announces that he needs to go home to pick up his ute before coming back to my apartment for dinner. 'We'll catch a cab there and you can see my place,' he says casually. I don't say anything. I can barely breathe. When we arrive in his suburb, he directs the driver to a spot on a poorly lit residential street and I see then that his Defender is parked just off the street, under a tree. I'm puzzled when Joe motions for me to get into the ute. I didn't see the name of the street, I don't know if it's the same one as that on his drivers' licence, and I'm puzzled – if this isn't where he lives, why is his ute parked here? But I have placed such store in this moment that I dare not ask questions. Joe accelerates slowly for a few hundred metres and then points out a brightly lit house. 'That's Mary's place,' he says. Some months earlier, he told me that after the separation, she had moved into a house close by his; the children use bush tracks to run between the two homes. He also volunteered the information that there was an AVO, an intervention order, in place to stop him going further than Mary's front gate. It was as though he wanted to be straight with me about his history. Instantly alarmed, I asked why. He'd done nothing, he said, absolutely nothing. The worst he'd ever done was send a stack of magazines flying during an argument, but Mary has an uncle who's a police officer and he made Joe's life difficult and facilitated the order. I saw no reason to disbelieve his story. The very fact he had told me about it seemed to indicate the veracity of his version of events. I didn't dwell on it.

Joe drives a little further, then points to the other side of the road. It's dark but I can just make out a driveway. 'My place is down there.'

I try to make my voice light and cheerful. 'So, are we going in?'

'No, not tonight. I'm sorry, not yet.' He tells me that Charlotte has started to ask him whether I've been to the house yet. She's anxious about me. He says the house has been a cocoon for the three of them through these difficult years; it's as much their home as his. He doesn't want to upset them by having me to the house for the first time when they're not there. After what they've been through he needs to protect them.

•

I was so tired, elementally tired. I didn't sleep when he stayed at my place. I was drinking too much. I was off-centre and discombobulated and a hum of unease was with me constantly. There would be a high – a wonderful night, words of affirmation confirming my place in his plans ('I am factoring you into my thinking'), a thrilling suggestion ('Come to Hong Kong with me' – something about an overseas bank account and money from property deals), then a low: another cancellation. I would feel then as though I'd slipped off a cliff edge, fingernails clutching at a crumbling rock face with a chasm below.

A high – we plan a weekend in Melbourne. Don't miss your plane, I say. A low – he misses the plane. I fly without him. When I turn on my phone at Tullamarine Airport there's a text message saying he'll be on the next flight. I wait at an airport cafe, try to practise yoga breathing. I've replied to his text telling him where I'll be, but when he arrives he strides past the cafe, a storm on his face. I grab my bags and chase him.

This June weekend, for the first time he is to meet one of my closest friends, and I am to meet one of his friends. These are the

things Joe has told me about his circle: after the divorce, most of
their friends lined up behind Mary. In any case, he's a loner; he
claims *Walden*, the nineteenth-century American writer Henry
David Thoreau's treatise on a simple life in nature, as his muse.
His two closest friends are Mike, a grazier with a property not so
far from his, and Jill, a friend from his schooldays who now lives
in Melbourne. This weekend we have been invited to dinner at
Jill and her husband's home. On the night of my first date with
Joe, many months earlier, it was Jill's husband who was sitting
on the other side of the bar, the balding man whose eyes I felt
boring into my back. At intervals since, Joe has told me of the
couple's chatter about my arrival in his life. He tells me that they
are insisting on having us for dinner because normally when he
is in Melbourne he takes them out. He asks me not to talk about
his various plans: money is tight for them – once, he bailed Jill's
husband out of debt – and he doesn't want them to feel uncomfortable. I am apprehensive about the scrutiny I will be under,
but delighted too: meeting them is, I feel, another significant
relationship milestone.

Jill and her husband are mixing cocktails when we arrive at
their home in a gentrified inner-Melbourne suburb, and keep
mixing them. There is teasing – 'He's always been flakey' is Jill's
response when I grumble about Joe missing the plane – and escalating laughter. Afterwards, I will think that she seems to know
very little about Joe's life, even the approximate ages of James and
Charlotte, but there seems no doubt about her affection for him.

As Jill starts to serve dinner, the conversation turns to Joe's plans.
Despite the fact he asked me not to bring them up, he seems happy
now to share details about his intriguing unfolding narrative.

Things have accelerated since the day of our drive into the country to visit the Southern Highlands property with the lake. Joe returned with an agronomist, whose subsequent report outlined a productive capacity far greater than Joe expected. He started to throw numbers around, to talk about herd sizes and cropping potential, and I was swept up in his enthusiasm. I built daydreams in which I rode my horse at dawn, turned earth for a vegetable garden, prepared lunches for him with yabbies from the lake and locked myself away to write a book.

Soon after his meeting with the agronomist, Joe announced that he'd put his treasured Southern Tablelands landholding with the shack up for sale and a neighbouring property owner had snapped it up immediately. He told me the small prefabricated house he'd designed for the property was still at the factory and could be moved to the property he eventually bought. Letting the land and shack go filled him with sadness, he said, but he couldn't manage it and the new place. I offered my own lament: 'I never got to see it!'

It soon became clear, though, that buying a new property was not a straightforward matter. One day he told me he'd missed out on the place with the lake – Chinese buyers had gazumped him, grabbing the land for its underground gas reserves. For a while he talked about another option – Mike was leaning on him to buy a landholding adjacent to his farm – but then he said it had been sold ahead of the auction. 'That's ridiculous,' I said. 'You expressed an interest; why wouldn't they have given you the chance to make a counter-offer?' Joe shrugged. He had no idea, he said. When I asked him what had happened about the land near the remote beach where we stayed earlier in the year, he told me the owner had withdrawn it from sale. And, on top of that, he'd discovered commercial flights would no longer service the alpine area where he'd been planning to build his little stone chalet.

Now, over Jill's tagine and glasses of red, Joe starts to tell the couple about a new property he has visited several times and which he's entered negotiations to buy. It's another Southern Highlands concern – I'll call it Happy Valley – of considerable lush acreage, cattle, a mansion, a self-contained flat in one wing, a fishing shack, dams, a commercial vineyard and an olive grove, peacocks. In this company, I try to appear a disinterested party in the purchase process and its outcome. But the truth is, I'm anything but. In phone calls, a friend and I have laughed about the idea of me as lady of the manor. Joe has revealed so much of the story and its hurdles (water rights issues, subdivision possibilities, council issues, contract inclusions) that I feel almost equipped to take over the negotiations.

These are the things Joe has told me: the wealthy owner of Happy Valley, a notable fashion designer, is unwell; the farm manager, the man responsible for breeding prize-winning cows, is going through a messy divorce. I know by name and anecdote two of the real estate agents involved, and the name of another investor, Liam, with whom Joe is vying to buy the property. I have seen an email from the owner's minder breaking down the components of the total price – the olive oil, wine, stock and furniture – and heard Joe's complaints about that price.

As Jill's husband clears our plates, Joe talks about his concerns that he knows nothing about the olive oil and wine businesses. One day recently he brought back samples of the estate's wine and olive oil and I sought out expert opinion: my brother, a sommelier, tasted the wines, judging them to be only average. I asked an Italian chef I know if he had time to share his thoughts on the olive oil, and one morning Joe and I sat with him in his restaurant while he sniffed and slurped the oil, finally declaring it to be ordinary. Joe showed me new name and packaging ideas for the wine and oil – some 'branding chaps' he knew had done a proposal for him. Tell me honestly what you think, he asked.

He started to talk about furnishing the house and I suggested he contact the stylist who had designed a string of restaurants, including the stylish city establishment where my brother works. In an antique shop Joe spent half an hour studying a seventeenth-century, twenty-seat oak dining table with a $35,000 price tag. He crouched on the floor and looked at its workmanship. 'Yes,' he said, and I thought he'd decided to buy it. A minute or so later he said he'd give it some thought. In a vintage emporium he sat and examined a strange antique contraption that he decided was a hand-made, gas-fired bird scarer. It was $250. He bought it as an ironic ornament for Happy Valley. We loaded it into my car.

I hadn't even seen the estate, but he seemed to have wrapped me up in his plans for it and secured the package tightly with a bow: he asked me if I'd like the study next to his or the one down the corridor. He wanted me to write. 'I want you to bloom.' He said he was putting the property's land in his children's trust fund, but the house itself would be in his name so Mary couldn't cause trouble if I lived with him there.

One night sometime after our dinner with Jill and her husband, I was falling asleep when I heard what seemed to be a sob. I rolled over and embraced him. He'd never thought, he said, that he'd find someone who wanted to share a country life with him.

•

Act I. Joe's mother is returning from New Zealand, where she has been staying with his sister. Her flight is due in around 4 pm. The plan is that she will go from the airport to his place and stay overnight to mind James and Charlotte so Joe and I can go out for dinner. Around 2.30 he texts to say his mother's flight might be delayed.

Act II. Around 4 pm he rings to say she won't be in until late that night and he'll have to stay with his children.

Act III. At 8.15 pm a text lands announcing that he and his sister have dropped into the restaurant where my brother works. My brother has been 'beyond the perfect host', Joe says. He suggests he and I take his mother there for a meal one day. The sweetener of his suggestion does nothing to stop the anxiety response that rips through me.

I do a search on 'New Zealand airports' and there are indeed widespread flight delays, but I'm still hysterical with questions. *I didn't know your sister was in Sydney, I thought your mother was visiting her in New Zealand, how could she get on a flight if your mother couldn't, who's looking after your children?* And . . . *is the woman you're with really your sister?*

I text him with a reply. 'Forgive me for being confused.' His response is as neat and light as the restaurant's dumplings. According to Joe, his mother is now due in at 10 that night. His sister has been having marital problems and made a spontaneous decision that when her mother returned to Sydney she'd come too for a break. She managed to get an earlier flight. He decided to take her to the restaurant so he could look at the notable stylist's design work. A neighbour's teenager popped in to mind his children.

I turn my phone off. I wash down a Valium with a glass of wine. I sleep, but the night is cut through with sinister dreams and moments of wide-eyed despair. In the morning my bedclothes are in chaos. I drag myself to a vertical position and call my brother. He is annoyed with me. Joe told him the woman was his sister. 'Of course it was his sister,' my brother snaps, adding that the body language was of sister and brother and he overheard conversational fragments suggesting they were discussing their mother.

I write one of my lists. 'Why I should stop worrying.'

- He knows my brother works at that restaurant.
- There *were* delays with New Zealand flights.
- My brother said they were clearly brother and sister.
- If he was going to take another woman, a woman who wasn't his sister, out to dinner, why would he go to the restaurant where my brother works?
- We had talked about the work of the stylist and he wanted to see it.

I fill a page. I stand in the shower for an eternity. I push the temperature up and up, desperate for warmth. Somehow, I make it into the office.

I confide in a close colleague who happens to work for Fairfax Media's investigative team. 'Let's do some title searches on him,' she suggests. I shake my head, roll on my chair back to my desk.

'No, no,' I say. 'I have to trust him.' This isn't a story; this is a love affair. Snooping would be a betrayal.

MY BED, A SATURDAY MORNING, JULY 2015: Joe wakes, sits upright, says he has to go. I've barely seen him for the past fortnight and have been excited about spending the weekend with him. 'I just need to be alone. I need to sit on my boat for a bit,' he says. I present as a millpond of serenity. He kisses me goodbye. 'I want to ask you a question soon,' he says.

He is gone. My apartment is silent and cold. I ball up and think of *Walden* and how Joe wrote in his dating profile that he sometimes needed to escape the world, but he always came back. At some point down the track I ask him what feeling he gets to make him need to escape. 'It's an enormous weight,' he says.

I try not to think about this question he might soon ask me – it would surely lead to disappointment were I to build up my hopes about what he could have meant.

It is days before I hear from him again. I do not manage well through that time. I visit my doctor and leave the surgery wearing sunglasses.

I have dinner at my brother's place and suffocate the conversation with my fears. 'Stop stressing,' my brother says.

'You're going to ruin it,' his wife says. I sign up for a Buddhist meditation course.

I WAS A SLAVE. BOTH TO THE DANGLING promises of Joe's intriguing unfolding narrative and my own sense of self-doubt. *Forelsket* had started all this, but now, immersed in intimacy, in hope for the future, extrication barely registered as a thought. If I didn't push, if I didn't ask too many questions, if I remained calm and loving, if I was patient with the complexities and challenges and hiccups of his life, the day would come that he would see into my heart, recognise my worthiness and finally break the bubble that separated our lives.

Then I might finally meet his mother. She wants to meet you, he told me. 'When am I going to meet your leftie journo?' is what he told me she'd said. One day he suggested that maybe we could visit her that afternoon. 'I'll ring her,' he said, and tapped a number into his phone. He talked for a minute or two and when he finished the call he said she was having lunch at a friend's home in the mountains but might be back in the city early enough for us to visit her that evening. I nudged him a couple of hours later. He called her again. She'd decided to stay in the mountains.

If I didn't push, if I was patient, he might take me to see the vintage wooden pleasure cruiser he was renovating. One Saturday he told me the boat builders were nearly finished their work on it and we'd be able to see it that day. Through the afternoon he made three phone calls to inquire about the work's progress. At the end of each call, he said the builders weren't ready for us. Another couple of hours, he said, explaining in some detail the challenges of a particular bit of joinery. After the last call he said the boat wouldn't be ready to visit that day after all.

If I didn't push, he might take me to see Happy Valley, which I'd dared to start thinking might be my future home.

JOE WON'T MAKE IT BACK TO the city for the dinner we'd planned. His offer for Happy Valley has been accepted and he's down at the property discussing which furniture and fittings will be included in the contract. The owner has opened a bottle of wine, then another, and is sharing his hopes, dreams and disappointments. He wants Joe to reassure him that he will continue what has been started and not let the place fall into the hands of 'cowards' who will divide it into weekenders. I ask him where he will stay. He's not sure. 'Slightly misty eyed atm.' He says the owner made a vague mention that he could bed down in the fishing shack or the flat. Dinner is being prepared.

In a message to a small group of friends on Facebook I lament how I pine; how I wait for him, forlorn and anxious. 'I know I'm doing *that thing* women do,' I say. 'I'm pathetic.'

My friend Alecia replies. 'I just read your post about you standing on the beach, wringing your hands and gazing at the trackless sea as you wait for your lover's ship to appear. It's such a grand misfortune this desire and love thing. We really must cocktail soon to get to the bottom of it. In the meantime, put your phone away. Sorry to be bossy, but I've so been there and they are wasted hours that you'll never get back.'

If I'd put my phone away I wouldn't have got his messages.

His daughter has had a fall and fractured her sternum.

The Defender has a flat tyre.

His dorpers are agisted at Happy Valley until settlement and one day the truck moving sheep here or there tips over on a bend and there is chaos.

A tree has blown down on a fence and the sheep are wandering.

I joke with Joe about my suspicions. In traffic one day I take a photograph of an advertisement on the back of a taxi for a private detective agency – Spousebusters – and text it to him. In some conversational context, he tells me he's a terrible liar. 'I go red,' he says. But as the year wears on, it becomes harder to joke. I am drowning in my anxiety and all that is left of me is my arms reaching above a waterline. I remind him of the effect his cancellations have on me. 'Are you playing me?' I ask him one day.

'No, I am not.'

'I need you to look after me – and I don't mean financially.'

'I know,' he says, pulling me towards him and kissing my forehead. 'I want you to tell me when you're feeling anxious.'

I return repeatedly to my psychologist and her tissue box and, through my snuffling, smell the musty pain of all the people who have slumped in this chair before me. We probe a chicken-and-egg, mountains-out-of-molehills riddle: is Joe's unreliability a spur to my anxiety, or is my anxiety turning small stuff into big dramas in my head that could sabotage the relationship? She knows how much I have wanted a relationship. She knows of my anxiety in certain family relationship situations. Sometimes she stands and draws diagrams on her whiteboard to describe the anomalies of my emotions. Sometimes she sits and without taking her eyes from my face taps on her laptop as I talk. She's not seeing red flags, she concludes. Children, ex-wife, farm, business, real estate – a degree of unpredictability is to be expected. It is not a world you are familiar with, it will throw up surprises, she says.

Yet there are things my psychologist cannot know: our sessions do not allow time for the sharing of the minutiae of the relationship, the to-and-fro of messages in text and word, the nuances of his language and declarations, the details that build up in increments to form a picture, the expressions on his face.

My testimony is hasty and impassioned and I do not remember everything I told her. I don't remember the vital signs I forgot to mention.

Leo, my mid-forties friend who chooses his shags from a teeming market of depilated younger women, knows more than my psychologist and me put together. He doesn't even need to know the details. One night we meet at a sushi bar in my neighbourhood. I pour my heart out to him. 'Steph,' he says, dipping into a bowl of edamame. 'How long are you going to let this go on for?'

•

But Joe and I were in this together, weren't we? And finally he wanted to take me to see Happy Valley. With his sheep in the property's paddocks, the owner was letting him use the fishing shack until settlement. He'd even bought me a pair of Ugg boots, which were waiting for me there, he said.

One Saturday lunchtime towards the end of winter, we stood in my hallway, hoisting bags up, ready to go. Packed: Blundstones, food to cook in the shack for dinner, red wine. I opened the front door. Joe's phone rang.

He listened to someone on the end of the phone. His face paled. He pulled the phone away from his ear. 'James has slipped and hit his head,' he said. The boy had been running around a friend's pool. 'He's in an ambulance on the way to hospital.'

'Go,' I said. 'Now.' And he was gone. His kelpie stayed with me. She circled and sniffed and whimpered.

He texted me from the hospital. James was concussed and they were keeping an eye on him. Charlotte was with a friend.

Mary, who he'd thought was looking after them, was not to be found. 'I think you might benefit from a cup of tea or coffee with some sugar in it,' I messaged him.

The dog and I had a long, quiet afternoon, interrupted only by the ping of Joe's text updates and phone calls: Mary was on her way, he'd stay with James until she arrived. She'd want to take over, he'd be pushed aside in the drama no doubt. Perhaps we might still be able to get away, he suggested. He texted me a photograph – a skull, a kangaroo skull, I think. 'How to educate a boy about skulls,' he captioned it. Later he would say he'd had it in the back of his ute and had taken it into the hospital to amuse James.

Hours passed. Mary was taking forever to reach the hospital. And then a subplot emerged: the boy had actually fallen because he'd been dizzy, a side-effect of inflamed adenoids. Mary had undertaken to organise for them to be removed but hadn't followed through. Joe had talked about the boy's adenoids before. Now they would be extracted tonight. Could he be operated on while concussed, I asked. It wasn't an issue, came the reply.

Joe returned to my place as dusk folded over my courtyard, where I'd been playing with his dog. Mary had arrived at the hospital but, he said, he needed to wait just a little bit longer before he felt comfortable about leaving for Happy Valley. We sat in my lounge room. Perhaps we watched some television. My thoughts were scattered and uneasy. Eventually Joe disappeared into my study to call the hospital. I couldn't help but hear his side of the conversation. 'Oh yes,' he said. 'She's behaved like this before. Yes. It's tough. Yes. Yes, there is a history of this. I'm sorry. Yes.' He returned to the lounge room. Mary was making a scene at the hospital and abusing the staff. They were going to throw her out. He would have to return to his son's bedside.

IN THE DAYS THAT FOLLOWED, I wrote more lists. About why he wasn't lying and why I should trust him and why I didn't need to be anxious. I considered a multiplicity of arguments and factors, events and circumstances, words and deeds. I wrote another list. I called it 'reasons to calm down'.

- Because 80% of the time he turns up when he says he will.
- He's said that after the school holidays we'll get into a routine.
- He's said he's planning to get a nanny so he doesn't have to rush off to attend to dramas with children, and at Happy Valley he'll have a farm manager.
- Because last month he said he'd been like a kid waiting for a party, itching to see me and engrossed in the thought of me.
- Because when we went out last week he said he wanted to show me off.
- Because if he wasn't into me, he wouldn't be hanging around.
- Because he talks frequently about the importance of honesty as a quality.

I had driven myself into a frenzy of worry that the reason Joe had not shown me his house was because he might doubt his feelings for me. But, thinking about the farms, how the purchase of one after the other had fallen over, that he had not shown me his city home or Happy Valley, another thought pushed itself forward. Could he be a *fantasist*? As quickly as the idea came to me, I shoved it away: who in the world would have the time and energy and motivation to weave such an extraordinarily detailed deceit?

•

Spring was nearly with us and Joe's various investment and property schemes seemed to be hurtling towards a climax. He appeared larger, more confident. When he bent his head to kiss my forehead, I felt his tenderness was suffused with a new strength. But perhaps I was imagining things. Perhaps I was imagining everything.

One Saturday he left his dog with me and went into the city for a meeting at which the final details of the south coast land sale were to be hammered out. He and his business partners, whom I still had not met, were selling their option on the land to a Chinese ball-bearing billionaire. Joe had told me the name of the Chinese businessman and his Australian agent, and the city tower in which he had his office where the meeting of lawyers and negotiators would take place.

Late in the afternoon he returned to my place and I started to finish the preparations for dinner – Chinese beef short ribs. They'd been braising for hours in a rich stock. Around 7, just as they sizzled to a crescendo under the grill and I reduced stock for a sauce, Joe took a phone call. He spoke for a minute or two, then stood up. The meeting was resuming, he said, signatures would be on paper before the end of the night. He had a special lucky pen that he used for such occasions, he said, as I kissed him goodbye.

I ate my ribs alone. Text messages arrived through the night from the city tower boardroom: burgers had been ordered in, rice wine was being opened, could I recommend a yum cha restaurant? Around 10.30, Joe texted to say he was half an hour away. At 11.30 I replied asking if he was still alive. He did not reply. I fell asleep, the sad-sick feeling enveloping me again. At 1.30 am my phone buzzed. He was finished now, he said, and would look for a cab. Around 2, he returned. Since the meeting had finished hours earlier with the signing of contracts, he said he'd been wandering around the city in a daze, barely able to comprehend the magnitude of what he had earned. He snuggled into me and kissed my neck.

THERE WAS ONE OUTSTANDING ISSUE TO be resolved before Joe's life could settle down. He was still consumed by the process of buying Happy Valley, and consumed by doubt. The property was too big, too much, too complicated. It would require him to poke his head up and build his profile in order to market the wine and olive oil, products about which he knew nothing. One night when I was expecting him for dinner, he texted to say he was staying down at the fishing shack. He said he was considering changing his approach to what he would do with the property after settlement. He was feeling anxious because it felt as though he was heading down 'the path of ego, which is not me'; he was concerned he was going to get carried away with 'the largesse of it all'. He finished the text by saying he hoped he made some sense and that he wasn't giving me too much frustration.

Frustration was the incorrect word for my state of mind. I was all jagged edges and sharp corners. I had started to jump at sudden noises. When I looked in the mirror I saw someone else, a pallid, puffy-faced shadow of myself.

In August, an article appeared in the real estate pages announcing that Happy Valley had been sold to Liam, the rival investor about whom Joe had talked on multiple occasions. He rang me swearing; the journalist had been fed fake information, he said. My anxiety spiked. I emailed the *Herald*'s property editor and asked if he had time for me to drop by his desk for a chat. And then I lost my nerve; I took Joe's explanation for the article and stashed it away and tried not to think about it.

And I kept putting a smile on my face for him. I smiled when he told me he had the final agreement in his hands and was 'skipping around'; when one settlement date after another fell over; and when he repeatedly said he was returning to the property to negotiate contract inclusions that he'd told me he'd already negotiated.

But when he told me one day in September that today we would definitely visit Happy Valley, I obediently climbed up into his Defender. Joe turned the ignition on, but before pulling away from the kerb, he reached across and felt around in the dashboard in front of me. I wasn't paying attention. I was trying to calm his dog at my feet. I was thinking about the state of the car – the seat under me was ripped and torn and covered with dog hair and crumbling foam and a filthy cushion.

'Oh,' he said. I shifted the focus of my attention to his outstretched hand. He was holding something, a brass cylinder, a bullet. 'I shouldn't have left that there with you in the car.' He made some comment about foxes. I asked him then where he was keeping his guns; after all, I joked, you're a homeless farmer now. The guns were in Mike's gun safe, he said. And then, a small correction. 'I'm a grazier, not a farmer.'

WE DROVE INTO THE COUNTRY. But on the highway, Joe sped past the turn-off to Happy Valley. First, he said, he wanted to show me J–, another property he'd inspected half an hour further south. It was frill-free but large and its lovely watercourse tumbled into a national park; some weeks before, he'd sent me a picture of the property's gorge and waterhole.

J– was his fallback should the Happy Valley deal fail. Today, though, he'd not arranged with the real estate agent to visit, so we sat in his ute on the edge of the property and he talked about its advantages. To me it looked harsh and barren. But it was proper sheep country, he told me. Sheep go better on brown, he said.

We drove back up the highway. Joe was hungry now. He stopped in a village and bought sandwiches. I thought then that I knew what would happen next. The phone would ring. He would need to return to the city. A child would be sick. A business deal would need his urgent attention. He was still not sure of his feelings for me and so would not take me to Happy Valley today. He turned the ignition on and pulled back out on to the highway. The dog squirmed. My backside ached. Wind whistled in through a gap in the door. I considered what I had in my fridge for dinner. And then the thin white needle on the round dashboard speedometer jerked backwards, the indicator clicked, the ute slowed. Joe turned off the highway again. A lush landscape opened up before us: a sweep up a long driveway, willow trees leaning close to a dam, a shield of closely grown pines, a glimpse of a steeply pitched roofline and dormer windows.

He pulled the ute into a driveway behind the house near a massive shed and a man wandered out. It was, I discovered, the farm manager going through the messy divorce. They had a brief conversation. It seemed Happy Valley's owner was home but unwell. We wouldn't disturb him then, Joe said, we wouldn't go in. He said goodbye to the manager and pulled away. He took a different route off the property, jumping out to open and close a gate, and then driving cross-country through a paddock. His phone buzzed. It was the manager. The owner wanted to see him, he said. Joe turned the ute around and drove back to the house.

I FOLLOWED JOE INTO THE HOUSE through a back door and down a passage. He stopped at the entrance to a large room. I hung back. I could see a grey-haired man in an armchair. But my attention was suddenly divided: a small, elegant woman had appeared beside me. She was asking me if I'd like to see the house. It was the fashion designer's wife.

I followed her as she led me away from Joe, chattering along corridors and into rooms bigger than my apartment, with stone fireplaces bigger than my bathroom and up stairs and down other corridors. Much of it is a blur now; I had seen the photographs, but the scale and ornamentation of the house that Joe had been negotiating to buy for months, and the fact he had finally brought me here, had thrown me into an altered consciousness. I heard the words the woman was saying but they weren't leading to coherent thoughts. I could hear her telling me about the packing progress. I could see the strewn boxes. I could see the open armoires two or more metres high filled with white linen. I could see the paintings, off the walls and leaning one against the other. I could see the French provincial style, the multiple living spaces, the fine bedrooms, another and another, but nothing made sense.

I looked at the rooms and I looked at the woman's hands. I couldn't stop looking at the woman's hands. She was, I thought, maybe seventy, maybe more. But her hands were those of a younger woman: elegant, slender, tanned and bearing multiple rings. Gold, rose gold. A thick ring like a man's signet ring, more petite rings on other fingers. Matched, but not matching. Refined, not gaudy. I was transfixed by the woman's hands. I tuned in to what she was saying. 'I don't know what's happening; I don't know what's going on.' It was clear she was talking about the property sale. 'I hope Joe gets it.'

And then suddenly he was at my side. He suggested we should look at the garden. He led me down a spiral staircase to a hallway, then out onto lawn. He showed me the vegetable parterre. It was circular, surrounded by a hedge, neglected. I held his hand and thought of what I could plant there. We returned to the car. We drove back down the driveway. Joe pointed out paddocks stretching into the distance speckled with his sheep. Perhaps he made some comment about the lushness of the grass and the drenching they would need. I don't recall. I do recall the dead beast we passed as we left the property, flyblown, head stretched at an odd angle, legs spread. It was one of Joe's. A fox had got it. He stopped the ute a few metres past the carcass and picked up his phone. He told the person at the end of the line to get rid of it as soon as possible. He finished the call and drove off again. The farm manager was on to it, he said. Bloody wily foxes.

'I COULD DO THIS ALL DAY,' Joe said, as we bumped down a rough country road between Canberra and the Hume Highway. I took his statement to mean driving in the country, where asphalt dissolves into dirt, soaking up the landscape: hilly, grazing land on either side of the road, sheep, an occasional rough property, the bony remains of ringbarked trees. A fortnight earlier we'd visited Happy Valley. Now we were on a multi-purpose trip: he needed to visit the real estate agent connected to the big land deal he'd first told me about, to address some matters, then we would head to his friend Mike's place to help with some farm work. Shearing? Crutching? I don't recall.

For an hour or so I wandered the streets of the town where the real estate agency had its office while Joe had his meeting, then we drove out to see the land. At the end of a suburban street lined with brick-veneer houses, he pulled off the road. Fenced-off vacant land stretched up a wooded hillside. Joe dug around in the dashboard. He was looking for the key to the lock on the gate in front of us. 'I hope I haven't left it behind,' he said. He found it, jumped out of the ute, unlocked the padlock and returned to the car. He drove on to the land. He stopped a little way beyond the gate to show me a patch of flowers, a little native daisy – the

Hoary Sunray, *Leucochrysum albicans*. He had been telling me about the flower for a while; it had 'endangered' status and local conservationists had mounted a court challenge to the housing estate he and his partners planned for the land. We had laughed about the name, about the impact of such a pretty little thing, its layered white flowers circling a dense yellow centre. Joe said the conservationists' argument was wrong and it wasn't under threat. I picked a flower and when I got back in the car perched it on the dashboard in front of me. What do you get a man who has everything? As we drove back down the suburban street, I thought that I might ask an artist friend if she would take a commission to paint a little watercolour of the flower. An ironic Christmas present for a man who knew the name of almost any plant at which you cared to point.

Now we were back on the road, on the way to Mike's place. Joe put his earpiece in; his phone must have buzzed in his lap. He had a brief conversation. It was clear that our plans would be changing. The farm work at Mike's was all finished, he said. They didn't need our help after all. We'd go instead to look at his old property, the land and the shack. We would spend the night at the motel.

I looked across at him in aquiline profile. Briefly, he turned his face from the road and smiled. 'You're the first woman I've ever taken there,' he said.

5

TWO WEDDINGS AND A FUNERAL

It is a joyful celebration. The grooms wear matching French-blue tuxedo blazers with contrasting black lapels. One wears a lopsided grey bow tie; the other, the muscle-proud, aesthetically adept of the pair, a black one that sits straight. The MC is one of the wittiest writers in the country. The guests have come from Sydney, New Zealand, France and Singapore, a collection of bright young minds. The cake is topped with two yellow rubber ducks in black top hats and tails. The photographer catches laughter and big hugs and small girls in pretty red and pink princess dresses and the grooms sliding gold bands on to each other's young hands.

Among the photographs in an online album are a few of me. I'm reacting to the speeches: in one shot my mouth is wide open laughing; in another I'm smiling broadly and affectionately, the way you do when two good people you love have just shared their determination to spend the rest of their lives together.

Now, I have trouble understanding these photographs. It seems impossible I was upright at any point during that Saturday evening in October 2015. It seems even more impossible my brain could command my mouth to activate a smile. I zoom in on my face in one of those photos to measure the integrity of my smile. The mask of make-up does not conceal the hot red evidence of my distress, my eyes' crimson trails, the swollen lids. Someone should have evicted me from that celebration, for I moved through it like a modern-day Magwitch, dragging a ball and chain of misery.

Some time after the beef or chicken, but before the grooms lay their hands over each other's on a sword to cut the cake, I flee. The wedding is in a hotel on Townsville's esplanade and I cross the road to the rocky shoreline. Kissing Point is to the north of me, Magnetic Island ahead, and some 2000 kilometres to the south lie Joe and the shoals of his intriguing unfolding narrative. Twelve hours earlier, he stood me up at Sydney Airport. Now it is as though my skin has been peeled back and a searing emulsification of every last salty teardrop, every burning moment of anxiety and stress, every prickling doubt of the past fourteen months has been applied to my raw flesh. I am a ball of pain and panic.

HE HAS, OF COURSE, PRODUCED A compelling three-act play. It starts with a prologue – the invitation addressed to 'Stephanie and Guest'. In those three words I see a sonnet. To be guests together at a wedding is surely a relationship milestone. But I do not push. I tell Joe of the event and book my own flight north.

I say nothing for weeks until an RSVP is required. One night when we're lounging on my couch I ask him if he can come. 'Oh yes,' he says, 'I can.'

'Shall I book your flight?' Casual. Don't dare reveal the pleasure this gives.

'No, no, I'll do it now,' waving his phone at me. 'I'll do it on here.'

I give him the flight details. 'Done,' he says a little later.

We are to fly on the Saturday morning. Joe stays with me on the Thursday night. On the Friday morning before we leave my apartment he holds me in a bear hug in my living room. Quietly, nervously, I ask him a question: 'Is it wrong to tell you that at the back of my mind I'm thinking of a life together?'

'No,' he replies, 'it's at the front of my mind.'

Over breakfast at the butterfly cafe Joe outlines his plans for the day: he will go home to pick up his suit, drop the dog at the kennels, visit his lawyer to deal with paperwork related to the Happy Valley deal, then be back at my place for dinner. He leaves his eggs to take a call outside and returns laughing: he's been telling his business partner about the wedding and now he knows what we should have got the boys as a gift – a lava lamp. I raise my eyebrows at his perception of a sophisticated gay couple's tastes and suggest he pack the nice blue-green-check shirt I gave him recently.

And then Act I. Totally weird shit. Mid-afternoon he calls. He's left the lawyer's office to take his dog for a walk. My stomach drops. 'I thought you were taking her to the kennels earlier?' I ask. 'Oh yes, I did, I got confused.' The heat has got to him, he says, and he's come outside for some air. It's likely he might be at the lawyer's later than expected. The weirdness escalates over the following hours with a volley of text messages. He's pulling out of the deal for Happy Valley and buying J– instead, so he'll be delayed at the lawyer's dealing with paperwork. I have half an hour or so to mourn the life I will not now have at Happy Valley before the next message arrives. He has to pick James up from the school disco and drop him at Mary's. Mary isn't home. It's late by now. He tells me to go to sleep, that he'll sort out 'this latest bit of WTF'. On and off through a night of shattered sleep, I reach for my mobile phone. A blank screen.

At 6.46 am the curtain lifts on Act II. 'And?' I text him. A minute later his reply lands: he's dropping off the children then will be on his way. Momentarily I relax. He'll be at my place in time. I shower, finish packing, have a coffee, but with each minute of silence my state of unease builds. At 8.24 I text him again. 'Am I going on my own?' A minute later he answers to say that he'll meet me at the airport. I tell him I feel unwell. My stomach seems weighted with jagged stones; I have the sense that the air I'm breathing is running over corrugations as it makes its way to my lungs. He replies telling me not to stress. I try to call him before I leave my apartment, and again in the taxi on the way to the airport. Each time, his phone goes to voicemail. At check-in I ask the woman behind the counter if the seat next to mine can be reserved for my friend, who is running late. She asks what name the booking is under. She looks at her screen, then glances at me with an odd expression. She makes some remark about privacy regulations. She can't tell me anything else, she says, and suggests I try calling my friend again. Joe's phone goes to voicemail.

In Act III I fly alone, huddled in a window seat. His text pings when I turn on my phone in Townsville around midday. 'Rebooking,' it says. I ask him to call me. My phone stays silent. I check into my hotel and curl up in a ball. My phone stays silent. His last text arrives at 3 pm. He's still in Sydney – 'stuck'. He can't call just now – his ex is being incredibly selfish and his children are caught in her turmoil. 'I'm very, very sorry.'

•

Dahlink,

I just fear that you're prolonging the inevitable. Fuck the oscillations and tempestuous feelings. You deserve to have someone who utterly adores you and who meets all of your needs – someone who commits. And they need to actually do this, not just to say that they will.

Love, Alecia

It was time, but it wasn't. Still I was unable to give up on the fairytale. I was the sucker at the bottom of the pyramid scheme, the fool thinking crystals can cure cancer, as silly as one of Joe's sheep. At some point I heard a radio interview with a woman who had lived through domestic violence. 'I was addicted to hope,' she said, attempting to explain why she stayed so long in her relationship.

Joe vanishes. In emails and text messages I ask him to call me. Days pass before he replies to my messages. 'I'm asking, just bear with me for a bit.' He's 'all over the shop'. He isn't getting things right with his children. He is thinking of me.

I try to keep working. I have stories to write, deadlines to meet. I drag myself from bed to shower to bus to desk. I stare at my screen and see nothing, try to re-focus my eyes and thoughts and find only fog. My hands are heavy on the keyboard; I type an ugly word, a clumsy sentence, then tap in slow motion backwards to delete. I pick up the phone and put it back down again. I keep my head low over my keyboard and fight tears. My editor sits ten paces away; I email him with faux excuses for my slowness. Joe, his story, this story, this pain pulse through my brain's every cell. There are no other stories.

One day I crumple. I'm at my desk, hunched over my keyboard, aware of the office chatter around me. Someone's child said something hilarious; someone's partner is taking them to Bhutan, where the government measures 'gross national happiness'; someone else is planning their Christmas beach holiday with their family. I am nothing, have nothing. There is now under my skin, running through my body, up my forearms and into my biceps, an insufferable tingle, a hot rushing swoosh. I haven't eaten. I am jelly. I grit my teeth, bite my tongue. Not here. Tears spill. I push back at them. I lower my head until it's almost touching my keyboard and thrust tissues at my eyes. Stop, not now. I reach for my bag, pull out compact, foundation, concealer, attempt a repair job. Breathe. Focus. Story. Screen. Focus. Breathe, yoga breathing. But my tear ducts are bursting. I run. Sunglasses. Bag. Corridor. Lift. Taxi. Home. Keys. Hallway. Door. As it closes behind me, I erupt. Heaving, gasping, choking.

I sleep for the day and the night. When I wake, it's all there again – the confusion, the uncertainty, the anxiety, the silence. 'The telephone becomes an instrument of torture in the demonic hands of a beloved who doesn't ring,' Alain de Botton writes in *Essays in Love*. My hair is lank, my weight is dropping. I email my boss with excuses for my absence. I call my mother, my weary friends, my brother. I lie in bed and listen to the spring rain. I lie in bed and listen to the radio. An Afghan asylum seeker has set fire to himself in Melbourne; a little girl whose remains were found in a suitcase dumped by the side of the road in South Australia has been identified; father-and-son murderers have been arrested. I crawl two, three times a day into brimming tubs of water close to scalding and sink into that womb until the temperature goes cold.

Two weeks after the wedding, on the last day of October, Joe emails me. 'Hello, I miss you terribly,' he writes. He's sorry. He's 'making sure of many things' during the next few days. He's nervous, but 'I know now I love you'. I read the last six words over and over. It is the fix I needed.

•

Sallie Belling is dying. For some months I have been working on a story about Sallie, a woman whose life and body have been ravaged by heroin. Her friends call her Mustang Sallie. She is forty-six years old. She has lived on the streets. Sold her body for drugs. Been in love. One day she tells me about her husband, Mark. 'The way he treated me, it was like I was the only princess on the planet.' She tells me they got married in a registry office and for their honeymoon shot up and went camping. But Mark died of cancer, and now Sallie is dying too: her kidneys are stuffed and only dialysis is keeping her alive. She is still using heroin. 'I think of it when I first wake up and it's the last thing I think of before I go to bed.'

I meet Sallie at the Wayside Chapel in Kings Cross. I take her to a cafe, where she orders steak and mashed potatoes. One day I sit with her in a hospital unit while she has dialysis. She's bedraggled and emits a scent of stale urine and old sweat. Sallie has lost everything – her dignity, her hope, her teeth – but she still has her story. She tells me about her twelve siblings; about her sister who is in jail and her brother who has transitioned to become a sister. She tells me about her stepfather, who started touching her when she was seven, the baby he fathered, whom she gave birth to when she was twelve and who was adopted out, and another baby she gave birth to years later, Anthony. Her mother stole Anthony from her when he was a toddler. Sallie wanted to raise him herself but her mother wouldn't let her. Sallie hated her mother. Now Anthony is at university, but she doesn't see him. She tells me about her life as a sex-worker: she preferred bondage work – 'fuck-all sex involved' – and it paid better. One client liked her to 'massage' him with her stilettos; another wore a slave outfit and cleaned her kitchen on his hands and knees with a toothbrush.

Sallie is dying and I'm running out of time to know her and her story. One day, in the middle of Joe's vanishing, I force myself to call her and arrange another meeting. I haul myself up, choke on a piece of toast, scrape my hair back into a greasy ponytail and catch a cab to the Cross. At Wayside, no one's seen Sallie. A tall woman with fluffy hair and a broad face looms at my side. 'I thought you looked sad; I thought you need a hug,' she says. Her face is lopsided and her eyes dart. She pulls me close. 'I love you but I don't know you.' She offers me a lolly from a red-and-white-striped tube.

My friend Graham Long, then the Wayside pastor, comes by. He has known something of my story and my despair. He hugs me and I burst into tears. We sit for a while and talk, with the life and chaos and pain of the Wayside crowd swirling around us. A dispute flares up: the woman with the red-and-white-striped lolly tube who loves me is in the middle of it. Voices are raised, chests puffed up, insults thrown. The row settles. The woman hisses last words at someone's back. 'Fucking toe-rag.'

•

November, and Joe's silence continues. I am dragging myself towards an acceptance of the idea that the situation can't continue. I text him to say that if he can't talk to me and explain his behaviour, it's over. I tell him I will return the pearls, and ask where I can send them. My message is determined and final; in truth I feel anything but, and when his reply lands the next day, my foolish heart flies out to him, wherever he is. 'I am sorry that I chose this moment to fall to bits.' He says he's pulling himself back together, but some days are 'very dark'. I had thought of him as reasonably mentally robust – this is the first glimmer that perhaps he's not. I email him to tell him I want to be there for him but he has to let me in. We're in the territory now of that common error, the ambivalent ending.

In a text message sent in the early hours of the morning a few days later, he adds a melodramatic flourish to our fragmented conversation. He wants me to keep the pearls. I can throw them back in the ocean if I really don't want them. Three-quarters of an hour later, he hits 'send' on an email to me. He is a poor sleeper and when I open it and see the time it was sent – 2.32 am – and read the contents, I worry again about his mental state. He wants to be with me, he says. But – 'and here's the big one' – he's damaged goods, not good for anyone. He's in the country pulling himself together and 'wondering how it is that people can be such utter shits to each other'. He promises to call.

He doesn't call. I am going out of my mind. I am Ingrid Bergman in *Gaslight*, the 1944 film that 'probes the strange emotional depths of one woman's heart'. 'You're not going out of your mind,' says the film's detective. 'You're slowly and systematically being driven out of your mind.'

A MONTH AFTER THE WEDDING, JOE arrives at my apartment looking stricken and pale. I have not met this man before. 'Oh god, what have I done to you?' he says when he sees me. I don't recognise his voice, either – it is higher pitched, frail. We sit on my couch and speak many words into the night. I tell him I don't believe he booked a flight to the wedding; he says he most certainly did, he had been looking forward to it. But I am so relieved to have him beside me again that when he embarks on a new extraordinary story, another about his ex-wife, a story with twists and turns to explain his absence, his distress, his damage, I instantly drop the interrogatory mode, abandon critical thinking. I forget that only days before, I had written the start of an email to him: 'Joe, I don't know quite what sort of fraud you are, but you are a fraud, aren't you?' Tonight in my apartment nothing matters other than that I have his touch again. 'Please will you stay with me tonight and just hold me?' Addicted to hope, to touch, to an illusion of love.

Now, years on, I can see that the ambivalent ending was only a delay of the inevitable and that nothing he said that night made sense. Nothing else about the remaining twenty days of our relationship would make sense either. Not the shifting excuses for absences – he was helping his friend Mike with shearing, but then he wasn't. Not the grandiose plan he outlined as we lay in my bed one night – now he wanted to buy a defunct bowling club and bring it back to life as a community hub with a large vegetable garden. Not the final two cancellations.

I told him again that I needed to see where he lived. He gave me another date to visit his home for a meal with his children. I checked my diary. It showed that my meditation class was exploring the subject of 'dealing with loss' that night. I told Joe that I could skip class and come to dinner. His text came through just after 5 pm. 'I've fucked up royally,' he said. He'd not realised that Charlotte had a school function that night to welcome the new girls starting the following year. He suggested the next night. The following day around lunch he called to say things weren't looking good. His dog was ill and he was on the way to the vet. A little while later a text landed with a pic of two plastic bags of medications. The label had a vet's name and that day's date. 'Haemorrhagic gastro'. It wouldn't be pleasant for me if I visited the house that night, he said.

On one of the last nights Joe stayed with me, we lay in bed talking about a range of scenarios that might make the logistics of our relationship simpler. We reached scenario three. 'For a fourth scenario, would you ever consider renting this place out?' he asked. I told him that yes, I would.

I threw a question at him: 'How would you feel if I lived in the country with you and discovered I liked working with the sheep alongside you?'

'I would like that very much,' he replied.

On the last night Joe stayed with me, he brought his phone to bed. As we lay talking, it beeped constantly. His daughter was upset. She'd been arguing with her mother again. He was worried about her. I shifted position to try to see the screen as he tapped out a message. He pulled the phone away. 'Are you always going to be looking over my shoulder at my phone?' he asked. It was another voice I didn't recognise, cold, mean. I rolled away from him. His phone beeped through the dead of night into the early hours of the following morning. I lay awake all night beside a stranger and his telephone.

A WEEK LATER, SUNDAY MORNING. I'M curled in a ball. I want the world to go away. I want my brain to stop. When I turn on my phone mid-morning there are several texts and two missed calls from my friend Leo. We had arranged to meet for breakfast and when I didn't pick up he started to worry. I call him and say that I can't meet him, that I'm nauseated and shaky. He replies to say he's on his way over. I beg him to leave me be but he is undeterred. He arrives twenty minutes later with coffee and pastries. I am a bad look. I'm in baggy leggings and a faded pyjama top. My hair is wild, my skin is blotchy and my eyes are swollen. We sit on my couch, I cry and a tower of sodden tissues builds beside me. 'Enough, Steph,' he says. 'You have to end this.' This is an intervention.

I know, I say. I will, I will. Leo pushes me. 'When?'

'Tonight,' I say. I'm ripping at the dry croissant he has brought me and stuffing it in my mouth. I can't remember when I last ate.

He hugs me when he leaves. 'Steph, I'm here for you. Call me anytime.'

For the first time in days, I open the door to my courtyard. It is the sixth day of the first month of summer and the sun is shining.

SUNDAY AFTERNOON. I AM UNSTEADY AS I descend the steps to my favourite ocean pool, the ladies baths, a magnificent Victorian relic cut into sandstone cliffs. Two topless women lean against a railing, their bodies pressed close; one woman caresses the other's lovely tanned arse. A Muslim woman in a neck-to-knee swimsuit, mirroring the black bathing gowns worn here a century or more ago, passes me on the stairs. The water is a glorious bolt of green shot through with shimmering brown-flecked turquoise. An ocean swimmer strokes strongly in the open sea. There are only a few women in the pool and they are standing in a shallow section in the sun, their arms folded and wrapped around their bodies. I stand at the edge, filled with trepidation – it will be cold – then dive. Deep, plunging towards the bottom, slicing through the dark frigid water. Then up, towards the surface, with my eyes open, and the shadowy green becomes translucent as I move towards the light and the sky, gasping for breath.

Sunday night. My fingers move over the keyboard. Words appear on the screen in a dramatic sequence that I cannot comprehend.

'Even taking into account your difficult circumstances, about which I have always been tremendously accommodating, you haven't given me any option but to think that you are a sad, hollow man full of empty words,' I write. 'Who are you, for heaven's sake? Do you even know? Where is your integrity? Do you really mean anything you say? I'm done.'

I know now that staying with him is an immeasurably worse option than going; that if I stay, I will never find myself again. *Still,* I can barely believe what I have written; words I have dared not assemble even into the vague outline of a thought. When I stand up from my computer I am shaking.

Joe's reply lands two days later. His tone is wounded. He thought there was more between us than an email send-off. He had to pick himself up off the floor when my email arrived. 'I'm not sad or hollow, my life is full and I'm living it very well.' Oh yes, he added, he was overly protective of his children, but he has nothing to be ashamed of. He is more than sorry he's hurt me, that sits uneasily but he hopes 'there isn't anything that lingers that would stop you from one day chasing me up'. He will go back to his world quietly and with plenty of sadness; it wasn't right that he thought he could try to place me in a different world. Go well, he concludes. The email is mannered, self-absorbed. It is completely disconnected from reality.

•

Biological anthropologist Dr Helen Fisher knows about the love rituals of albatrosses, mud turtles, baboons, Papua New Guinean men with multiple wives, and western millennials. Her curriculum vitae lists hundreds of scholarly papers, magazine features, journal articles, and books she has written or co-written, with titles such as 'Love Is Like Cocaine', 'The Tyranny of Love: Love Addiction – an Anthropologist's View', 'When to Trust Your Gut' and 'Bereavement and Reactions to Romantic Rejection: a Psychobiological Perspective'. In ground-breaking research, Dr Fisher has put people who are madly in love into functional magnetic resonance imaging (fMRI) tunnels and watched as their brains flicker with life, as the little factory of the ventral tegmental area sparks with activity and sends dopamine surging. She's seen how a brain in love is high on 'natural speed'. As Jacqueline Olds and Richard Schwartz first suggested to me, Dr Fisher says that romantic love and attachment are addictions – 'wonderful addictions when the relationship is going well; horribly negative addictions when the partnership breaks down,' she writes in her book *Anatomy of Love: A Natural History of Mating, Marriage and Why We Stray*.

I want to know what Dr Fisher has to say about romantic heartbreak. One morning I call her in New York. 'Every single time you feel anything, something is going on [in the brain],' she tells me as I gulp strong coffee. I have watched her TED talks about love, and seen her in a powerful documentary about heartbreak, *Sleepless in New York*. She is a beautiful and brilliant blonde dynamo who lives alone and jogs in Central Park and dates another writer. She is in her mid-seventies. She has tried online dating. She has known heartbreak.

In *Sleepless in New York* the cameras follow Dr Fisher into a laboratory where she puts men and women who have recently been dumped into an fMRI tunnel. As with the test subjects who were happily in love, the scans of the heartbroken show activations in regions of the reward system deep in the reptilian core of the brain. Their loss, and their rumination on their loss, are experienced as both physical and mental pain.

Dr Fisher and I discuss my situation and decide that although I was the one to call time on the relationship, it's likely my brain responded in much the same way as that of someone who has been rejected. 'I would think that if I put you in the machine I would have found pretty much the same thing,' she says. 'You had begun to figure it out, begun to realise, *this guy's using me, this guy doesn't like me, this is not real*, and I think that's a form of rejection.'

She talks then about the science of rejection. 'Rejection seems to have two stages, the first being the protest stage, and the second being the resignation and despair stage.' In the protest stage, dopamine levels continue to soar, giving a jilted lover the energy, focus, motivation and craving to woo back the object of their affections, 'life's greatest prize which is a mating partner and a parenting partner'. In the second stage, the addicted brain realises the neurochemical reward will not be forthcoming. Dopamine-producing cells decrease their activity. There follows that well-worn path through lethargy, despondency, melancholy and depression – the withdrawal effects the broken-hearted must endure.

But this is the path I have been on for months; it's clear now that almost from the start of the relationship with Joe my reptilian brain was aware of what was happening even if I was unable to acknowledge it; that from the outset I must have been going through a form of withdrawal.

And now something I lost has been found – control. I do something I should have done after my first date with Joe in that city wine bar more than a year earlier. On Facebook I write a private message to the woman Joe mentioned, the woman he said had confronted him at a function years before – the food celebrity's wife, Susan. I write to her and ask her if she knows Joe. Who is this man? What is this man?

She replies immediately. 'Oh my god,' she says.

•

Joe claimed to dislike social media. His Twitter account had been left idle. He did not have a Facebook account. I respected the privacy he claimed to crave and through our time together took few photographs of him. I was even more reluctant to put anything of him on social media. I posted only three photos of him on Instagram. He was a faceless man in each: a hint of striped shirt, a section of arm, a lead running from his hand to his red dog's neck; a silhouette beside the blazing Tasmanian fire pit, a sliver of illumination down neck, arm, abdomen and leg; a headless figure in a chair on the jetty, legs, boots and jeans, arms, a fishing rod.

I will forever be grateful to social media. I had met Susan only once or twice a decade or more before; I had 'friended' her on Facebook long before I met Joe. In the cacophony of my newsfeed I rarely saw her posts and we'd had no cause to communicate directly. Now, through the social networking service's private messaging function, Susan becomes an instant source of information.

She tells me he has been going out with a friend of hers for three years. 'You poor girls.'

I am hurled into a rabbit hole: I am Alice, who, having heeded the words 'EAT ME' marked in currants on a cake, is farewelling her feet as she grows and grows until they seem a great way away. Curiouser and curiouser! I am looking at this new information and I am here and it is there; it is as though I have put the wrong end of a telescope to my eye to study the facts and they are reduced and distant. I can see it is shocking information but I feel no surprise. How can I be surprised? The rabbit hole is where this story really starts. Now, in possession of a name, I can become a journalist again. I can return to what I know. I can turn Joe into a story to investigate, a subject to understand.

SUSAN SHARES HER FRIEND'S NAME, KIRSTIE. Google searches of the name draw a blank and I can find no likely woman on Facebook, Instagram or Twitter. I take a different approach: Susan has several thousand Twitter followers and I scroll through every one of them, studying profile pics and bios, and zooming in on any woman whose name starts with 'K'. After hours, as the faces and names and miniature biographies of hundreds and hundreds of women start to blur into one, a likely candidate pops on to the screen. A Kirstie, an attractive woman with big eyes and a lovely smile. The surname doesn't match the one Susan has given me (I will later discover that Kirstie now uses her maiden name) but the bio does. I find her Facebook and Instagram pages.

As recently as a decade earlier, social media was in its infancy and few would have dreamt there could be such an avenue of private investigation. Now, in this new era of privacy awareness, many people have switched their social media account settings from public to private. But, in that window in time, Kirstie's accounts were public. And they offered extremely helpful details about Joe's double life. As he used photographs to fabricate his world, now the photographs Kirstie has taken will knock it over.

Like me, she was sparing in the number of shots of him she posted. But she'd had fewer reservations about revealing his face and there were enough pictures spread over time – of Joe at a winery, holding her hand at a restaurant table; in a swimming pool; shots with hints of his presence (a recognisable shirt sleeve, his pudgy hands resting near a wine glass) – to make it clear their relationship had started a year before I'd met him and had continued throughout my time with him.

That weekend when Joe told me a snake had bitten his dog? He'd been with Kirstie at an expensive Central Coast resort. Storms threatened, but he enjoyed a swim and quiet time on their veranda, reading the book I'd given him for his birthday, Don Watson's *The Bush*. Later, in the Hunter Valley, they stopped at wineries and a pub. It must have been a nuisance for him to keep me informed about his dog's wellbeing. Or perhaps it was sport: through the days they were north of Sydney, and I was at home in Sydney fretting about his dog and his honesty, he sent me fourteen text messages spinning a bush yarn about the unfolding veterinary emergency in which he said he was immersed south of Sydney.

On the night before my friends' Townsville wedding, as I pictured Joe picking his son up from a school disco and looking at his watch, worrying when he could get to my place, he and

Kirstie were having drinks at a bar overlooking Sydney Harbour. Around the time I was crying in a Townsville hotel room, they were enjoying grilled scallops and a prosciutto salad at a northern beaches restaurant. At some point that spring weekend, they headed into the country. They drove along red-dirt tracks under a grand blue sky and through glades of leaning eucalypts. They came upon a fat red-bellied black snake; Kirstie took a photograph. The snake's mouth was agape; it looked like it was laughing.

I EMAIL JOE ONE MORE TIME. I send him two screenshots pulled from Kirstie's social media feeds. The first is of a wedding party. The beautiful bride and her ponytailed groom are flanked by family members. Kirstie, who I guessed was the bride's aunt, wears a pretty dress and holds a posy of flowers. Joe stands stiffly behind her in a pale moleskin sports coat, the image of an affluent country gentleman. It was Easter. Joe told me he was in the country with his children. I was in Queensland with my family; on Easter Sunday we had finally managed to assemble family members, and we scattered my father's ashes in the ocean.

The second shot was taken a couple of months later. It shows a steamer basket of dumplings. 'Thanks for complimentary dim sum and Veuve,' Kirstie captioned it, naming the restaurant where my brother worked. She posted the picture on the night Joe cancelled dinner with me and then spun the elaborate story about his mother being stuck in New Zealand because of flight delays, and he and his sister dropping into the restaurant.

I type two questions under the screenshots. I'm not expecting him to answer them.

'Did you enjoy the wedding with Kirstie?'

'Wasn't it nice of my brother to give you complimentary dumplings and champagne that night at the restaurant?'

I hit 'send'. It is more than a year before I hear from Joe again.

•

I take time off work and flee home to my mother. I lie on the couch, bereft and buried under a blanket, for hours at a time. I feel my mother's eyes on my back and her concern as I retreat to my bedroom and ball up for hours more. She cooks for me. I push the food around my plate. On the way to the kitchen I pass a photograph of my father that he had framed for her shortly before he died, with his handwritten message: 'Always remember how much I love you.' I flick listlessly through my phone. I immerse myself in Dorothy Parker's poetry and her taut, bruised words about love and the death of love, 'a trodden lane to woe'.

I can see that nothing will ever work again, be pure again, make sense again. I have never felt lonelier. The sense of control I thought I had regained, the rage and investigative resolve, is dribbling away. I do not, for now, have the capacity to parse this story into its component parts, to even attempt to understand what has just happened to me, to understand how such a man can be. My mind flits across Dorothy Parker's razors and rivers and acids and guns, the nooses that give and the gas that smells awful.

I ruminate over a series of images of Joe: beside me on the couch booking a flight to Townsville on his mobile phone; taking a call on the footpath outside the butterfly cafe before returning to the table and talking about lava lamps; the odd expression on the face of the woman behind the counter at the airport. One thing is clear: Joe did not book a flight to Townsville. He sat next to me and pretended to do so, then, a week or so later, watched me over breakfast, knowing he would not be returning to my apartment later with his suit, knowing that I would be frantic at the airport the following day, knowing that I would go to the boys' wedding alone.

Why did he not simply say he couldn't make the wedding? Did he premeditate the pain he would inflict? Did he script the story he would weave or did it come to him spontaneously, text by text? I cannot now stretch my mind to form images of what I did not see, but they will appear in the months ahead: Joe naked and reclining beside Kirstie, tapping out a text that would lead me to continue to think he could make it to the airport in time, throwing the phone aside, pulling Kirstie close to him.

And something else is dawning on me. I have been subject to something far more sinister than mere infidelity. This is no ordinary breakup.

ONE AFTERNOON I DRAG MYSELF UP and walk to the rocky headland at the end of the beach where we scattered my father's ashes. In the waves rolling up around my bare ankles and in the salty wind I imagine my father's thoughts, his horror at this turn of events, his despair for me.

'You are so precious, Daddy,' I whispered to him in the days before he died.

'You are so precious too,' he said, slurring a little; his kidneys were failing and he would soon lose consciousness. 'I worry about you more than I do about your mother or brother; perhaps I let you lean on me emotionally too much. Your mother has had me. Your brother has his family.'

•

In the cab from the airport to my apartment, the driver wants to chat. In the way of immigrant cabbies everywhere, he asks me if I have children, for what other use for me could there be? I make the mistake of telling him I don't and mutter something about 'bad men'. I have unleashed a monster; the driver has opinions he wants to share. Through his heavy accent, I understand that he is comparing women to fruit. You want a fresh one, not a dirty one, from the tree, not from the ground, he says. But he does not spare his sex or himself. 'Man is always like a dog,' the cabbie says. 'Man like me, I've been no good man.' I lose some of his words, but not the sense of them: it seems he has had a wandering eye and treated his wife poorly. As we pull up outside my apartment block, he has reached the point in his story where his children have thrown his bags out on to the street and have said to their mother, 'Don't trust him, Mum, he's a bad man.' The driver is chuckling to himself as I pull my suitcase from his car and slam the door.

I unlock my apartment and a wave of desolation hits me. There are reminders everywhere of what has passed. Joe's stubble runs down the basin in a dried-up soapy drizzle. A dozen dead red roses droop out of a vase, their dried-blood petals litter-ing the table – he sent me the flowers during the ambivalent ending. A smell is coming from the kitchen. I fled without emptying the compost container on the bench and the stench knocks me sideways when I lift the lid; fruit-fly maggots have hatched and a writhing mass of them are feeding on the decaying scraps.

Dorothy Parker and the worms that wriggle their way through her bleak verse are on my mind as I empty the container. Poor, sad, frail Dorothy Parker, whose love life was a tragedy, who wrote of a brittle heart 'torn and maimed', and who died alone in 1967 in an apartment in Manhattan's Upper East Side. She imagined herself laid deep in her grave; she imagined petals tossed and marble urns and weeds growing above her corpse, and 'busy worms' kinder to her than love ever was.

I HAVE A FUNERAL TO GO TO. Sallie Belling is dead. She died alone in her public housing flat. It is unclear whether her death was the inevitable conclusion of her disease, or an overdose. I hope she went gently.

In the Wayside Chapel I take a seat some rows back. Pastor Graham Long is leaning over a woman in black who is crying quietly in the front row. A young man rests his head on the woman's shoulder. A pianist plays Cyndi Lauper's 'True Colors'. I study the graffiti art on the chapel's walls and try to hold in my tears.

'There is no hole so deep that God is not at the bottom.'

'It's all about grace.'

'God chooses the foolish things of this world.'

Cyndi is followed by a blast of R&B – the 1965 song 'Mustang Sally' – before the ceremony begins. 'Sal was more Kings Cross than the El Alamein fountain,' Graham Long tells

141

his congregation. He calls for eulogies from the floor, open-mic style, as is the way at a Wayside funeral.

Sallie's friend Dave gets up. It was he who found Sallie dead on her bed. She used to call him her 'street brother'. When things in Dave's life turned to shit, she was always there to pick up the pieces, he says.

A well-dressed woman speaks. She explains that she volunteered at a local drop-in centre and that's where she met Sallie. A few months ago they'd crossed paths again and with great pride Sallie told the woman that her son was at university.

The woman passes the microphone to 'Taz', a tall biker with a neat beard and black waistcoat. He says he and Sallie were an item in the Cross in the early nineties when she was 'a little redhead, a foxy little piece'. He remembers Sallie's honesty.

Sallie departs Wayside in a box in the back of a black hearse in the rain. 'Ride, Sallie, ride,' a woman bellows as the car crawls down the street.

I join the crowd inside for lunch. Graham Long has explained to Sallie's family members that I've been working on a story about her; they are, he relays, happy to talk to me. I introduce myself to a well-dressed woman in black and ask if I can sit with her. Her name is Rachel, she is one of Sallie's sisters, and she is dazed but welcoming. She introduces me to a young man – it's Anthony, Sallie's son, the man who had been beside her in the chapel.

I ask gently about her other siblings. Could they not make it, I ask? She looks puzzled at my question. 'Well, there's only Martin and me,' she says.

'Oh,' and I'm blundering around a bit now. 'Sallie told me she had twelve siblings.' We look at each other and a flash of understanding strikes us at the same time. Rachel glances towards Anthony; he's talking to someone else and she moves a little closer and lowers her voice.

'There were only three of us,' she says. 'Sallie, me, and Martin, our brother.' She presses me to tell her what I know – she last saw Sallie more than fifteen years before, and Anthony, now twenty-five, hadn't heard from her since he was eleven. Rachel did not recognise the person eulogised in the service. Her face widens then falls as I share the story of Sallie's life as I understood it: the twelve siblings, the sister in jail, the trans brother, the sexual abuse she suffered at the hands of her stepfather, pregnant at twelve to him, the mother she hated who stole her second child.

'None of it is true,' Rachel says. 'None of it.'

THE DAY AFTER THE FUNERAL, I meet Rachel and Anthony at Sallie's apartment. They were planning to clean it out but are overwhelmed and emotional. No one told them Sallie was a hoarder who lived in squalor. The smell in the apartment is a punch in the nose. A pet food bowl on the floor holds desiccated cockroach carcasses. The sink is a foul tower of dishes. The rubbish-strewn path from front door to Sallie's dirt-blackened bed is treacherous. Rachel and Anthony have found a small box of photos and must accept they are all that is left for them of Sallie now.

We retreat to the courtyard to talk. Overnight, Rachel has told Anthony how his mother crafted a story about her life. Now anger and hurt are muddling Rachel's grief; her mind has not stopped working since our conversation at the funeral. Her dark hair is pulled back from her face and she is pale. She clasps and unclasps her hands as she tells me that Sallie started to fiddle with the truth when she was a teenager. Her sister's disputes with their mother and stepfather echoed through the family's life. Sallie fell pregnant to a local boy when she was fifteen, had an abortion, and within a year or so had moved out to live with a different boyfriend. In her early twenties she gave birth to Anthony. She did not put his father's name on the birth certificate. At some point, Sallie asked her mother to mind the toddler for a month or two. It's then that a thick Department of Community Services file emerged. It included reports that Anthony had been asking neighbours for food.

Rachel says that Sallie made no attempt to retrieve Anthony from their mother. Rachel wrote to her sister care of Wayside but got no response. 'There was no contact; we didn't know where she was.' When Sallie's mother died, Anthony's step-grandfather, the stepfather Sallie claimed had sexually abused her, took over Anthony's care. Rachel knows not to dismiss a claim of sexual abuse lightly, but no matter which way she looks at it, she doesn't believe there's any way her stepfather was abusive. 'He's a bit of a gruff old man, but I love him for it,' adds Anthony. His mother was never in contact; when he was a teenager he attacked the only photograph he had of her with a stapler. He sensed during the Wayside service that something was odd. 'Well, that's a load of shit,' he thought when the woman said that Sallie was proud of her son at university. Anthony works at a fish and chip shop.

Rachel is devastated by Sallie's allegations about their mother. 'Mum did so much for all of us.' She is grappling now to understand why her sister built a false self.

Perhaps, she thinks, Sallie understood that a junkie with a background of poverty and sexual abuse would be a more sympathetic character than a junkie who had made some poor choices.

I HAVE AN ARTICLE TO WRITE, a deadline to meet. Rachel and Anthony are happy for me to tell Sallie's story. I call Graham Long – I feel that, in a way, he is now Sallie's spokesperson, and I need to check he is comfortable with me proceeding.

We talk for a while about how the story has unfolded, about lies and the facades people build around themselves, truth as the collateral damage. 'We are all constructs to one degree or another,' says Graham. 'You build what you need to build to justify the path you're on.' I think of Joe, of how he corrected me when I described him as a 'farmer'. 'A grazier,' he said. I think of Sallie and the bondage work she told me she preferred; of her filthy flat, and how unlikely it is that she ever had a client there dressed in a slave outfit, on his hands and knees, cleaning that floor with a toothbrush. I form a theory: Sallie just wanted her fair share of glamour and excitement and control, and in her world bondage work was the best she could see. When she had nothing else, she still had her stories.

My editor and I discuss how I'll treat the article. I tell him I cannot now write the straightforward story about Sallie's life that I had planned at the outset. There is no black and white to it; it is complicated, full of unexpected twists, dark depths and immense pain. I can see now that the story I must write is about much more than a woman's life. It is about the profound, unknowable elements of a human soul.

6

A CABINET OF CURIOSITIES

I reach and pass certain milestones in my private, post-truth world. Christmas Day 2015 goes by. I try not to ruin it for everyone. There is champagne and seafood in my brother's backyard, familial peace and goodwill, and a ruthless ice-cube battle with my nieces and nephew. For now, they are the only ones who can get a smile out of me. The New Year's Eve that Joe said we'd spend watching the fireworks over Sydney Harbour from his vintage cruiser looms then is mercifully over – I open a bottle of champagne for my mother and me at dusk and am in bed long before midnight. In the first week of January I return to my normal work routine.

But there is no normal now; I might as well have stumbled into one of Enid Blyton's surreal lands at the top of *The Magic Faraway Tree*, the Land of Topsy Turvy, the Land of WTF. On the morning of my first day back at work, I visit a man who has attracted a large following on Instagram for the shots he posts of his unusual offal-laden breakfasts. I have convinced my editor at *Good Weekend* that a story about this man might be entertaining. He has been at work in his kitchen since dawn and, with a sly grin, he serves me and the videographer smoked cow's udder and ram's testicles cooked in cream and single malt whisky, and seared fish semen. 'Now I know you swallow,' the cook says as I taste his food, and his snicker is high and smutty. On the drive back to the office, a red light stops me at the turn-off to Joe's neighbourhood; the nausea only abates when the light changes and I can accelerate away.

In the afternoon of my first day back at work, I do a title search on the address on Joe's driver's licence in that neighbourhood, the place he called 'my Tintagel'. When I open the documents that land in my inbox, my stomach plummets. The reaction has nothing to do with anything I have eaten. I sit and stare at the documents on the screen; perhaps I have misunderstood them. I read them again. I have not misunderstood. The name of Joe's ex-wife Mary is the only one on the title.

I look a little further and see that in 2003 he transferred his interest in the property to Mary, presumably for business reasons. Another document shows that, for the most part, she paid the mortgage. It's clear now that Joe does not live in the house, probably hasn't for years. Had I decided to pay a surprise visit during our relationship, he would not have been the one to answer the door.

I have a box in my head in which I have stored the fact of Kirstie, the images of her with him, the knowledge of his romantic betrayal. I can see now that I'm going to need more than a box in which to store such things. I assemble a cabinet with shelves, a Wunderkammer, a cabinet of curiosities. I put Kirstie on the top shelf. I put the title search result on the shelf underneath. There are empty shelves waiting to be filled.

Two colleagues, Kate McClymont and Michaela Whitbourn, are chatting near my desk. Michaela is a lawyer and the *Sydney Morning Herald*'s legal affairs reporter. Kate is the newspaper's venerated investigative journalist, a woman whose formidable work through decades has brought down corrupt politicians, race-fixing jockeys, dodgy union bosses and grubby scammers. My need to unpack the information I have uncovered now overrides my need for privacy and I join their conversation. They are astonished as I explain the story. We discuss how I might find out where Joe really lives. But what's the point, I ask, what would I even do with the information – stalk him? My question is flippant. 'Absolutely,' says Kate. 'We'll be your wing girls.' She's not being flippant. She has no sympathy for flim-flam men and charlatans. 'These people shouldn't be allowed to get away with it.'

I stay in the office late that night working, searching, filling in applications for information from public records. I take a break and ring my mother to tell her about the title search results. She is aghast. 'I couldn't put my finger on what it was about him when I met him that night at dinner,' she says, 'but . . . he didn't seem to be with us.'

THE SHELVES OF MY MENTAL WUNDERKAMMER start to fill. 'I have a disgusting amount of money,' Joe told me. Now, underneath Kirstie, underneath the title search results, I store the documents that arrive in my inbox revealing that Joe is an undischarged bankrupt. It will take time to process all the implications of this fact but some things are clear: a man who is bankrupt faces impediments in the pursuit of a high-net-worth lifestyle; generally, a man who is bankrupt is not in the business of buying and selling multi-million-dollar properties, or of renovating expensive wooden boats. I do a quick Google search: a man who is bankrupt faces certain legal limitations on the vehicle he is allowed. It was a dyslexic reading of the situation to see the decrepit Defender as a statement of Joe's understated nature.

I study his upper-case handwriting on a form on which he listed his assets (one bank account with a current balance of $120, 'tools of trade' with a resale value of $500). The handwriting is cold and lovely. It is the uniform upper-case lettering of the old-school architect and reveals nothing of his character. I think of the one thing he hand-wrote to me – a birthday card. I remember how soulless it seemed, how I clamped down on the disappointment that rose when I read it.

'MY DEAREST STEPHANIE, A VERY HAPPY BIRTHDAY TO YOU! ALL MY LOVE, JOE XOXOXO'

And now another curio has landed – a document on which Joe's full name is typed in capital letters. Words jump up at me but take time to settle into an order I can absorb: 'date of listing', 'accused', 'plea of not guilty', 'convicted', 'good behaviour bond', 'the offender'. It appears that Joe is a man in possession of a criminal record. The date is December 2011. The offence is 'use false instrument'. A 'false instrument' is generally a forged document.

I think about the article I found in the early days of our relationship, the one about Joe's former business partner, Peter, who was struck off the architects' register for professional misconduct. When I asked Joe about it, he said he'd known Peter was a problem and he shouldn't have stuck by him for so long. I have another conversation with Kate McClymont. We look at the documents relating to Joe's bankruptcy. She has never seen anything like it: a trustee was appointed to manage Joe's affairs in early 2009, but it wasn't until he was summonsed to court nearly a year later that he provided the required asset and liability statements. As a result of his lack of cooperation, the trustee objected to his discharge from bankruptcy and he was not due to be released until February 2018. Unless there was a change to that date, he would be in bankruptcy for around three times as long as normal.

You have to call the business partner, says Kate. I have known for a while I would need to make this call. I return to my desk. As I pick up the phone, I am shaking.

'HE'S A COMPULSIVE LIAR.' JOE'S NAME has barely left my lips before Peter is off. 'When things go wrong he will never tell you. He will try to patch up behind the scenes, never show he's wrong, never show he's made a mistake. Basically, he can't accept failure or setback, so he will hide and hide things from you until he can't hide things anymore.'

After nearly twenty years in business with Joe, everything was over almost before Peter even knew there was a problem. And now on the phone he can't stop talking; talking about his history with Joe, about things he has stewed over for six years. 'It was just like a divorce. It was devastating. We were like brothers.'

They met at a major Sydney architectural firm in the mid-1980s. Old architecture – the striking art deco Rural Bank Building with its rams' head plaques, the Regent Theatre, which opened in 1928 with a gala showing of the silent Greta Garbo film *Flesh and the Devil* – was coming down. New architecture – office towers like Harry Seidler's Grosvenor Place and the Capita Centre in Sydney's Castlereagh Street – was going up. Gordon Gekko and *The Bonfire of the Vanities'* Sherman McCoy would soon become emblematic characters of the greed-is-good, greed-is-right era. Before the stock market crash, Joe and Peter and a bunch of other workmates took a course at the stock exchange; they'd gather in the morning at work and pore over the market listings in the newspaper. 'Buy this,' they'd tell their broker on the phone or, 'sell that'. French-born Peter put a sign above his desk – 'La Bourse'.

Joe was only a few years out of school and still at university studying architecture when they met. Peter was older by ten years but he was drawn to the younger man's amiability, by his knowledge and broad interests; Joe could talk about anything – architecture, art, politics, animals, nature, even flowers. He knew the botanical names of every plant they passed on their bush-walks – Joe, Peter and his wife, Rosalie, tramping together. Joe was a bit stiff, both in bearing and behaviour, but the couple liked the values he espoused and his earthy sense of humour – he expressed, for example, a preference for women with big tits.

On weekends they'd often head south to a beach house owned by Joe's affluent family. He'd go spearfishing and bring back fish for the barbecue. Rosalie remembers his perfect recipe for 'ear shell' – abalone. She'd pick wild blackberries and make pies. Joe mixed the G&Ts. They talked about one day buying some land in the area and designing and building their own simple place. 'We had a lot of fun,' says Peter. 'Joe was a lot of fun.'

A friend of Rosalie's thought he was hot, but Joe never brought a girlfriend with him on their outings. He talked about a girlfriend only once; he was, he said, helping her out with a few things. At one point he told Peter and Rosalie that he was painting her parents' house. Then the relationship was over: Joe told them he'd found her in bed with another guy. Apart from Jill, who they saw occasionally, he didn't seem to have many friends, either. But Peter and Rosalie got to know Joe's family and regularly headed through his mother's back garden past the pool to reach his grandfather's house, where they played tennis. They could see how much he adored his grandfather. 'He was like an ideal for him,' says Peter.

Mary was a friend of one of Rosalie's friends. After Joe met her in the early 1990s, everything changed. He was besotted. Mary went to Europe and he chased after her. He had started to build a house of his own design on the harbour-front block not so far from his grandfather's place. But he was doing almost all the labouring himself and it was taking forever. Mary told him that if he wanted to marry her, he'd have to finish the house – she wasn't going to live in a hovel. The weekends away and the tennis and the bushwalking came to an abrupt end. He dropped everything for her.

The black-tie wedding was big and costly and churchy. Rosalie bought a posh frock and Peter was the best man, and they looked at each other and raised their eyebrows and wondered at the change in their friend, who had often told them he didn't believe in marriage or religion. Afterwards, a photograph of the bride and groom appeared in a glossy magazine. And by then Joe had said something that Peter would remember. 'He used to say that if he married an Irish-Catholic girl she would never leave him.'

IT WAS ALMOST AN ACCIDENT THAT Joe and Peter ended up starting their own business. Joe moved to another architectural firm in the late 1980s, and when he told his friend they were looking for other new architects, Peter followed. But it didn't last long: within a year or so they had both been booted out. They formed a theory about what had happened: a jealous colleague had told their boss that they were hatching a plan to steal away clients and set up on their own. It wasn't the case at all, but they thought, *well, if he thinks we can do it, let's do it.* Joe was smart and knew the planning and property title systems intricately. He worked his butt off. He could find ways to make jobs work that nobody else could have dreamt of. And his drawings were exquisite – in those pre-computer days most architects would have killed to draw like he did.

But architecture was a mug's game. If you wanted to make money, property development was the thing. So as the years wore on, and the new century rolled in, Peter kept the cash flow going with bread-and-butter architectural work while Joe's attention was increasingly diverted towards the business and its growth;

to research, land-spotting, feasibility studies, development. He liked Canberra as a money-making prospect, and spots on the south coast and the Southern Highlands – only one set of traffic lights out of the city and then you're on the highway. But so much came to nothing and some things gave them great big bloody headaches. After three years' work on one multi-million-dollar city warehouse apartment development, their builder went bust and they were forced to put themselves into administration. The banks took over, sold off the apartments dirt-cheap, and when finally things were done and dusted, Joe and Peter were left with only a few thousand dollars to pay the solicitors.

Peter thinks it destroyed his partner. Joe just couldn't accept that the development had failed: he thought he was going to make money, he thought he was going to *make it*. He consulted lawyers and went round in circles with his arguments and stories about where responsibility lay for the fiasco, and no matter how many times Peter told him he should move on, he would not let it go. It was clear he held grudges, but no one could see what was really happening; they couldn't see the ball of humiliation and rage that was growing in his belly, they couldn't see just how much he was locking away from them. And there was no respite from the financial pressures. When their business downsized and moved offices, Peter found a pile of Lotto tickets in a drawer – Joe had evidently been gambling on other sources of income.

But the partners had been together for so long that Peter didn't question him; he wouldn't even harm a fly, he thought. So in 2009, when Joe told him that he'd sold the option on a development site – an imposing 1927 church in Darlinghurst built in the Greek Ionic style – and a large cheque would be arriving when it settled, Peter believed him. He and Rosalie organised a year-long sabbatical overseas; they had their bags packed to go. But there would be no cheque and no sabbatical, only a slow-motion train wreck.

NOW PETER KNOWS THE WHAT, if not the why, of the events that unfolded from 2007 and would eventually bring both men down. At the time, though, he was oblivious. 'I don't know what I was thinking. Something was wrong with me there, too,' he says. 'I was stupid. I was just not looking at what he was doing.' Besides, Peter came from a tight family where there was almost an honour code of trust between him and his four brothers. He considered Joe to be his fifth brother. It did not occur to him to be remotely suspicious.

In a few months through late 2009 and into early 2010, Peter discovered he had been bankrupted, the firm had gone under and his professional organisation was suspending him for misconduct. The foundations of his life collapsed. 'I went bananas.' He had to save his home, his family, himself, get a job, get his head around what the hell had happened, what Joe had done.

Joe, it turned out, had been playing the omniscient lead role in his own little theatre of the absurd, and, of all the multiple characters, he alone knew the plot. It didn't take long after everything fell apart for Peter to see the fabrications and fantasies, the scale of the deceit. Joe kept detailed diaries; now Peter understands why – it was so Joe could remember all the pieces in his puzzle. 'He wrote absolutely everything down; he had a diary that you could not imagine. Everything is in there, everything he does.'

The meetings Joe had set up to discuss the church project, bringing together the vendor, lawyers and investors, were choreographed farces. Emails that flew between the parties slipped down to the bottom of inboxes. Joe would miss deadlines, stuff that was meant to be happening wasn't, and all the while he led Peter to think the cheque would soon be in the mail.

Peter requested meetings with solicitors or bankers to ask 'why this?' or 'why that?'; Joe would be hovering outside when Peter arrived, with a story to explain why the appointment wouldn't be going ahead: the solicitor or the banker had been early, he'd met with them already, everything was fine. Odd things happened in the office, too. Now he realises that emails he received from solicitors and others were fabricated and sent from fake mail accounts. Joe had started to insist that he be the one to collect the mail each day. Phone calls Joe made within earshot, in which he talked about delays or problems, or which appeared to be evidence of progress or resolution of one thing or another, were figments of everyone's imagination. No one was at the end of the line. 'So many fake calls, so much bullshit, bloody good actor.'

But Joe's conjuring acts were not just designed to make it look like a project was happening when it wasn't; they were concealing problems that were hurtling towards the two men like a killer asteroid. Mounting debt, including an ugly tax office bill. A fraud investigation. Piles of urgent letters addressed to Peter, and he had seen none of them.

PETER STILL CAN'T UNDERSTAND HOW HE could have been so blind to his old friend's actions. He can't understand why Joe did what he did. He had good ideas, he got people to the table, but he seemed not to be able to follow through with anything. When things went off the rails, everything he did thereafter was counter to his own interests. All Peter can think is that his behaviour was a twisted form of face-saving. No, it was more than that: all he can think is that Joe went crazy.

In mid-2006, in a departure from his more typical research and development work, Joe took on the design work and overall responsibility for a residential job. But month after month passed and still there was no sign of council approval for the development application. The clients, a married couple, grew increasingly frustrated. They hassled Joe. They'd paid more than $25,000 in fees to the firm. Their marriage imploded in the middle of everything. They hassled him some more because now they wanted the approval in place when they sold the land. Finally, in January 2008 Joe gave them what he said was the council's development consent. It was on council letterhead. It had a council officer's signature on it.

The clients were suspicious and took it to council for verification. It was a forged document. Council referred the matter to police and the Independent Commission Against Corruption. The clients' lawyer referred the matter to the NSW Architects Registration Board. Through 2008 and 2009, the board executed its processes, held hearings and sent a flood of correspondence to Peter. He was oblivious. Nor did he know that Joe's estate had been placed in the hands of a bankruptcy trustee, and that soon his would be too. Even after documents were served to his residential address, he went to Joe: he was furious. 'You got us into this mess,' Peter said. 'Now fix it.' Joe said he was on to it. Peter trusted him like a brother. It wasn't until mid-2009 that Peter discovered he had been found guilty of professional misconduct. He was the architect nominated legally responsible for the firm's work.

Peter knew that Joe had never gone through the process to register himself as an architect, but he'd never had cause to be troubled by the fact. In the course of the Architects Registration Board deliberations, it emerged that Joe had likely never even completed his university architectural studies. Peter didn't know that. In early 2010 Peter lost his registration as an architect. He did not regain it until 2016.

In December 2011 Joe stood before a magistrate in the Local Court of New South Wales and defended himself against charges of using a false instrument. Joe had, says Peter, lied to so many lawyers that no one would represent him. 'Not guilty, your honour' was his plea. But he was found guilty, given a good behaviour bond, and ordered to pay compensation to the clients.

One day soon after Peter's world had come crashing down, he opened his front door and a bottle of French wine was sitting on his veranda. There was a card attached to the bottle. It was signed – 'La Bête Noir'. The Black Beast.

●

I had wondered if Joe could be a fantasist. But no paths of thought could ever have led me from that concern to this bizarre and malignant outcome. My mind churns over Peter's story. Every detail of his casts new illumination on mine; my cabinet of curiosities is going to need an annexe.

Peter has revealed at least one of the magician's tricks, and it is remarkably simple. The fake phone call. I build a mental inventory of the occasions on which Joe might have performed the trick in my presence.

So often a phone was attached to his ear, there were so many calls: the one he took when we were on the road from Canberra to Mike's to help with some agricultural pursuit, and during which Joe claimed to have been told our labour was no longer needed. Google had long ago proved to me that Mike existed, but even if they were friends, was the suggestion that we might visit his property another prop in Joe's attempt to stay in character? He would not have wanted Mike and I in the same room in case one of us raised something at odds with the other's understanding of his story. The call to his mother to inquire if we might visit her. (Did she even know I existed?) The call informing him his son had fallen running around a pool, and the conversation with hospital staff during which they told him crazy Mary was making a scene and he was needed; calls that summoned him back to meetings; calls to boat builders working on the joinery of his vintage motor cruiser.

One sultry summer's day, I decide it's time to visit the boat. Joe had sent me photographs of it, including two showing his children on board, and told me where it was moored – at the Point Piper Marina, down the road from former prime minister Malcolm Turnbull's harbourside home. Someone going into the members-only marina has left the gate open and I slip in after them. And there she is, the *Blue Goose*, blue-hulled and golden-timbered, the sort of pretty vessel one might imagine that other spectacular fantasist Jay Gatsby piloting on Long Island Sound.

The *Blue Goose* was built in Los Angeles in 1927. She is 50 feet long. Her exterior brass is painted with twenty-four-carat gold. She is considered to be one of the five most classic motor cruisers in the world. She's priced at $135,000 because she needs some work. Her joinery hasn't been touched in years.

A day or two later, I call marine broker Henry Minter. He tells me he has been trying to sell the *Blue Goose* for years. 'I don't know what it is about that boat. All the weirdos want to buy it.' He remembers Joe well. He visited the *Blue Goose* on several occasions – with his children, with a woman with black hair who Henry took to be his wife. (Who was *she*?) The children crawled all over the boat's fine Cuban mahogany interior. The woman looked bored. Henry thought Joe was a bit odd, but noted his R. M. Williams boots and how relaxed he was, like a country bloke. Joe told Henry that he was just about to settle on some property he was selling and wanted to buy the boat for his family. He dropped names. 'Oh, look, I've got to go,' he said after taking a phone call at the end of one visit. 'I've got Bob E– screaming at me.' Henry knew the man he was talking about, a billionaire property developer. Bob E– screamed at everyone. So that rang true.

Henry watched when Joe drove off in the beaten-up old Defender. *Well, that's odd*, he thought, *but don't judge a book by its cover*. And Henry had sold boats in some very odd situations to some very odd people: once, he'd met a woman in the city to pick up the payment for a yacht sale and she'd handed him two shopping bags full of cash. Later, when the Australian Federal Police came knocking, Henry discovered that the infamous Melbourne crook Tony Mokbel had escaped the country on the yacht the woman had paid for.

Joe told Henry that he wanted to have covers made for the *Blue Goose*. One day, Henry went through the rigmarole of bringing the boat in from the mooring. He called in a contractor to measure her up. 'Send me the quote when it comes in, and the contract of sale,' Joe told him. 'I'll transfer the money,' he said, and wandered up the road to the Defender. Henry never heard from him again. Joe was nothing more than a skilled tyre kicker.

WE TAKE CERTAIN THINGS IN LIFE for granted; things that are, if you like, planks in the great structure of civilisation. We think that when someone picks up a phone in front of us and has a conversation, another human being is at the end of the line. We think that when someone says they own a boat and has a photograph of their children lounging all over that boat, they are indeed the owner of that boat. But pull one or two planks out of that structure and it starts to wobble.

I take another look at some of the photographs Joe sent me. I look again at the shot of the Defender axle-deep in mud with the caption, 'my day'. I turn to Google again. Its reverse-image search function unearths the complete shot from a Land Rover owners' forum. Joe pinched the photograph and did some work on it, cropping out the central body of the vehicle and two blokes looking at it. The photo was taken in Queensland in 2012. The vehicle is the same model and make, but the full picture shows it doesn't have the blue-striped doors of Joe's ute. He embellished his self-portrait as a rugged man of the bush with a doctored photograph of someone else's ute, someone else's day in the mud.

I make some more phone calls. The nice woman on the end of the line at the abattoir where Joe claimed to have his dorpers slaughtered looks up her books. 'Sorry, love, can't find any record of him or his sheep.' The head of the private equity firm at which Joe claimed to have worked in his Savile Row suits tells me that my ex-boyfriend brought a joint-venture proposition to the firm, an interesting proposition, but in the middle of discussions he disappeared. He was never employed by the firm. 'My guys, when they were dealing with him, they don't hold him in any regard – as in, he's flakey; you can't get hold of him. He's a very strange unit,' the man says. At my end of the line, I flush with embarrassment that I was ever connected to such a person. 'Look, there are a lot of people in the world, and particularly in the world of real estate, masquerading as having large amounts of capital.'

MY CONVERSATION WITH PETER HAS GIVEN me another lead to follow. 'He managed to manipulate people you could never imagine you could manipulate,' Peter said. I pushed him for more information. 'There was a very well-known man who spent time in jail,' Peter added, seemingly reluctant to say more. I thought for a minute. A man who had spent time in jail? It clicked. Did he like to go fishing, I asked?

The clarity that comes when facts are in hand. When, the year before, I returned from the winery café's bathroom, there was a good reason that Joe had vanished. He wanted to avoid a conversation with Howard Hilton, the man sitting across the room he had pointed out to me; the former lawyer who once had the biggest criminal law practice in the country and who spent time in jail in the late 1980s for bribing the New South Wales prisons minister. The nonchalance with which Joe sat there and told me Howard's story, and suggested he might invite him to fish on his lake one day, belied the agitation he must have felt at the idea of Howard spotting him. Joe owes him rather a lot of money.

Kate McClymont laughs when I share this new intelligence. Joe is far too inconsequential for her, but she has Howard's number in her contact book and she calls him on my behalf. He agrees to see me.

A few days later, Howard Hilton and I meet at a cafe in Sydney's east. I know who I need to look out for: I've found a photograph of Howard standing in a river, a bald man holding a large spotty trout and looking delighted. In the flesh he is taller than I imagined and doesn't look delighted at all. He orders a coffee and, with a little prompting, embarks on the story of how he got mixed up in Joe's shenanigans.

So, Howard says, there was a guy called Barry Goldman, a real estate agent and developer. Howard had known Barry since they were children, and although they weren't close, they knew each other well enough to have a chat. Goldman, who would eventually end up in jail for fraud, had been doing a development for which Joe and Peter were both the architects and investors. Goldman asked Howard for informal advice in relation to some issues around the development. A meeting was held in Joe and Peter's offices. Howard recalls that they were very personable. He even got paid for his advice. Howard's conversation with Joe continued in the months and years ahead. 'I'm not a developer myself, but everyone's interested in real estate. You chat about this and that, and how you make a quid.'

Around 2002, Howard decided he liked the look of a project that Joe and Peter were trying to get up – the development of a heritage-listed church built in the Greek Ionic style in Darling-hurst. 'It looked like a very good deal,' he tells me. Howard's face is lugubrious, with deep crevices running from nose to jawline. It's a face built to tell stories about the shifty characters he has known. 'And I was greedy. I put $180,000 in and I was supposed to get a million dollars back.' But as Peter would eventually discover, the deal wasn't moving forward. 'Joe would manage the meetings, talk about things. It all looked plausible, but in the end it never happened.' On a few occasions, Howard caught Joe out giving different versions of events to different involved parties. Years passed. Nothing. 'And then he sort of ran away, and I was chasing him and threatened to sue him but . . .' Howard shrugs, then offers a complicated explanation about the nature of the loan he had signed which, ultimately, prevented him pursuing Joe for the money he was owed.

I ask him why he would have signed such a document. 'Because I was an idiot,' he replies. 'I've always been an idiot. I'm quite smart but credulous. It means you go faster down the wrong path. I'm a complete klutz in many ways and part of it's caused by greed. I'm reasonably smart for other people, fairly dumb for myself. Probably a bit like yourself.'

'I've been very dumb,' I say. 'It's a relief to discover that other people have been dumb too.' I don't tell Howard of the greed that made me vulnerable to Joe's wiles. I don't tell him how greedy I was for love, for connection. I think of Joe's greed. It's becoming clear that his was far more complex than a simple hunger for money or love of one description or another.

'I wouldn't have thought he'd be that attractive?'

I squirm. Howard is right. 'Um,' I say. It is hell to have to explain myself but I feel as though his candour calls for an equal measure in return. 'It's complicated. Women who haven't met men at my age are told we shouldn't be so picky. I didn't look at him and think he was an Adonis, no, but he seemed decent and kind and emotionally uncomplicated. He was interested in the environment and history, and some of the things I'm interested in.'

'Con men hold the mirror up to you and you see reflected back at yourself your own desires, simple as that,' says Howard. 'You wanted that. I wanted to make a million dollars. I've met lots of con men and I've been ripped off by them.' He tells me about one he met in Long Bay Jail: Phillip Kingston Carver, legendary in the catalogue of Australian con artists. 'He cost me about a million dollars. Of course, in prison you're worried about not making any money, and how your family will get by, and how useless you are, so you feel if you can do something, you can validate yourself.' He tells me Carver swindled Kerry Packer, too – the tycoon invested hundreds of thousands of dollars in a bogus wonder drug Carver was peddling, a capsule that promised eternal youth.

Later, I will find a 1994 *Sydney Morning Herald* article about Carver, headed 'Is This Australia's Greatest Conman?' At the time the article was written, Carver was in court facing charges related to a $65 million theft from two life insurance companies that were controlled by the late Melbourne billionaire Richard Pratt. 'Phillip is charismatic, attractive, friendly and totally amoral,' a former girlfriend of Carver told the article's author.

'He is very businesslike, with a strong and commanding speaking voice. The thing is, though, that he lies so well even he believes it is the truth. That's why he's so convincing.' In the now-defunct *Bulletin* magazine, journalist Adam Shand said of Carver: '[He] was a dumpy, rumpled medium sized man, not much more physically than a boiled egg on toothpicks.' In the piece, Shand wrote about how the best con men have the skills of a salesman. 'They can sniff a man's "unique selling point" – that hidden weakness, vanity or conceit.'

I ask Howard another question about Joe but he has lost interest in the subject of swindlers. 'I find him a boring turd,' he says, standing to leave. Before he goes, I ask him what he might have done if he had spotted Joe that day at the winery cafe. 'I would have asked him, "Where is my fucking money?"'

•

My best instincts fail me – I become a social media stalker, obsessively watching Kirstie's Facebook and Instagram pages for signs of Joe. I am torturing myself. I am still deranged. There he is in the blue-green-check shirt I gave him, with a broad, goofy grin, holding her hand, sitting at a restaurant table in a group of ten for her birthday. She glows, she's lovely, she smiles, she's happy, and he seems to be a familiar member of the group. That bites. 'Thank you, Joe,' she has captioned the photograph. Did he pay for the occasion? But how? Where does his money come from? Does Kirstie know the facts I have uncovered? Has Susan not told Kirstie about me, or has Susan told her about me, and she and Joe have thrashed it out and she's forgiven him? Or did she know about me all along and allowed him his freedom? Is he missing me? Is there even a thought in his head about me? (Was there ever a thought in his head about me?) There they are again, at another restaurant, evidently an intimate dinner, red wine, fancy desserts, Joe's hand resting on the table in the corner of the shot. Why is she still with him if she knows about me? Surely Susan has told her about me? Or should *I* tell her about me?

Then there's a break. No sign of him for months. What's happened? Have they parted? Has he vanished? Is he doing to her what he did to me? One day on Facebook Kirstie posts a link to an article: 'Signs You're Dealing with an Emotionally Manipulative Man'. I clutch at it. It must mean something. Something's happened. I am a bad person because I am relieved. My punishment arrives swiftly. Within days he reappears on her Facebook feed. They're in the country; she's taken a photograph of him in the grand reception room of a country house hotel – chandeliers, velvet, polished antiques. It's *a wedding reception venue*. He's taken a photograph of her in the hotel's garden. A month or so later comes one of his dog: somewhere in the country, at a fence, looking towards a lake. I miss his dog.

Then, nothing. Joe vanishes from Kirstie's pages completely.

SO, THIS IS A WEIRD THING. Given what I have discovered, it is screamingly weird that I should feel any sense of what can only be described as jealousy. But in these months, I move through hypercharged emotions as a Formula 1 driver switches through gears. I am jealous and sad and self-flagellating and bewildered; I am up and down and tied in knots and caught in a twister of questions. I am sinking into a cesspit of rage and disgust and horror.

One or other version of Joe's face appears in strange places: at Central Station on a homeless man curled on the ground with a cup in front of him – I consider kicking him, or taking a photograph, before dropping some spare change in his cup and walking away. There he is in a street in my neighbourhood, his shoulders sloping, his hair shaggy, muttering to himself and scratching his balls, something wild and lost in his eyes.

And I just can't get him out of my apartment. The reminders are heart-stopping: a photograph I missed when I moved all trace of him off my computer; a packet of razors I bought for him, fallen to the back of a bathroom drawer; the receipts for this or that restaurant meal we had, which tumble out of a folder at tax time. In an article in the *Observer* I read about the Museum of Broken Relationships. 'What can one do with the frail ruins of a love affair?' says Olinka Vištica, co-curator of the museum with her ex-partner Dražen Grubišić. It has permanent installations in Zagreb and Los Angeles, pop-up shows, a virtual museum, a Wunderkammer of exhibits: a silk wedding dress patterned with butterflies and flowers scrunched up and stuffed in a glass jar. An envelope holding a single human hair. An answering machine playing the voice of a woman calling her ex-boyfriend an asshole. A black dildo. I consider what submission I might make to the Museum of Broken Relationships. I vacuum and vacuum and still his dog's red hair remains. A vacuum-cleaner bag of a red dog's hair? But then I think, *how can a heart be broken for a man who was never there?*

I HAVE A NEW EDITOR, AMELIA LESTER. She has come home to Australia after years as an editor at my favourite magazine, the *New Yorker*. When she starts work in early 2016 she takes me to lunch and we have an intense and thrilling discussion about story ideas. We talk about this and that; I tell her I think there is an important story to be written about the increase in prescription opioid abuse and addiction in Australia. I suggest, nervously, that I could consider writing something about my experience of being a woman without children, although I'm terrified about the personal exposure it would require. Amelia likes both ideas and wants me to start on them immediately. As we walk back to the office, I mention another story I could perhaps write for her, although not for a long while yet. I outline the barest of details, and, infuriatingly, start to cry. Perhaps, I say, I shouldn't have mentioned it. I don't know whether I'll ever be ready to write it. Amelia tells me that she wants the piece the moment I'm ready. 'What a story,' she says. 'And I know you have the reportorial chops to pull it off.'

I SIT AT MY COMPUTER IN MY STUDY and start recording memories of the relationship. With each word I write I want to slam my head on to my desk at my idiocy. Every writer knows they must show not tell, yet I let Joe tell me everything and show me practically nothing. I find an article that offers a line which should be distributed to every high-schooler in the country: 'When you find yourself becoming a detective within your own relationship, it's time to call it quits.' This time I do slam my head on to my desk. I wasted swathes of time being a detective, but what an ineffective detective I was! I checked weather reports when he said it was raining on his alleged farm. I scoured a school website to find mention of a function his daughter had forgotten to tell him about. I googled for flight delays, and incidents of sheep-drench poisoning, and the names of his business associates. And yet I set aside searches that would have immediately revealed the truth. Why? It's obvious, now: I just couldn't bear to find out that it was all a fairytale – that he wasn't a prince, he wasn't *the one*; he was a hollow man living in a world of make-believe and peddling fake dreams.

From the vantage point I have now, it is completely clear. I am, in the words of the con man 'Colonel' Harry Harrington in the 1941 romantic comedy *The Lady Eve*, 'as fine a specimen of the sucker sapiens as I've ever seen'.

But, please don't be too hard on me. I think Alain de Botton might empathise with my situation. In *Essays in Love* he conjures up both the force and the deficiencies of the whirlwinds of love: 'a certain wilful exaggeration of the qualities of the beloved, an exaggeration which distracts us from our habitual pessimism . . . we base our fall into love upon insufficient material, and supplement our ignorance with desire'.

When I spoke to anthropologist Helen Fisher, she was empathetic. In addition to her university work, Helen is the chief scientist for the online dating behemoth Match Group, the parent company of brands including Match, Tinder and okcupid. She has both a scholarly and personal perspective on love and heartbreak. 'You shouldn't beat yourself up too much,' Dr Fisher says on the phone from New York. 'It's amazing what we overlook when we really like somebody. It's called "positive illusions" and, you know, when you're madly in love, activity in brain regions linked with decision-making begins to shut down, they begin to de-activate. We're very well built to deceive ourselves when we love.' I think of what psychiatrist Jacqueline Olds told me about love's effect on our cortical circuits, how our ability to judge someone else's character flies out the window.

ONE DAY I STUMBLE UPON AN ARTICLE on *The Conversation*, written by American cognitive scientist Vera Tobin about how writers exploit our brains with devices such as plot twists. In the article, Tobin referred to *The Sixth Sense*, that terrifying 1999 film in which Haley Joel Osment's character confides in psychologist Malcolm Crowe, played by Bruce Willis. 'I see dead people,' the little boy says. Then comes the wicked twist at the end – Crowe is one of the dead people, too, and it's all so obvious you kick yourself you didn't see it at the start. 'Remember that once we know the answer to a puzzle, its clues can seem more transparent than they really were,' Tobin writes.

On a gloomy Sydney winter's day I have a Skype conversation with Vera. She's in her study in Cleveland, Ohio, where she's an associate professor at Case Western Reserve University. I catch a glimpse of the American summer streaming in the window behind her.

Vera tries to console me: any reasonable person with the partial knowledge I had might have been persuaded to believe the stories I did, she says. She's warm and vivacious and I immediately feel comfortable talking with her about these difficult things. 'Seeing somebody's address on their driver's licence most of the time is a pretty good indicator that they live there,' she says. 'All those clichés about hindsight being 20/20 and so on really are true. Everything seems more obvious when you have the answer; you can't even remember what it was like not to know, now that you know.'

In Vera's book, *Elements of Surprise: Our Mental Limits and the Satisfactions of Plot*, I learn for the first time about a raft of cognitive concepts, unconscious cognitive biases, which can lead us astray. I grab at them eagerly. 'The curse of knowledge' and 'hindsight bias', for example, in which – and let's make this personal – the more information *you* have about something, say the outcome of *my* bad relationship with Joe, the harder it will be for you to understand how it would have been for me *not* to have that information, meaning you might overestimate how easy it should have been for me to predict the outcome that he was a bankrupt liar with a criminal record and a fantasy life. And 'anchoring', whereby someone relies too heavily on certain pieces of information to make decisions and form beliefs.

I relied on multiple anchors: certainly on that address on Joe's driver's licence, as evidence of his place of residence; on the fact of his antecedents – his successful grandfather, by all accounts a most decent man; on the information contained in the photographs he sent me; and, fundamentally, on his story that his ex-wife was crazy and erratic, which meant his never-ending stream of dramas and disappearances were plausible. I used as an anchor his business knowledge and interest, which I assumed he had inherited from his grandfather and saw in practice over countless breakfasts when he read the *Australian Financial Review*. A finance journalist wouldn't have needed five minutes with him to work out he was talking rubbish; a real grazier would have taken one look at him and laughed. Lies are easier to get away with when the liar is telling them about a specialist subject to a non-specialist.

Instead of thinking it strange that an affluent man drove a decrepit Defender, I relied on misleading thinking about it – first, that it was a signifier of Joe's frugal, understated ways; second, that it was an object of desire: in addition to his comments about it being a collector's item, my brother had always enthused about the model. I relied on the huge volume of highly specific detail Joe shared – people's names, and intimate stories about them, and minutiae such as his talk of *Leucochrysum albicans*, that troublesome little native daisy.

I believed erroneously in another anchor, too – that most people in the world are fundamentally truthful.

'Once an anchor is set, it can be very difficult to break away from its grip,' says Vera. She writes in her book about magicians' techniques and what we can learn from them. 'The tricks they have painstakingly developed to mislead and delight their audiences are also beautiful laboratories of perceptual and cognitive psychology. They show us when and how people will reliably notice some things rather than others, where they will see things that aren't present and miss things that are, and how they can be induced to believe they have been given free choice when only one option was ever available.'

In *Wilful Blindness: Why We Ignore the Obvious at Our Peril*, English author Margaret Heffernan adds to what I have learnt from Vera: '[Wilful blindness] is a human phenomenon to which we all succumb in matters little and large. We can't notice and know everything: the cognitive limits of our brain simply won't let us. That means we have to filter or edit what we take in. So what we choose to let through and to leave out is crucial. We mostly admit the information that makes us feel great about ourselves, while conveniently filtering whatever unsettles our fragile egos and most vital beliefs.'

Heffernan offers any number of examples of wilful blindness, both institutional and individual: the 'blind intransigence' of the Catholic Church about abuse of children by priests. The sun-damaged patients who get angry when their dermatologist explains to them that the tanning sunbeds they use could kill them. The mother in a relationship with a man who is abusing her children; she knows he has a past conviction for sex abuse but has convinced herself he has changed.

'It's a truism that love is blind; what's less obvious is just how much evidence it can ignore,' says Heffernan.

Nev Schulman's story proves how much evidence it's possible to ignore. When I learn about it, I'm further reassured that I'm far from the only one to have suffered temporary blindness. Schulman, a young, good-looking American actor, producer and photographer, was the subject of the 2010 documentary *Catfish*. In his mid-twenties he began an online relationship with a woman, a pretty young musician named Megan. In his book, *In Real Life: Love, Lies and Identity in the Digital Age*, he writes of how he spent eight months enraptured by Megan, 'texting daily, spending hours on the phone every week, exchanging a huge volume of email and Facebook messages'. He never met her. Eventually he discovered that Megan didn't exist. But Angela did: she was a frumpy, unhappy middle-aged woman who had conscripted Schulman as the unwitting lead character for her world of fantasy.

Such was the success of Schulman's documentary, such was (and is) the global epidemic of catfishing, that he went on to produce a follow-up and highly rating MTV series. 'Catfishing' has entered twenty-first-century dictionaries as a term to describe the activities of a person who builds a fake social media profile, usually appropriating someone else's photos and biographical details they've found online, to trick someone into falling in love with them – the one fished never actually meets the fisher-person. In some instances, the person doing the fishing is like Angela, lonely and building a fantasy world, but catfishing is also perpetrated for financial gain. As ABC's *Four Corners* revealed in early 2019, any number of young West African men, posing as dashing cyber suitors, are systematically breaking the hearts, bank balances and lives of women around the world.

In his book, Schulman explains how it is that the catfishing stories which a viewer can see are outlandish are so believable to the victim. '[In our series] we don't have the advantage of showing our viewers the slow, piece-by-piece trickle of how each relationship developed,' he writes. 'When you talk to someone every day, you feel like they care about you . . . But when you fast-forward and sum up an entire digital relationship from the outside, it often looks totally implausible.'

I can only inadequately show you the trickle of the develop-ment of my relationship with Joe. We exchanged countless texts and emails and, unlike a catfishing victim such as Schulman, had dozens of moments of physical contact over nearly eighteen months. For the purposes of this retelling I have abbreviated the details of the love I felt and instead lingered on the details of his inconsistencies and inconstancy. You did not feel the intensity I felt in his embrace, know the looks we shared, nor the sincerity with which he seemed to speak, his commanding voice.

7

DISORDERED

For everything the Harvard professors, the famous anthropologist and the kind cognitive scientist have told me, I remain enfolded in a shroud of shame. It is a double-edged embarrassment: if I share the story more widely, people will see how foolish I have been; they will see what I fear: that for a man to have treated me in such a way, he must have recognised my limited value.

But a stronger instinct starts to assert itself: I *must* reveal this story. When I slip away from myself and look back at it as an outsider, as Amelia has done, I can see its gothic, bodice-ripping potential: the brooding, self-confessed villain ('La Bête Noir', no less), a wan and weakening heroine, the treachery and horror, the web of deceit, an ancestral curse, the pervasive aura of impending doom, the slowly dawning sense of wonder . . . It's magnificent! It's hilarious! Joe has given a writer a greater gift than some silly old silver-cased Victorian pencil; in fact, it is as though he laid this fabulous material out for me deliberately, as though he wanted me to tell this story.

I start to share with friends what has happened.

Oh my god, everyone says, you should write a novel.

Of course, fiction and film have long adored the malignant narcissist, the tragic fantasist, the conscience-free con man. Joe is hardly original. He is the appalling Gilbert Osmond in Henry James's *The Portrait of a Lady* with his demonic imagination and egotism 'hidden like a serpent in a bank of flowers'. He is Walter Mitty dwelling in the 'remote intimate airways of his mind'. He is Gatsby telling Nick Carraway how he lived like 'a young rajah in all the capitals of Europe . . . collecting jewels, chiefly rubies, hunting big game, painting a little'. It is as though Joe has assembled himself from bits of others – from Nicholas Cage's Roy in *Matchstick Men*, from Steve Martin's clownish Freddy Benson in *Dirty Rotten Scoundrels*, from Matt Damon's talented Tom Ripley, who 'always thought it'd be better to be a fake somebody than a real nobody'.

On a putrid summer's day, I pull the blinds down in my study to block the heat and play around with an opening to my own fictional venture.

For a time after the scream there was silence. The rosellas squabbling over eucalyptus blossoms ceased their chatter; the traffic hum from the highway stopped. It was as though the air had been sucked out of the atmosphere. Now the red dog moves. Her chain clanks. She sniffs the ground at the bottom of the door, whines, circles the veranda as far as the chain will allow and returns her nose to the door again.

A ruby flow is seeping from inside the cottage, out under the door, on to the veranda. Now the rosellas restart their mad screeching; a distant truck changes gears as it comes down into the valley. The dog whines and scratches the ground until her paws are wet and sticky. She puts her snout down, sniffs again, and, tentatively at first, and then with increasing enthusiasm, starts to drink from the pooling blood.

I am hot and listless and I don't know where to go from here. Who is the murderer? Who survives? What reckoning will there be? Besides, in my story, truth is stranger than fiction. As the sun lowers, I abandon my keyboard and drive to the ladies baths.

A languor lies across them; women – large, small, voluptuous, elfin, plain, pretty, gnarled, pubescent, clad, half-clad, brown, white – are draped on the grassy patches above the water and the baking rocks at the edge of the sea below. I join others lolling in the water; I starfish on my back, and as the sky softens and a hot wind brushes my exposed skin, things come to me: a picture of Joe waiting for me in a bar or restaurant, and he is a different beast. Not the affectionate, affable fiction, but the cold, hard reality. His eyes are slits and he is watchful and his slow glance grazes across people as he looks and waits. Here he is now, walking towards me, erect posture, feet thrown out slightly and then solidly returned to the ground. My mind's eye is drawn to his sloping shoulders and sagging jawline. I compose an email to him in which my vicious rebuke is so perfectly pitched that he melts like an ice cream into a summer footpath. I reach my arms out further in the water, move my fingers and they collide with flesh. I tread water again, reel in my imaginings.

The woman I have bumped into seems entirely constructed of curves and warmth. We bob together and talk. She is exotic and her dark hair tumbles from the top of her head; I picture her in a *hammam*, a bath-house, steamy, shards of light piercing the golden-arched dimness, the sound of gently trickling water. She comes to the ladies baths almost every afternoon, and they have helped her through grief. Four years ago she lost her wonderful husband of sixteen years. Within seven weeks of being diagnosed with cancer, he was dead. Now she finds comfort in the water, in meditation, and in her women's drumming group. They drum and chant. 'It's very shamanic,' she tells me. 'We call it ooga-booga.' I start to share something of my own story. Perhaps, I venture, I should join her ooga-booga group. My eyes prick with tears. Another woman, wrinkled, grey, topless, enters our water circle. She is loud and agitated; she wants to talk about how her handbag was stolen. She goes on and on about the violation of it, the stress . . .

•

Consider the dismal context in which we find ourselves. A woman a week is murdered in Australia by a current or former partner. One in five women reports having been physically or sexually assaulted and/or threatened since they were fifteen. Eighty-five per cent of Australian women over the age of fifteen have been sexually harassed. A woman lodges a sexual harassment complaint against the then deputy prime minister, Barnaby Joyce; he resigns, then publicly throws doubt on the paternity of the unborn child that his girlfriend, a woman for whom he has abandoned his wife, is carrying. In the US, the *Washington Post* releases a recording of Donald Trump saying that if he wants a woman, he doesn't wait, he just grabs her by the pussy. A month or so later he's the leader of the free world. Like skittles, some of the creepy guys topple – Bill O'Reilly, Harvey Weinstein, Bill Cosby, Larry Nassar, Don Burke. Hashtag MeToo. *New York* magazine advice columnist Heather Havrilesky nominates 2017 as the 'Year of the Sociopathic Baby-Man'. 'It feels,' she writes, 'like we're cursed by an increasingly grotesque subspecies of this infantile beast at every turn.'

Havrilesky is talking about apex male predators of the most egregious kind and prefers not to use the term 'toxic masculinity'. But it works for me: everywhere I go now, one degree or other of toxic masculinity slaps me in the face. The driver who shakes his fist at me when I'm out on my bicycle and he's forced to slow his Ferrari. A small man in an expensive suit in an elegant city bar I overhear giving a hissing commentary about a woman to his chuckling buddies ('fucking big tits' and 'fucking that' and, in his mouth, the word is a hard and nasty thing). The most pleasant, gentle man at a dinner party who, the hosts later tell me, talks in the crudest of terms about women when his wife or other women are absent. All men do it, says the male host, shrugging.

I interview a number of girls for a story about their lives online – Amelia makes it the cover story of *Good Weekend* and headlines it 'How Social Media Changed Everything for Teenage Girls'. I learn that boys throw dick pics at girls like confetti and make comments on girls' selfies like, 'Take that dress off then I'll do you.' *Vanity Fair* headlines an article 'Tinder and the Dawn of the Dating Apocalypse' and interviews young men at a bar in Manhattan's financial district who take it for granted they'll have multiple dates running at once, often in the course of one night. One young man compares young women to restaurants: 'You can't be stuck in one lane,' he tells the author, Nancy Jo Sales. 'If you had a reservation somewhere and then a table at Per Se opened up, you'd want to go there.' Sales interviews young women who take it for granted they'll get texts from men they've never met asking things like, 'Wanna fuck?' or 'Come over and sit on my face.' In a text or email or on Snapchat or Messenger you can be whoever you want to be, and you can say whatever you like, because you don't have to look someone in the face when you say it.

A Perth judge sentences a man called Leigh Abbot, a thirty-seven-year-old one-time footballer, to three-and-a-half years' jail after he extorted about $160,000 from twelve women he'd met on dating sites including Tinder and Plenty of Fish – he threatened to release sexually explicit photographs of them if they didn't pay up. A psychologist's report said of him: '[He] could be gracious and charming, but underlying that facade was a person who could be cruel, malicious and fear provoking . . . [and] who lives by the law of the jungle.' Scamwatch, an arm of the Australian Competition and Consumer Commission, reports that in 2018 Australians lost $24.5 million in dating and romance scams. In the US, the Federal Trade Commission announces that in 2018 romance-related scams generated more reported losses than any other consumer fraud type. Losses quadrupled from $33 million in 2015 to $143 million in 2018.

Los Angeles Times journalist Christopher Goffard spent nearly a year working on a true-crime podcast series called *Dirty John,* about a relationship between an interior designer, Debra Newell, and a sinister, 'black-hearted Lothario' she meets online, John Meehan. 'It was as if he was finding victims and feeding them into the void where his soul ought to be,' Goffard told *Rolling Stone*. Within six weeks of its launch in October 2017, *Dirty John* had been downloaded an estimated ten million times. Actor Eric Bana plays Meehan in the TV series based on the podcast. At the Oscars a few months later, shortly before *The Shape of Water*, a film about a woman's relationship with a strange scaled river creature, won Best Picture, host Jimmy Kimmel told the audience, 'We will always remember this year as the year men screwed up so badly, women started dating fish.'

A number of women in Port Lincoln, South Australia, are stalked and terrified at night by drones hovering outside their bedroom or bathroom windows. The *New York Times* reports that South Korean women are protesting against an epidemic of hidden cameras across the nation – the cameras are perched inside public restroom toilet bowls or disguised as smoke detectors in shop fitting rooms, and the images taken often end up on pornographic websites. Los Angeles writer Alexandra Tweten sets up @byefelipe, an Instagram account in which women contribute the violent/misogynistic/pathetic messages they receive from men via online dating apps. The account quickly gains nearly half a million followers. Tweten sorts the emails she receives into categories: dick pics, fat shamers, fuckboys, mansplainers, trolls. A friend tells me of the night she took home a man she'd met online. Eventually, after some time in her bedroom, he told her he couldn't have 'normal sex' because he'd watched too much porn.

It's little wonder that the famous five of *Queer Eye* pack a certain smugness in their pick-up truck as they tour Georgia giving makeovers to sad men struggling with the weight of life and bad hair. These guys are gentle. They hug each other. They've got their shit together. 'In each new installment of the reboot, queerness is gently suggested as an antidote to the hot mess of toxic masculinity under late-stage capitalism,' writes the English journalist and critic Laurie Penny for *The Baffler* magazine. 'The gimmick is that heterosexuality is a disaster, toxic masculinity is killing the world, and there are ways out of it aside from fascism or festering away in a lonely bedroom until you are eaten by your starving pit bull or your own insecurities.' Perhaps someone should let the incels know.

Of course, popular culture plays the moment, plays women, for the laughs; I binge watch the Jill Soloway creation *Transparent* – wall-to-wall sad and damaged humans – and roll around my lounge-room floor laughing when a female dominatrix tells one of the characters, as she pays for her services, 'It's really not that hard for a woman to find someone to treat her like shit for free.' And what fair game women over forty are, even more so if they're single. In *Veep*, the slimy lobbyist Sidney Purcell fires the deputy director of communications, Dan, for being 'basically as useless to me as a forty-year-old woman'. In the Laura Dern vehicle *Enlightened*, a character makes the comment, 'Look, picking up a single woman in her forties? Please, it's like shooting fish in a barrel. Old fish.' By the time I see Brooklyn illustrator Emily Flake's *New Yorker* cartoon – a woman sitting over a martini lamenting to another woman, 'Every guy out there is either married, gay, or a human suit zipped around a column of ants' –

I'm waving the first white flag I can find – most likely Bonds comfy classic full-brief cottontails because I'm not ever going to let anyone see them.

I COMPLAIN, OF COURSE I DO, about being single again, about the lonely sound of Saturday nights, of every other night. My friend Alecia thinks I should start dating again. She thinks I should consider a younger man. She's found one on Tinder. She thinks that's where I should look. 'Steph, at this point I think you need to make friends with your spit-flecked rage,' she texts me with characteristic eloquence. 'There's no better way to cure longing and nostalgia. J–, he's truly great, and you too must embrace a younger lover. K– was seeing a 26-year-old at the age of 44; P– has a 39-year-old in her 60s. I'll work on getting you yr own. Xx'

Alecia's J– is lovely. Her message sparks just a little curiosity in me. I take a look at Tinder. I set up a profile and choose a pseudonym, 'Annie', which is at least half-true – and a photograph of myself in shadow so as to remain incognito. I swipe left and left again, over and over – reject, reject, reject, reject – and wonder what it is that makes a man looking for a date think a tattooed bare torso and a come-hither trail of abdominal hair will do the job. Perhaps I swipe right once or twice, I can't recall, but in any case, soon enough I have a message. A man with an equally shadowy photograph, but who seems to be fully clothed, has written to alert me to the fact that my Tinder settings are such that anyone looking at me can click straight through to my Facebook profile and see who I am. Panic! I go into privacy lockdown. I message the man to thank him for the warning.

We catch up at a cocktail bar one night. I don't want to go, I curse myself for having agreed to do so. Before I arrive, all I know is that he works in a creative field and can spell. When I arrive, after I have suffered his clammy, tiny handshake, I discover that his shadowy profile neglected to mention a vital piece of information: his speech, his face and his movements make it clear that he has some neurological damage. Almost before I sit down, perhaps as an apology for not revealing the information earlier, he explains that he sustained a brain injury that has left its mark. I sip my drink and smile and do my very, very best to be empathetic and interested, but I get lost trying to keep up with his conversation, a Jabberwocky of lines that gyre and gimble and duck and weave off on tangents. All I can think about is an escape plan.

I go on a date with a man I have met through a friend. He arrives at my apartment with a bunch of flowers plucked from a convenience store's bucket. How lovely, I tell him, and I mean it. We walk to a local restaurant and I think as we walk that even nerves can't explain why he's so jittery, so weird. 'Are you okay?' I ask.

'Oh, it's the Ritalin and the painkillers,' he says. 'My back's been bad.' I consider giving him a shove and making a run for it. At the restaurant, he boasts about his wine knowledge to the sommelier and then settles in to talk about himself. He has a passionate interest in himself. Such is his enthusiasm for his special subject that I barely need to adopt the customary position of asking questions, although I venture one – do you have children? Perhaps he's in a drug-induced delirium because he tells me then about his teenage daughter who has cut marks up and down her arm.

He tells me that, one day when he was still married to her mother, his daughter said to him, 'Mum doesn't like you very much, does she?' My mind wanders to past first dates, to other over-sharing suitors: the skinny doctor who told me all about the tantric sex ashram in Goa from which he'd just returned and where each new visitor was required to submit to an STD test; the small public servant, grey in colour and character, who wanted to tell me all about his ex-girlfriend's kooky sexual proclivities.

When, finally, I manage to tear myself away from the man who needs to find a good therapist, and am home alone again, I close my front door and lean back against it and scream very loudly and think it will be a cold day in hell before I date again. I think that the world and all the people in it are teetering, damaged, broken, held together by safety pins and staples; that the centre is not holding.

•

I'm not sleeping. I wake at 2, 3, 4 am, and roll and toss and stretch my arms and legs at diagonals in my empty bed; throw one pillow and grab another one and get tangled up in the bedsheets and eventually sit up and reach for my laptop.

In these past few months, this has become a habit – looking for illumination in the early hours. The first terms I searched were 'pathological liar', 'compulsive liar' and 'relationship'. The collective knowledge of humankind wasted no time in offering me insight. Pathological liars are frequently possessed of a personality disorder, possibly narcissistic personality disorder. Pathological liars have, at the very least, strong narcissistic traits.

Narcissists are usually pathological liars. So are sociopaths. Psychopaths, too. Con artists likely have 'dark triad' traits – psychopathy, narcissism and Machiavellianism. I'm on a quest for understanding now, travelling through eerie, cognitively dissonant territory and into a warren of goblin caves towards Gollum.

Perhaps I am not alone in having mistakenly thought the term 'narcissist' generally described a person's self-absorption, particularly in relation to their physical appearance: the word derives from the preening, prideful obsession of the beautiful hunter Narcissus in Greek mythology, who is said to have fallen for his own reflection in a pool of water, a level of self-involvement that equips him well for the age of the selfie. But now I believe that our understanding of an often malignant personality type is diminished when we use the terms 'narcissist' and 'narcissism' lightly. In the fifth edition of the American Psychiatric Association's *Diagnostic and Statistical Manual of Mental Disorders* (DSM-5), a reference point for psychiatrists, psychologists and counsellors internationally, narcissistic personality disorder is one of ten personality disorders.

According to the association, 'personality disorders are associated with ways of thinking and feeling about oneself and others that significantly and adversely affect how an individual functions in many aspects of life'. About 6.5 per cent of Australian adults are estimated to have a personality disorder – a greater number than have diabetes.

The DSM-5, which I read feverishly as the city sleeps, breaks the ten personality disorders into three clusters:

- Cluster A: odd, bizarre, eccentric (including paranoid and schizotypal personality disorders)

188

- Cluster B: dramatic, emotional, erratic (including anti-social, narcissistic and borderline personality disorders)
- Cluster C: anxious, fearful (including obsessive compulsive personality disorders)

Psychopathy and sociopathy are not listed as disorders and when I dig further I learn they are considered to be covered by Cluster B's 'antisocial personality disorder' (APD). Indeed, I am enlightened when I examine the Cluster B disorders, especially antisocial personal disorder and narcissistic personality disorder (NPD). According to the DSM-5, APD is marked by 'a pervasive pattern of disregard for and violation of the rights of others'. This might include a 'failure to conform to social norms with respect to lawful behaviours'; 'deceitfulness'; and 'lack of remorse'.

Reflecting the fact that this is an evolving research field, the manual also includes an alternative model for diagnosing personality disorders. As I read, I'm struck by a line in the alternative model for APD: 'Incapacity for mutually intimate relationships, as exploitation is a primary means of relating to others, including by deceit and coercion.' The alternative model for APD lists seven personality traits that might be evident, including manipulativeness; deceitfulness ('misrepresentation of self; embellishment or fabrication when relating events'); hostility (anger or irritability in response to minor slights; mean, nasty, or vengeful behaviour); and risk taking.

I find revealing information too in the description of the characteristics of narcissistic personality disorder. According to the DSM-5, NPD is characterised by 'a pervasive pattern of grandiosity (in fantasy or behaviour), need for admiration, and lack of empathy'. Someone with NPD is likely to be self-centred and have a 'grandiose sense of self-importance' and a sense of entitlement.

The alternative model for NPD lists impairments in a person's functioning, including 'excessive reference to others for self-definition and self-esteem regulation', and a pattern of having relationships that are 'largely superficial and exist to serve self-esteem regulation' or which are rooted in a 'need for personal gain'.

A vision of Joe comes to me. Look, now he's a paper doll, naked and pink: so light he will blow away if I don't hold him down. I proceed to dress him in paper-doll clothes. To start, I cover his vulnerabilities with a pair of blood-red boxer shorts and fold over the paper tabs to keep them in place. I give the boxers an identity tag, labelling them 'disregard for, and violation of the rights of others'. I think of the trail of damage Joe has left in people's lives over years. I put a singlet on him and pin a label on it with the APD trait of 'failure to conform to social norms'. I fold paper moleskin trousers on to my paper-doll ex-boyfriend and label them 'deceitfulness, misrepresentation of self, embellishment or fabrication when relating events'. All the grand tales – the harbourside house, the acquisition of property, meetings with the former treasurer Wayne Swan and the Chinese president's delegation, the call from Google in Silicon Valley. I button up his blue-green-check shirt and tag it 'risk taking': surely he knew that one day I would come to discover what he had done and feel compelled to use my journalism skills to tell this story?

He needs something to cover his feet now, and I look at the list of traits for narcissistic personality disorder. I give him yellow socks and designate them as the narcissistic trait of 'a grandiose sense of self-importance', for all the stories and fantasies he used to mask his own lack of anything. I see now a pattern of condescension and contempt: one day a 'squadron of chooks' disturbed his coffee; another time he referred to 'impressively thick' members of the 'handbag and hot-flush club' who were only interested in money – their husband's money, anyone's money. Real estate agents were 'lower forms of life'. He had only disdain for his father, his brothers and his ex-wife. I put a pair of R. M. Williams boots on him and tag them 'excessive reference to others for self-definition and self-esteem'. I think of the times he said, 'Let's go out – I want to show you off,' or told me proudly that other men had cast admiring glances my way.

I could keep playing paper-doll dress-ups. There is so much of Joe in the DSM-5 descriptions. But I am puzzled because he doesn't fit neatly into either narcissistic or antisocial personality disorder, and I am heartsick that, no matter what he is, this is the disfigured destination to which this quest has led me. In my head I strip the paper doll of its layers of paper clothing and behaviours. And now I can see there's nothing left, nothing left at all but an old piece of paper in the shape of a person. I scrunch it up and throw it away.

THE AMERICAN PSYCHIATRIC ASSOCIATION is a sage looking down on a rabble of pop psychology. But for the time being it is pop psychology's translation of the dry academic language into relatable, human terms that I find most helpful. I can barely believe it but as I move from one site to another, it becomes apparent that the specific dynamics of my relationship with Joe are by no means unusual.

I am one of tens of thousands, maybe hundreds of thousands, of bewildered women and men around the world huddling in online communities desperate for empathy and explanations; who want to know who behaves like that, how can he or she even *be*!? So, so many of them, so many hair-raising stories. There to help, dispensing pithy slogans, you-go-girl-style motivation and 'affordable healing sessions', are countless clinical psychologists, life coaches, counsellors, survivors and amateur experts. On Facebook you'll find them at Psychopath Free (half a million followers), the Covert Narcissism group, the Refuge Survivors ('empaths surviving narcissism and sociopath abuse') and After Narcissistic Abuse ('there is light, life and love'); on Instagram are, among others, Narcissist Free (24,000 followers), Narc Knowledge (60,000) and Narcissist-Sociopath Awareness (135,000). There is a sickness in the soul of an inestimable number of relationships; an inestimable number of people are suffering at the hands of lovers or family members with personality disorders.

To be sure, it's likely that a number of the aggrieved following these accounts and commenting on their posts are overwrought and, in their grief and rage, exaggerating, mislabelling or wrongly maligning their former lovers. But even accounting for that, there is a remarkable consistency in the large number of testimonies that reveal distinct patterns of abominable behaviour.

Research has established that personality disorders occur at the same rate in males and females, but in these communities, perhaps naturally enough, it is women more often than men who are telling their stories, sometimes about same-sex partners. By taking their stories in unison and using the dialect of this territory, it is possible to assemble a template, an identikit image, if you like, of a typical pathologically toxic, personality-disordered lover, and how a relationship with him might progress.

LET'S CALL HIM NIGEL, NIGEL THE *NARC*. There's just something about Nigel – he's so damn charming. He tells you about his dazzling resumé and about a promising venture he has in the pipeline. But he's humble, too; nothing he says ever seems like bragging. (Later, you'll learn about covert narcissists, creatures who have perfected the art of appearing gentle, vulnerable, modest.)

With Nigel, things move fast. In the idealisation stage, he love bombs you – you've never had such an intense relationship! You're soulmates, he says, there's no one else in the world like you. Actually he's not feeling anything. But he's a very good actor and he studies everything you say and do so his responses are perfectly pitched. Quickly you're moving in together, or are married.

Just as quickly, though, Nigel changes. He's surly or silent or threatening. He says work is tough, or his ex-wife is being a psycho-bitch. And his life is so complex: there are legal battles – over this, over that, over the property settlement, over custody arrangements. (Later, you'll discover that people such as Nigel love tormenting their former partners with protracted court battles that have nothing to do with their children's wellbeing and everything to do with their need for power and fondness for the dramatic.) Now he's waiting for payment for some work he's done – can you help him with some money to tide him over?

Once or twice Nigel breaks down and cries. He's a good man who's been through a rough time. It wasn't his fault he was sacked; he was entitled to a partnership but his idiot boss was jealous of his talent.

You're in love with him, but you're confused. The venture Nigel talked about doesn't seem to be happening, and one day a friend sees him having coffee with a woman. You ask him about it and he tells you not to be stupid, it was his lawyer. 'Are you crazy?' is what he starts to say when you ask him about things that don't add up. 'You're imagining things' or 'There's always drama with you, isn't there?'

He doesn't seem to have many friends, but now he's telling you about a woman he's met at the gym and how he's confiding in her about relationship issues. He talks about her so much; you don't know that he's 'triangulating' you with her.

Your best friend is worried: she doesn't trust him, but you fiercely defend him. You don't see her so often after that. You don't see your family much either because Nigel doesn't like them. His manipulations are now isolating you from your support network.

And Nigel has started to scare you. One day during a discussion about something minor he stands over you and his eyes are cold and you think he might even hit you. Other times, he ignores you for days: everything's your fault, he says. You don't know it, but his angry responses are narcissistic rage and you're in the 'devaluation' stage now.

Often, Nigel vanishes. He doesn't tell you where he's going, and when he comes back – sometimes days later – you don't dare ask. His stories are constantly shifting, his excuses are weird and if you dare question him your conversations go in circles.

You don't see the breakup, the 'discard' stage, coming. Maybe on the way out he says he can't stand to look at you anymore. Your relationship has probably lasted about three years. Afterwards, you discover how often relationships with narcs end after about three years. You learn that they need more stimulation than normal people, they get bored easily. Perhaps that's why it's over so soon, or maybe they're just tired of putting in the work to maintain their persona.

You gradually discover that almost nothing about Nigel or his story was real. Every last little thing that bothered you was actually part of a puzzle that you can only now assemble. You'll learn other things about Nigel as time goes on. Perhaps there's a string of mysterious events in his past, or an addiction he hid, or even the hospitalisation or suicide of a former partner. He's likely to owe money.

And you learn about *gaslighting* – you watch the old black and white movie *Gaslight* and see how Charles Boyer's character torments Ingrid Bergman's Paula, telling her that she's imagining mysterious noises in the attic, a gaslight dimming unaccountably, until she starts to doubt her own reality.

Soon Nigel has a new girlfriend and you learn she was around before he walked out on you. Narcs like to have new 'supply' lined up before they get rid of the old. They need constant attention and adulation – everything in their life is about being seen to be a winner. But one day he knocks on your door. He's sorry – he's realised what a terrible mistake it was to leave you, there is no other woman in the world for him but you. He's 'hoovering' to get you back. But you know now that Nigel has ice where normal people have blood and, in his utter self-absorption and single-minded pursuit of self-gratification, he'll say anything to get what he wants. He is devoid of a conscience. You know that you have been a victim of an emotionally violent form of abuse. You tell Nigel the Narc never to contact you again. You shut the door on him. You maintain NC (no contact).

One day on @narcissistfreenow there's a post that gives you a chill. It's a photograph in which a sleeping man lies curled up in bed with a grotesque creature that looks like something out of *The Walking Dead*. 'If you could see people's energies you wouldn't sleep with just anyone,' reads the caption. Then, on another of the Instagram accounts you follow, @Narcissistic_abuse, you read a quote that makes you weep. 'We eat lies when our heart is hungry.'

•

Around the time I was in Tasmania with Joe and feeling like the world was all before me, Josie Charles's world was crumbling in Florida. In May 2015 she had the locks changed on her house in a beachside community near Jacksonville. She spent a week crying. She lost 10 kilograms in a month. An ulcer ruptured and she started to vomit blood. She thought she was losing her mind. 'And then I said, "I'm done. I'm not crying anymore. I have to figure out what happened."'

By August 2015 Josie had started an Instagram account, Narcissist-Sociopath Awareness (@narcissist.sociopath.awarenes2). It was a way of keeping a journal, a way of healing, but it was something else, too. In the bio she wrote, 'This is for you SC. I'm praying for you.' SC were the initials of the young woman whom Josie's former partner Simon had moved on to. The Instagram posts were a way of warning SC. Josie posted aphorisms such as 'Don't be misled: lust is not love, anxiety is not excitement, control is not devotion' and 'In order to hook you, narcissists will appeal to your deep sense of compassion; they will initially appear humble and wounded, proclaiming that only you can heal them.' They were insights Josie would have liked to have had when, as a divorcee in her early forties with two children, she embarked on a relationship with Simon.

In a long conversation on the phone from Florida, Josie tells me all about Simon. 'The guy, I got to tell you, he was hilarious and he was easy to talk to; super-charming, but, like, really laid-back – the whole Aussie, no-worries-no-drama mentality.' Simon was an Australian footballer who had moved to the US to play in a small Florida league. In early 2012 she met him at a gym where he was employed part-time – they started flirting one night when she was the last one working out. He was ten years younger than Josie and he told her that he was married to an American woman he barely knew – he'd married her so he could get a green card, and they didn't live together. Josie didn't want a bar of a married man and straight away she thought, *close that down*. But their friendship grew after Simon told her his current employers were giving him a hard time. She started to help him set up his own personal training business.

Within six months Simon had moved in with her. 'I mean, the sex was insane and was constant,' Josie recalls. 'I had been in a rut; he was the first person I dated after my fourteen-year marriage dissolved in 2010.' She thought there wasn't much more to the relationship than sex. She knew he'd taken drugs in the past and was wary. But then he started to get under her skin.

'He was never anything but 100 per cent supportive, doting, loving, kind, generous, helpful. I mean, honestly, I never had such a wonderful relationship with someone.' He played football with her son. Her daughter adored him.

Josie, who has a degree in business communications, stepped up to handle his immigration paperwork, his business and his taxes. She introduced him to friends, who tipped tens of thousands of dollars into his new business and encouraged others to take him on as their trainer. 'He was absolutely the centre of our universe, my kids' and mine.' And he wanted to marry her. He was at her all the time to get married. While we're on the phone, an email from Josie pings into my inbox. She's sent me a photograph; they look so good together – she, petite and pretty and blonde; he tall and dark with a lovely smile. But as good as everything was, Josie thought, *The hell I'm getting married. I just got divorced two years ago.*

Her business started to go through tough times and it got to the point that she was no longer able to support Simon's life and business. 'It was like the light went out of his eyes when that happened.' At the time, she put the change in his demeanour down to his stress about the immigration process: the woman he'd married had filed for divorce. He discovered that his application for conditions on his green card to be lifted had been rejected and he was told to leave the country. He increased the pressure on Josie. 'Show me what your ideal engagement ring is,' he said. But she could see the light in his eyes had dimmed further and his behaviour was becoming weird.

One day, Simon asked her to check something on his old Facebook account. In doing so she found historical messages between him and scores of women – 'Ten or eleven conversations going on at the one time, bouncing between girl to girl to girl and him just soaking up the adulation and the validation.' One message stood out: in escalating sex talk with a woman he had outlined a horrifying, violent rape fantasy. 'When I saw this, I was like, *who the hell is in my bed?*' When Josie confronted Simon, he told her he had been high on drugs at the time. 'I was really fucked up,' he told her. But he wasn't his normal assured self as he made his excuses; it was the only time she'd seen him off-kilter.

After that, it was a swift collapse. Her next discovery was a text on Simon's phone: 'Yeah man, you just really need to cut your losses and get out of there,' the message from one of his buddies said.

JOSIE CAN SEE EVERYTHING CLEARLY NOW. 'I loved this guy, but I also knew, if I'm honest, that from day one there was something quietly and slightly off about the whole thing,' she tells me. 'The inconsistencies, ever so slight, but inconsistencies – they troubled me.' There were red flags around his immigration status. She'd pushed them away, thinking, *what do I care – I don't work for Homeland Security or Immigration!* There were red flags when he moved in with her. Initially he was housesitting for her and looking after her dogs while she was travelling. When she returned, he stayed one night, then asked if he could stay another, and all of a sudden he was living with her. 'I could not get the guy out of my house, and as uncomfortable as I was and as much as I was knowing that this was a bad decision . . .'

She was hysterical when she confronted Simon about the text message from his mate. 'I had his phone in my hand and started punching him with it, basically like pounding on his back and going, "*Cut your losses?!?!*"' She demanded to know why he had still been proposing to her. He just kept saying, 'Things went south.' The last time he was in her home, he'd been taking steroids, he was pumped up. 'He looked at me in a way that I thought he was going to murder me. He scared the crap out of me.' She took out a restraining order.

Josie is still dealing with her losses: hundreds of thousands of dollars in alimony payments gone, plus tens of thousands she and her friends lent Simon. Her children, too, are still trying to come to terms with what happened. 'Three years later, it's a work in progress. My daughter was suicidal. These kids really had put all of their hope and their future and everything invested in Simon. To this day, my children say they don't know how they'll ever trust another man – like, ever, in any capacity. It's devastating.'

After it was all over, Josie became a detective. She contacted an ex-girlfriend of Simon in Australia. 'I said to her, "You don't know me but this is what's going on in my life." And she said, "Dear god, whatever you do, start protecting yourself now."' She told Josie that Simon had been married twice before. His first wife had ended up in a psychiatric ward. The woman he said he'd married to get his green card, the woman he said he'd barely known – he'd been living with her for years in Australia before they'd moved to the US. Simon had been a serious drug user and dealer and had ended up in hospital on more than one occasion after opiate overdoses. He'd been pursued by dealers to whom he owed money.

As we talk, I bring up Josie's Instagram account on my screen. It has gained 7000 followers since I last looked. The account that started as a journal for herself and a warning to Simon's new partner, SC, a nineteen-year-old nearly half his age, has become something else altogether. As it built a following, Josie started to get messages from people around the world begging for her advice. She started to speak with people on the phone to try to help them through the process of understanding what the fuck had just happened to them. She got a certification as a life coach. 'I felt like, I'm supposed to do this, like I have to do this.' She says that since 2015 she has talked to thousands of people. Fifty per cent of her clients are men. Every day she answers seventy to eighty direct Instagram messages and thirty to forty emails. She's rarely away from her computer. She charges people who can afford to pay for her phone consultations. Australia is her second-biggest market; she tells me we can't talk for much longer because she has a phone appointment with someone in Adelaide.

'I look at it like triage: I'm going to patch you up and stop the bleeding.' She frequently hears of situations where the victims of these toxic relationships have attempted or succeeded in taking their own life. 'I tell people, "I can't diagnose your ex-husband but I can tell you that he sure sounds like a very toxic human."' She talks to people for as long as they're dealing with the immediate aftermath of a specific situation and then urges them to see a qualified therapist. 'And you know what's funny – they're all the same. People will say, "Well, you wouldn't believe it, he did this and he did that," and I'll be like, "Yeah, and then did he do this?" And they're like, "Oh my god, how did you know – are you a psychic?" and I'm like, "Nope, I'm more of a mathematician: it's a formula."'

Josie has learnt many things about personality-disordered men in particular. 'They love to impregnate women,' she says.

'They sort of spread their seed everywhere and then promptly abandon their partner.' They also love to drop hints about their true nature. She describes it as a 'psychopathic tell'. Simon sometimes told her he was a 'monster'. She thought he was talking about his past, when he took drugs, and she'd reassure him he was anything but and think, *oh my god, this guy's an angel.* She thinks it's why he gave her access to his Facebook page, where such incriminating messages resided.

'These guys are so charming, they're very believable. I don't think we're naive, I don't think we're gullible. I think it's that they are incredibly good at what they do. I will definitely take personal responsibility for a lot of stupid things that I did along the way. But, god, they're good.'

Now I reflect on Simon and Joe's behaviour through the prism of cons and con artists. 'You don't seem like a bad guy,' the character Angela says to *Matchstick Men*'s Roy, a small-time grifter. 'That's what makes me good at it,' Roy says.

Josie and I talk about how isolated and alone women feel after these relationships collapse. 'You've been protecting his image and you've been making excuses for him to your friends and family, and I think that's why we sort of crawl back into the hole whence we came, and try to get over this in a solitary, isolated, confused state,' she says. 'I don't think that anybody should ever have to do that. We need to call it what it is. This is fraud. It's just fraud.'

8

WHO THE HELL ARE YOU?

About eight months after Joe's passing from my life, in mid-2016, I show the world my wounds. I write an article for *Good Weekend* magazine about being a circumstantially childless woman. I have always wanted children. I wanted four children, maybe five. Since forever this was the picture: *the one* sitting at the end of a long table, gazing adoringly at me; the children lined up and down each side, gazing adoringly at me. A roaring hearth, a golden retriever; and nightly I would cook and ladle out meals of incomparable deliciousness. It seemed a straightforward enough idea, an automatic, adult progression. See how crazy and fucked-up fairytales are.

It wasn't in my picture that, at the age of forty, after breaking up with a man for whom I'd moved from Hong Kong to Melbourne, I'd be sitting solo in an IVF doctor's office asking how I might have a child on my own. The options were limited and unpalatable. It was 2005; at the time, Victorian law barred single women and lesbians from IVF treatment. For access to donor sperm and the disagreeable associated procedures, I would need to travel back and forth across state lines into New South Wales, a clucky outlaw. In the same week, I sat at home one night face-palming as I watched an interview on a current affairs program with a sperm donor who had fathered dozens of children around the country. When he talked, a whistle blew through the hole in his mouth where a couple of front teeth should have been. I didn't go back to the IVF doctor. Three or four years later, most likely too late, drinking beer and shelling peanuts in a Sydney bar with a gay friend, I teetered on the edge of a precipice, words away from asking him for a donation. Then, in the flash of a peanut shell, I stopped. Too late, too old, too isolated, too terrified, too much at stake, too everything. And what if he said 'no'?

It wasn't in my picture, either, that one day I'd find myself sharing with a million or more readers of *Good Weekend* the messy grief lodged within me for the children I'd never had, and a secondary grief, the effect of the exclusion from much of adult society. For, when you reach a certain age, it's in the all-consuming world of parenthood – in playgrounds, parks and mothers' groups, at school pick-ups and fetes, on sidelines and at end-of-year concerts – that new connections are forged, invitations issued, circles cemented. Alongside that exclusion comes the tertiary effect – the looks, the questions, the outrageous commentary, the fallacious judgements. *How selfish, putting her career first,* or *My stake in the future is bigger than yours because I have a child,* or any sentence that includes 'As a mother', or 'A woman's purpose is to have children' . . . ad infinitum.

On the morning my article is published I lie in my bed feeling sick. Why, oh my god, *why*, have I volunteered to reveal this deeply private information about my regrets and vulnerabilities? I have painted a sign on myself for all to see – 'Sad Childless Woman'. I am a lunatic. I put a pillow over my head.

Later, I open my computer with trembling fingers. There are a dozen messages waiting for me. Hundreds more will arrive in the days ahead. Through them, I will discover the quiet despair of so many women without children, the little empty graves they keep hidden in their hearts, the daily tortures they endure. The women who contact me tell me how diminished they cannot help but feel – by 'the media hollering about the virtues of motherhood', by the 'invalidation of my views on so many topics and issues'. Others share their desperation, the tears that fall 'wondering if I will ever make peace with my situation'; the suicide constantly contemplated for 'feeling like such a loser in my own mind'.

And there is a subset of correspondent: women whose prime child-bearing years were spent with men who evaded or postponed discussions about babies. More than one woman tells me of having been in long-term relationships with men who were adamant they didn't want children but who went on to have them in subsequent relationships. 'My nurturing tendency has so far only benefited a series of damaged men who seem to be drawn to me and who I feel compelled to look after and "fix",' one woman writes, acknowledging the futility of such an exercise. 'Problem-riddled men . . . using up the 20s and 30s of empathetic, selfless women.' Says another: 'I spent from 22 to 29 putting a charming narcissist through uni, then when I met a "decent bloke" he didn't want to have children.' A woman emails to say she was trapped in a violent marriage and resisted bringing a child into that environment; finally she found the courage to leave but by then it was too late. Too late, too late, too late.

'For the first time I feel like I'm not alone,' someone says in an email thanking me for my article. The power of sharing a personal story.

I FEEL SAD AND EXPOSED but I put on a bright, strong face for an interview on ABC's *Lateline*. I reply individually to every one of the hundreds of people who email me. And still, if I dare, there is another personal story to write. It has not left me, not for a minute. 'You're not ready,' a friend counsels me one night. 'It's too soon.' It is true that I tamp down a volcanic rage. I am quick to tears. I am still, despite my increasing understanding of pathological personalities, huddling at odd hours with the bewildered on Instagram and in Facebook groups.

And I keep one eye on Kirstie's life online; I'm terribly curious to know more about her. One day she posts a video on Instagram and I hear her voice; it's a bit posh, sexy, strong. If I write the story, I will need to call her. I feel sick at the thought. But if I tuck away the story about Joe and the lessons I've learnt, mend my broken self, move on . . . Well, then there will be no need.

'I'm still thinking about it,' I tell friends when they ask if I'm going to write the story. I'm torn: haven't I shared enough now? I risk a great deal – my privacy, my pride, my dignity, my future romantic prospects. Nevertheless, my mind moves constantly towards the idea, on the magnificent potential of the material Joe has given me. I start to set up interviews. I map a story structure.

And I continue to look for signs of him on Kirstie's social media. He has not been there for months. Are they still together? Does she know who he is?

•

There are so many of him. He is, in one form or another, everywhere. I set up a string of Google alerts and the articles pour into my inbox from around the world. In St Paul, Minnesota, divorced flight attendant Missi Brandt met Richie Peterson through a dating site. An article in *The Atlantic* headed 'The Perfect Man Who Wasn't' relays the story. Peterson told Missi that he was 'a career naval officer, an Afghanistan veteran who was finishing his doctorate in political science'. He was tall and charming. He liked the good life. He paid for restaurants, hotels and took Missi out on his motorboat. But their relationship was plagued with dramas and weird stuff and constantly cancelled plans: he had to get his daughter into rehab; he had to get his dog, Thumper, put to sleep; his mother died; he was in a motorbike crash. One day Missi snuck a look in his wallet. She found his photograph on an ID card with a different name – Derek Alldred – and credit cards belonging to a woman called Linda. When she googled 'Derek Alldred', mug shots popped up. He was 'a career con man with a long history of deception'. Among multiple misdemeanours, he'd dated a Californian woman and stolen almost $200,000 from her. Missi and Linda finally met. Turned out, Derek had been siphoning money from Linda's savings. Thumper was still alive and living with Linda, an engineer at a nuclear power plant. Richie's mother was alive, too. They discovered he'd been seeing another woman, Joy. He'd told Joy that he was a professor who volunteered at a homeless shelter. In fact, he'd lived at the shelter for a time. Other women who had been in relationships with him emerged, including a doctor and a couple of tech workers.

'He used different names and occupations, but the identities he took on always had an element of financial prestige or manly valor: decorated veteran, surgeon, air marshal, investment banker,' journalist Rachel Monroe wrote in the *Atlantic* article. 'Con artists have long known that a uniform bolsters an illusion, and Derek was fond of dressing up in scrubs and military fatigues. He tended to look for women in their 40s or 50s, preferably divorced, preferably with a couple of kids and a dog or two. Many of the women he wooed were in a vulnerable place in their lives – recently divorced, fresh out of an abusive relationship, or recovering from a serious accident – and he presented himself as a hero and caretaker, the man who would step in and save the day.'

In 2018, in the Federal Courthouse in Sherman, Texas, Alldred was eventually sentenced to twenty-four years' jail for using dating websites to scam women. A busload of women arrived at the court to hear the sentencing. A documentary, *Seduced by Evil*, was released in early 2019 in which nine of around two-dozen women connected to Alldred were interviewed. Collectively they lost more than US$2 million.

Here's another: an unemployed man and wannabe actor called Brett Joseph, who lived with his parents in their modest brick-veneer home in Mudgee, convinced multiple women he was a wealthy pastoralist. He had multiple fake names. He told some he was Brett Ingham, a member of the poultry family, others that he was Hunter Baillieu, part of the department-store-founding Baillieu-Myer family, and others again that he was Brett Inglis and had serious racing connections. According to *A Current Affair*, as 'Hunter Baillieu' he made dummy offers on at least two mansions overlooking Sydney Harbour. He inveigled his way into wealthy circles in Sydney's eastern suburbs, including into the home of 'public relations queen' and charity fund-raiser Jane Ferguson, the sister of sidelined royal family member Sarah Ferguson. He claimed to have $15 million he wanted to put towards a worthy cause. A St Vincent's hospital spokesperson told the program that 'in good faith we explored a number of projects with him'. Eventually, the hospital discovered there was no family fortune or generous donation.

On 1 September 2016, after a six-month relationship, Griffith woman Daisy Armstrong booted Joseph out when she learnt about his egregious history as a scammer. 'He was literally every-thing I had dreamed of – or so I thought,' Daisy says on her website 'Stop Brett Joseph'. As she picked up the pieces of her life in country New South Wales, artist Stephanie Hoskins was about to fall into 'the Tinder love rat's' trap in Collin County, outside Dallas, Texas.

In November 2016 Stephanie met a man called 'Brett Goodman' through the dating website Plenty of Fish. Goodman told her he was 'the son of moneyed Australian ranchers' and an Exxon oil executive on a US working visa. It was a whirlwind relationship: he moved in with her and they set a wedding date; Goodman wanted the wedding to be held at Southfork Ranch, where *Dallas* was filmed. He loved *Dallas*. Photographs show a blonde Stephanie holding a small fluffy white dog and nestling into Goodman, who wears a very large white stetson. Good thing Stephanie happened to see her fiancé's ID a few days before they headed to the courthouse to get their marriage licence. The man she thought was Brett Goodman was actually Brett Joseph. Soon enough, she found Daisy Armstrong's website. 'It was very painful,' Stephanie told the *Dallas News*. 'I was in love with him. He was very clever, very detailed. Whenever he tries to convince you of something, it's like he's casting a spell over you. He really does his research.'

On the other side of the Atlantic, British media report the story of a striking, fifty-four-year-old divorcee, Carolyn Woods who fell in love with a man called Mark Acklom. She knew him as Mark Conway. He claimed to be a Swiss banker and MI6 agent, and during their year-long relationship took her on shopping trips to Harrods, moved her into his house in Bath's famous Georgian street The Circus and convinced her to lend him money for his business ventures. The house was rented and Acklom vanished with Woods' £850,000 life savings. In July 2018 he was arrested in Geneva and is facing multiple fraud charges. 'I was in love with the man Mark Acklom created. He hooked me and reeled me in,' Woods told Sky News in 2016. 'It was all a charade . . . I did wish that he had actually killed me, that's how I felt . . . I was suicidal.'

And then I'm alerted to a *Vanity Fair* magazine article headed 'The Celebrity Surgeon Who Used Love, Money and the Pope to Scam an NBC Producer'. In early 2013, New York-based journalist Benita Alexander fell in love with Dr Paolo Macchiarini while she was working on a two-hour television special about regenerative medicine. He was a pioneering, globe-trotting surgeon who gave critically ill patients new plastic tracheas embedded with stem cells to spur new tissue growth – the only surgeon in the world doing such operations. Doctors who had worked alongside him described him as a 'Renaissance man'.

I barely take a breath as I read the *Vanity Fair* story and absorb its extraordinary ending. When, some time later, I learn that Benita has produced a documentary about her experience, I email the production company and request an interview with her and a copy of the film. It's called *He Lied About Everything*.

'PAOLO WALKS IN AND HE'S LITERALLY like a knight in shining armour.' Late one night I have a Skype conversation with Benita Alexander, who was born in Perth and retains her Australian passport but was raised by her nuclear physicist father and art teacher mother in Detroit, Michigan. Benita's apartment is near the Brooklyn Bridge and I can see the New York morning skyline behind her. In her documentary, even when she is collapsed in grief, Benita is glamorous. She's fifty-two but looks a decade younger. She adores salsa dancing and her body is slim and strong; her film includes a sequence in which she and her teenage daughter do cartwheels on a beach – Paolo Macchiarini had taken them to the Bahamas.

When she met Macchiarini, Benita had been an NBC producer for nearly two decades, and while her career was dynamic, emotionally she was in a 'rocky place'. She was in her late forties and struggling to cope with the breakdown of her second marriage and the fact that her daughter's father, her first husband, was dying of cancer. Even though she knew that as a journalist it was wrong to get close to a subject, her friendship with Macchiarini grew through the months it took to film and edit the NBC special. Over long dinners, she poured her heart out to him. He seemed such a sympathetic ear, he gave her such soothing advice. In hindsight, she can see that she was 'giving him a playbook' for his later manipulations.

Benita became increasingly intoxicated by the surgeon, a multilingual, high-flying charmer with something of the George Clooney about him. He was employed by Stockholm's prestigious Karolinska Institutet, home of the Nobel Prize in Medicine, and told her that he commuted between the institute and his home in Barcelona, where he lived alone. He told her he had been separated from his ex-wife for years but had never got round to filing for a divorce: she lived with their two children in Italy. As their friendship rolled into physical intimacy, he flew Benita around the world – to London, Greece, Russia. He showered her with flowers and jewellery. He wrote poetry for her. He left husky Italian-accented voice messages on her phone – 'I love you so much,' he would say, over and over. In June 2013 he took her on a surprise trip to Venice. A ritzy hotel, champagne, gondola rides. They attached love locks to the Ponte dell'Accademia bridge. 'This means we're forever now,' Macchiarini whispered in her ear. 'I felt like Cinderella,' she says.

Her friends, gay men and women, all fell in love with Macchiarini too; they dubbed him 'Mr Big' after the *Sex and the City* character. Her single women friends were envious: they wanted one like him. On Christmas Day 2013, less than a year after they'd first met, Macchiarini asked Benita to marry him. The pace and the excitement picked up: in the summer of 2014 he took her and her daughter to meet his mother at her home in Lucca, Tuscany. She didn't speak English so Macchiarini translated as they ate her homemade gnocchi and looked at family photographs, at baby Paolo. He was physically demonstrative towards Benita during the visit. At one stage, his mother started to cry.

In June 2014 NBC aired *A Leap of Faith*, the documentary Benita had produced that focused on Macchiarini's work. She hosted a viewing party; she and Macchiarini held hands as his face loomed large on the big screen. Afterwards he gave a speech in which he gushed to the guests about the 'love of his life' and how he couldn't wait to marry her. Around this time, he told her his divorce had come through. The wedding was a year away – in Italy on 11 July 2015 – and Benita sent save-the-date notes to more than three hundred people around the world. But she knew little about other arrangements: Macchiarini told her that he'd engaged a wedding planner and wanted to surprise her. He made her promise she would not ask any questions. He gave her instructions, though. He told her she needed four frocks for different wedding events, including a white wedding gown and a custom-made ball gown for a dance they would do; the dress was to be designed so that when he dipped her, he could easily rip it off to reveal a skimpy, sparkling dancing costume underneath. Don't worry about money, he said.

With great humbleness Macchiarini had told her that he was one of a number of 'highly classified' doctors around the world who treated VIP clients; once, she'd seen a letter of recommendation in which another doctor had cited the fact that Macchiarini had treated the Pope. Macchiarini wanted a big Catholic wedding but he and Benita were both divorcees and she wasn't even a Catholic. He told Benita that he would talk to his Vatican connections. In October 2014 he left a message on her voicemail: 'His Highness Pope Francis will marry us.' The moment she got the message, she called him back. 'Give me a fucking break,' she said. 'You are pulling my leg.' He told her that Pope Francis wanted to thank him for being his personal doctor and to make them a 'poster couple' to show how he was modernising the Church. She went straight to her computer. Did the Pope even do weddings? There it was: he'd recently married twenty couples in a single ceremony. Macchiarini told her the wedding would be at the Pope's summer residence, the Papal Palace of Castel Gandolfo.

But Macchiarini hadn't finished with the surprises: the guest list was growing. VIPs who were now planning to attend the ceremony included President Obama and Hilary Clinton; they too had been his patients, he said. Vladimir Putin was another one – the Russian government had supported one of Macchiarini's clinical trials in Kazan. He told her that Andrea Bocelli, John Legend and Elton John would perform at the wedding. In *He Lied About Everything*, a friend of Benita's, Amanda, talks about a dinner she hosted at her home for the couple. Amanda and her husband were astonished by Macchiarini's plans. 'It seemed ridiculous that it was happening, but it also seemed more ridiculous that somebody would make it up,' Amanda says in the documentary. 'He didn't come in here and present as a crazy person at all.'

ON 10 JANUARY 2015, WHILE I was in Sydney worrying about Joe's snake-bitten dog, in Brooklyn Benita received a delivery of six long-stemmed red roses from her fiancé – one for each of the months before they would be married. But she was worrying, too, and on multiple fronts. In November 2014, she'd read an article in the *New York Times* that revealed the Karolinska Institutet was investigating 'serious and detailed' accusations against Macchiarini. The article claimed he had not received 'ethical approvals for experimental operations on patients and misled medical journals about the success of the procedures'. Macchiarini explained it away by telling Benita that he was the victim of a witch-hunt by jealous colleagues.

Meanwhile, he still hadn't shown her his house in Barcelona. 'It just was not sitting well with me,' she tells me during our Skype conversation. For a moment she turns her head away from her computer's camera and her lips form a thin, hard line of bitter memory. 'Why can't I see the house where I'm supposed to be moving with my daughter? This is absurd.' Every time she was booked to fly to Spain to visit, he would be called away to perform an emergency surgery. She asked him repeatedly for the wedding planner's details but Macchiarini kept saying everything had to be a surprise. 'It was just weird,' she says. And she was deeply concerned about his increasingly fractious relationship with her daughter.

The passionate romance had stalled and the couple started to argue; Benita knew they were clashing over serious issues but, swept up in a maelstrom of stress and excitement, on 13 May 2015 she resigned from her job at NBC in preparation for her new life.

On 14 May the dream disintegrated. An email from a colleague landed in her inbox. Subject line: 'The Pope'. The email included a link to an article documenting the Pope's forthcoming itinerary.

On the day he was meant to be marrying Benita and Paolo in Italy, the Pope would be in South America. 'I literally buckled, I almost fell to the floor,' Benita tells me. In that moment, sick and shaking, she could see everything as it really was.

She called the castle where he'd said their guests were booked to stay; the hotel had never heard the name 'Paolo Macchiarini'. She called him. Initially he had answers for everything: it must be a mistake, Vatican politics, he would sort things out, the castle staff couldn't talk because of VIP security, blah blah blah. And, good grief, he even told her that his role as surgeon was a front and he was a CIA operative. Benita hired a private investigator. Paolo was still married and had been for twenty-nine years. His estranged wife did live in Italy but he was living in Barcelona with another woman and their two children.

Benita unravelled. She barely ate or slept for a month. 'I kept figuring things out and I was apologising to my daughter, probably like every ten minutes, that motherfucker, and then I'd be on the floor, you know, in a ball crying.'

Working with the private investigator, Benita discovered that the Vatican had never heard of Macchiarini; nor had the Michelin three-star restaurant in Florence he said he'd contracted to cater for the wedding. Nine months later, while reporting the *Vanity Fair* article, writer Adam Ciralsky reached out to Andrea Bocelli's manager – he'd never heard of Macchiarini either. When contacted, the doctor who had written the recommendation letter citing Macchiarini's treatment of the Pope acknowledged that the source of that information was Macchiarini himself. Benita still wonders what he told his mother about her the day they visited her in Italy and he translated the conversation.

'God knows.' Perhaps, she thinks, his mother wept because he told her that Benita was one of his patients and she was dying.

Benita attempted to explain to Ciralsky why she had believed Macchiarini's stories. Primarily, she had an anchoring knowledge about him. 'This was not some guy I picked up in a bar. This was a renowned, accomplished, established surgeon whom we had followed all over the world,' she told the reporter. 'The very prospect of him making all of this stuff up . . . seemed too ridiculous to give it any credence. Why would he risk his reputation by doing that?'

There's more. Macchiarini's professional reputation, already on shaky ground, was about to collapse. The *Vanity Fair* article picked holes in his CV, finding multiple exaggerations and discrepancies. He was a surgeon, but the research community started to describe the work that had made him a medical hero as a hoax. Seven of the eight patients who received Macchiarini's plastic tracheas are now dead; many died in excruciating pain. (The one who remains alive had the synthetic trachea removed.) In early 2016 he was fired from the Karolinska Institutet for breaching 'KI's fundamental values' and 'scientific negligence'. In September 2017 the *Guardian* published an article about Macchiarini: 'Dr Con Man: The Rise and Fall of a Celebrity Scientist Who Fooled Almost Everyone'. In June 2018, two years after he was fired, the Karolinska Institutet announced that he was guilty of scientific misconduct. Prosecutors reopened an investigation into his role in the deaths of an Icelandic man and a Turkish girl in December 2018.

In an interview with an Icelandic television station Macchiarini, with quivering lip and wounded puppy-dog eyes, defended himself. 'No one can understand what it means being vilified,' he said. 'I have been treated like I would never treat even the worst animal.'

IN THE WAKE OF THE *VANITY FAIR* article and the documentary, Benita heard from hundreds of women who suffered at the hands of similar serial fabulists. One had given birth to Macchiarini's child during his relationship with Benita. She and Benita eventually communicated. 'She kept saying, "You're lucky, you don't have a child with him."'

Benita has continued to use her personal knowledge of con artists for professional purposes: she and the production company for which she works, Efran Films, have recently produced *Seduced by Evil*, the documentary about conman Derek Alldred and the women who fell for him.

We talk about Macchiarini's possible motivations. 'I think it's the adulation and the adoration,' she tells me. The extravagance, the grand gestures, the romance – everything was about him. Her reactions fed his ego; he adored the way she adored him. Maybe, Benita thinks, it was also about the thrill, the risk. '[He] was always driving the boat a little bit too fast, or driving the motorcycle a little bit fast . . . everything was always on the edge, and the same with his surgeries.' In one of her last conversations with Macchiarini, she asked him why he'd picked a journalist who would eventually start asking questions. He cocked his head on the side, smiled a little, and said, 'I know, that's why I love you so much.' It gave her the chills.

She realises now that men like Macchiarini don't think the way normal people do. 'How do you not feel any guilt, or any remorse, or any empathy? I don't think they understand what they've done. It's just like pieces [of the brain] are missing. I keep joking that nothing will drive you crazier than trying to get inside the mind of a crazy person.'

In the days after her discovery that the wedding plans had been a fantasy, she emailed Paolo. 'Who the hell are you and what the hell is wrong with you?' I think of the email I sent to Joe when I finished things with him some months later. 'Who are you, for heaven's sake? Do you even know?'

The fact is, they don't know. Their sense of self is broken.

•

We all have a sense of self – a personality and patterns of behaviour – but at issue is how well they work for us. How much do they help or hinder our attempts to live comfortably in the world, to be our best selves; how much do they contribute or detract from our ability to form and maintain strong relationships? Paolo Macchiarini's personality seems to have worked like a charm for him – in attaining a medical degree, building a high-flying career, conquering multiple hearts; in earning enough money to maintain a playboy lifestyle – until it didn't. Until his house of cards toppled and his manipulations and deceits were exposed. Joe's personality, similarly built on a termite's nest of falsehoods, worked to a degree for a time: he had jobs, then started a business, bought his land on the harbour, built a house, found a wife, had children. But as he grew older, more and more seemed to slip from his grasp. Over and over, he seems to have conspired against his own best interests;

his behaviour appears at times to have amounted almost to self-harm. And then, in engaging with me, a journalist, exposure was almost guaranteed.

The more I have read and heard about men like Macchiarini, men like Joe, the 'narcs' of pop psychology, with their deceptions and treachery, their fantastical grandiosity, their callousness and absence of empathy, their insane risk-taking, the more I feel they elude understanding. I can see that their ingrained and often formulaic behavioural patterns match, to varying degrees, the traits listed in the DSM-5 manual of personality disorders, particularly the antisocial and narcissistic personality disorders. But why do they behave as they do? Why are they so?

'WHAT IS A PERSONALITY DISORDER? It's really a vulnerable sense of self, and problems in relationships with others,' Professor Brin F. S. Grenyer says. We're taking tea on the sunny terrace of a University of Wollongong cafe and the professor's next statement stops me mid-sip. An issue for people with personality disorders is 'identity diffusion', or having a diffuse sense of self. 'That is the problem – if you have a diffuse sense of self, you actually don't really know who you are.'

For my benefit, the professor of clinical psychology breaks down the components of a human personality into two major elements: first, a person's relationship with themselves – their sense of self, identity and self-esteem, their values, their goals and dreams, their likes and dislikes, the things that bring meaning to their lives. Second, their relationships – how effective their relationships are with other people, how they understand others.

He introduces a new acronym to our discussion – ICD-11, the 'International Classification of Diseases', a World Health Organization document that classifies all known diseases and medical conditions. Those who work in mental health are generally guided by either the ICD-11's mental, behavioural and neuro-developmental disorders section, or the American Psychiatric Association's DSM-5.

'Both the DSM-5 and ICD-11 are quite similar in their consensus that the relationship to the self, and the relationship to others, are really core, fundamental components of a personality, and in a disordered personality both of those things are usually the problem,' says Grenyer. '[Those with personality disorders] can be quite disordered in their capacity to understand the impact of their behaviour on other people, and in severe or antisocial kinds of attitudes and behaviours there is a real lack of empathy towards other people.'

The eleventh edition of the ICD was released in June 2018 and features a substantially overhauled section on personality disorders. The changes are significant because they go some way towards resolving an issue that has divided mental-health experts – the unsatisfactory historical approach of splitting personality disorders into categories such as narcissistic, anti-social or borderline. 'Individuals are complex combinations of categories,' Grenyer tells me. 'When you have a categorical approach, a typical person will end up with four personality disorders because they have so much overlap.'

The ICD-11's new model has jettisoned categories in favour of one descriptor – simply, 'personality disorder', which it classifies as mild, moderate or severe in six 'prominent personality traits or patterns':

- 'negative affectivity', in which a person tends to experience a range of negative emotions 'with a frequency and intensity out of proportion to the situation', as well as poor emotional regulation
- 'detachment', a disorder in which someone tends to maintain both interpersonal and emotional distance and detachment, often avoiding social interactions and friendships
- 'dissociality' – the core feature of which is 'a disregard for the rights and feelings of others', and might also include a sense of entitlement, manipulative, deceptive and exploitative behaviours, and physical aggression
- 'disinhibition', in which a person has 'the tendency to act rashly . . . without consideration of potential negative consequences'
- 'anankastia' – a 'narrow focus on one's rigid standard of perfection and of right and wrong' to the point of trying to control the behaviour of others, as well as situations, 'to ensure conformity to these standards'
- and 'borderline pattern', which is 'characterised by a pervasive pattern of instability in interpersonal relationships, self-image, and affects' and might also include impulsivity, self-harm and fear of abandonment.

'There's a lot of controversy in the field around personality disorder and a lot more science needs to happen,' says Grenyer, the director of the University of Wollongong-based Project Air Strategy for Personality Disorders. The strategy's aims include improving treatment options, supporting carers, and increasing the understanding of the condition through research. Grenyer points to the prevalence of personality disorders in the community. 'This is not a boutique area; there are a lot of people out there who are very vulnerable and who are really struggling and suffering.'

I ask the professor why he thinks people are so fascinated by personality disorders. 'Because we've all got a bit of it in ourselves,' he says, and smiles. He is a neat man in a dark suit with chic square spectacles, slicked hair and pale hands. I ask him if he does. 'Of course,' he says, but when I ask how he might categorise himself, he laughs. 'That's too personal.' He changes tack to talk about the film industry's fondness for dark, disordered characters. 'It preys on people's fears that there are actually real monsters out there . . . it probably taps into people's primitive experience.'

Professor Grenyer's interest in his field grew from his work with clients, especially prisoners, who had chronic depression and substance dependence. He found himself returning to the same question: 'Why is there this group of depressed people who don't improve?' He came to realise that for many of his clients a personality disorder was the fundamental issue underpinning a range of other problems, including chronic depression and criminality. Up to 60 per cent of people in psychiatric units, drug and alcohol treatment facilities and prisons have a personality disorder. 'I really started to understand just how complex the interaction is between sense of self, self-concept and relationships with others.'

Experts believe that all personality disorders have the same underlying causes: first, a hardwired genetic component; and second, environmental factors – how someone has been shaped through their life experiences, particularly in early childhood when the serious psychological process of 'attachment' takes place. 'Very early on in our lives we need to learn whether or not we can trust others and ourselves enough to feel secure,' says Grenyer. It is no surprise to learn that the types of environments that can lead to other mental-health issues are also implicated in the development of personality disorders: childhoods in which trauma, chaos and fear are frequent visitors; childhoods in which there might be physical or sexual boundary violations or abuse, or intense bullying, or being witness to domestic violence, or verbal and emotional abuse, or stress because of poverty or absent parents or abandonment in one form or another. Childhoods in which a growing person's sense of self and trust in others have been continually violated.

WE ARE ALL, TO ONE DEGREE or another, narcissistic. It is a protective and adaptive behaviour, an element of the conceptual, social and practical skills we have in our survival kits to navigate everyday life. 'All of us need to have a certain sense of self-preservation which could be called narcissistic,' Professor Grenyer tells me. But at a pathological level, there are two subtypes of narcissistic behaviour – the grandiose, entitled way of behaving in the world, and a more subtle, covert form. 'There are some people who consume a lot of other people's resources through their intense neediness and their over-engagement . . . they keep a lot of attention on themselves but not in a grandiose way, in more a subtle way, but it still has a narcissistic function of maintaining a weak self-esteem, a weak sense of self.'

Our discussion circles back to the term 'identity diffusion'. Grenyer observes that people suffering the effects of a personality disorder often have a palpable sense of emptiness. 'It's a terrifying experience.' He has counselled clients in that desperate space. 'How do you feel alive and how do you feel real in this world if your sense of self is broken or empty?' And, he says, 'If the person feels empty inside and they feel like they're a tiny person, then are they trying to create a false image of themselves to feel bigger and stronger and more important?' Grenyer believes that personality disorders have been 'much maligned in psychiatry'. 'We need to be more compassionate and we need to do a much better job recognising these problems in people of school age before they become severe issues in adulthood,' he says. 'Left untreated and unrecognised they can inflict significant pain and suffering – on the people with the disorder, on those close to them, and on the community itself. Yet there are good psychological treatments.'

I ask Grenyer about elements of Joe's behaviour that have mystified me. Joe's former business partner, Peter, told me of Joe's brilliant ideas but how he frequently seemed unable to take the practical steps required to bring them to fruition. Others told me of the meetings Joe missed and the phone calls he ignored; how he would go missing in action at crucial moments. Again, it seems to all come back to a diffuse sense of self. 'One of the sad things about people with the disorder is that they find it really hard to follow through with things and follow desired directions in life.'

I wondered too why Joe and Paolo Macchiarini, and so many other men I know about now, leap to blame others, to be the victim, when they are so clearly the architects of their own misfortunes. 'They're too vulnerable. It takes a lot of ego strength, a lot of self-esteem, to admit your own mistakes.'

I ask Grenyer about something Peter told me. He said that on one of the last occasions he ever saw Joe, when Peter confronted him about his deceits, Joe's body appeared loose all over, a jelly body. The professor nods as though he can picture the scene. His work has given him a glimpse of the inner movements of disordered minds. Sometimes, he says, people report a feeling of sheer terror. 'Literally you're one step away from losing your mind, from crumbling. And it's scary, it's awful.' He offers a small smile then, and a metaphor. 'You know in Harry Potter when the Dementors come and suck your soul out of you . . . you're still alive but you don't have a soul anymore . . .'

As I return to my car the day is dissolving into dusk and I suddenly feel cold. I sit for a moment and think about Joe before I turn the ignition on. I recall one day telling him of my frequent feeling of 'imposter syndrome' – that sense of self-doubt, that your accomplishments have been overstated or have come through luck, that you don't deserve them, and that eventually you will be exposed as a fraud. He had never heard the expression before and leapt on it. 'Imposter syndrome,' he repeated. 'That's how I feel all the time. I feel, *how could this be me?*' It was clear he was turning the idea around in his head. He would return to the subject again: 'I've been thinking about imposter syndrome,' he would say, as though the discovery of the concept had clarified everything for him. Later I wondered if in that moment he was brazenly telling me who he really was, that he was a real imposter.

I remember something I read in American psychologist Martha Stout's *The Sociopath Next Door*. She questions why so many sociopaths have not achieved their innate desire to be successful and dominant. 'Given their focused motivations, and granted the freedom of action that results from having no conscience whatsoever, they should all be formidable national leaders or international CEOs, or at least high-ranking professionals or dictators of small countries,' writes Stout. 'Instead, most of them are obscure people, and limited to dominating their young children, or a depressed spouse, or perhaps a few employees or co-workers. Not an insignificant number of them are in jail . . . Having never made much of a mark on the world, the majority are on a downward life course, and by late middle age will be burned out completely. They can rob and torment us temporarily, yes, but they are, in effect, failed lives.'

Was Joe sitting warm and clean in one café or another as he crafted his pastoral representations so vividly in text and email? Torrents of rain and newborn lambs and nasty foxes and mud and felled fences with a cappuccino and a nice piece of cake beside him?

I realise I am crying. I miss the man I thought he was; I am mourning the life I thought we could have together. I cry for the man he is, a man whose life force is directed towards doing everything possible to keep alive the illusion of a superior wholeness. I remember now a night at home. We sat on my couch. The television was a background hum. We sat close. He asked me a question. 'Can I put my head on your lap and will you stroke my forehead?'

•

It is more than two years since I drove down the highway to a cottage in a valley and hoped I might have found true love. It is more than a year since my email to Joe in which I showed him the evidence for his imposter self I'd found on Kirstie's social media pages. I know now that I will not tamper with the truth of my story by turning it into a work of fiction. I tell Amelia I will write it as a non-fiction article for the magazine. I try not to think about the new sign I'm painting on myself for all to see: 'Sad Childless Woman Falls for Con Man'.

Generous friends let me use their holiday house on the south coast to write. It rains for days. I sit at my friends' kitchen table and study my notes from all angles. I write nothing. A neighbour's dog, Buck, a kelpie, comes and goes, nudges the screen door open with his snout, watches me dolefully, resists my attempts at friendship. I wander through my friends' silent house and feel alone and desolate. I flick through the happy snaps of Instagram, past someone's puppy lying in front of a fire, past a couple who have just announced their engagement, past someone else's family holiday. I scope Kirstie's Instagram feed: she is at a wedding in Byron Bay, one of seven attendants to the bride; a shot shows them lined up and laughing and wearing sweet watermelon-hued slip dresses with flowers in their hair. And each day I feel emptier, of words, of self. One day, I go to Jervis Bay. Photographs show it as a blue-green paradise. They lie. I pass through the late-summer scrub and drizzle to Honey-moon Bay. The sand is white but the sea is grey. I turn around and drive the hour back to the house, arguing with tears all the way. I pack up and head home, days earlier than I intended. I have written a sparse and unsatisfactory paragraph. Stopped at traffic lights coming into the city, I watch a beautiful young couple pressing against each other outside a cafe. They touch noses. Back in my apartment, I plug my phone in to charge and a list of my neighbours' wi-fi networks jumps on to the screen. There's a new one – 'TheLoveNest'.

I TRY WRITING IN THE OFFICE. Even without conversing with colleagues, I feel as though I am stripping naked before them. I try writing in a cafe, but the clatter kills my concentration. I try writing in the Mitchell Library. Here, anonymous but in human presence, words finally start to emerge. What matters is the work; the work always matters. And now another memory returns: Joe told me that when he did due diligence on the properties he was interested in buying, he'd sometimes devote time to exploring historical material related to them in this library's special collections. He had, he said, eventually organised multiple boxes of uncatalogued and chaotic archival material, and as a result had been given an honorary library title – library 'sheriff', which allowed him unimpeded access to collections. I pause at the end of a paragraph and go to the information desk; I ask the woman behind the desk about the 'sheriff' system. She looks at me as if I am mad. There is no such title.

AS IS EVER THE CASE IN the weeks before publication of a major feature article, there is a frenzy: discussions with Amelia about structural issues, queries from sub-editors, a barrage of proofs, fact-checking. I am bone-tired and ragged. I jump at small noises.

I'm lonely and frightened. I am remembering the bullet he showed me one day. Amelia arranges for the company's security executive to visit my apartment and look at its vulnerabilities. He's a big, amiable former police officer. He looks around, suggests I get a peephole for my front door and better blinds for my bedroom window. He wants to natter. I'd rather he didn't but to be polite and grateful I sit down with him at my kitchen table. He tells me about his wonderful wife and children. 'Look,' he says, and reaches for his wallet. 'She's as gorgeous as the day I married her.' He produces a photo of her, and another of their children. He studies them affectionately. 'Couldn't survive without them.'

ON A TUESDAY IN APRIL 2017, Anzac Day, I go into a meeting room at work, close the door behind me, and make the hardest phone call of my life. I call Kirstie. She needs to know that in four days an article will appear in *Good Weekend* telling my story, and that it will include hers – the story of her cheating long-term partner's double-life. I do not name him or her in the article – he is 'the man' and she is 'another woman', 'the other woman' and 'the woman', but there are enough identifying details in my piece that she will recognise herself. She cannot open the newspaper on Saturday and discover her story there without warning.

Ripples of panic run through my body as I dial her number. She answers almost immediately, that husky, strong voice. I talk. She doesn't speak. I continue. She doesn't speak. I talk and talk and talk, and try to explain this whole damn mess – his bankruptcy, the criminal record, the house he doesn't live in, the countless deceptions; I try to explain how I'm so sorry to have to be making this call. I start to wonder if she's hung up on me.

Finally she says something. 'He lives on the harbour.' It is a statement, not a question. The voice is cold, an Arctic front. I think I might pass out. 'He looks after his children.' I redouble my efforts. I tell Kirstie that I can show her documents; I say that the article could not be published if I did not have evidence for the things I am telling her. She asks a question and her voice wavers a little. I answer it: no, I tell her, I do not know where he lives. I venture a question of my own: are you still in a relationship with him?

9

ALL THE SIMILAR STORIES

Saturday 29 April 2017, morning. I'm still horizontal. Images arrive in my head of those who are blithely vertical. I see people in cafes, soy decaf lattes and skim caps, avocado on toast, sharing newspaper sections, slipping the magazine out . . . They will be struck by its cover: long-stemmed red rose on white backdrop, blood dripping from a thorn on to red serif type – 'Love Lies Bleeding'. Distracted as I have been during the week, it took me a while to see that the art director had riffed on the rose image alongside my words in the magazine: inside, the rose wilts.

Perhaps the people in the cafe order another coffee to carry them through to the end. Perhaps they say something to their companion across the table – 'You won't believe this story . . . this silly woman.' Or do they skip it altogether and turn to the restaurant review? Finally I wiggle one hand out from under the bedclothes and reach for my phone. I look at the screen through cracks in my fingers, open my inbox. My stomach lurches. For the first time in sixteen months Joe's name is there. The subject line is 'Well I never'.

I need to read the email a few times before I settle on an interpretation of his words. He starts with what I suspect might be a veiled threat, referring to privacy being 'a two-way street'. What, I wonder, does he have in store for me? But his writing is nothing if not tonally diverse and he moves on to exercise his comedic muscle – he compares what he says is my 'self-centred' power and influence (as evidence of that he refers to my appearance on ABC *Lateline*) with his 'generosity and dedication'. I laugh out loud. Then the ludicrous turns sinister: I was on to him early, he writes. I am chilled by the clarity this brings: I can see now the calculation, the disregard that underlaid each and every one of our interactions over eighteen months, from bed to table and beyond.

But make no mistake: Joe is the victim. He is upset, he says, that his voice will never be equal to mine. He continues in what can only be interpreted as a smug tone: he's met someone else, they 'get on', he's told her about me, he's told her to expect the article, so any warning I might have hoped it would convey has been in vain. He's 'grateful for being accepted,' he adds. He shares a little more information: he is writing now, too – about his farm and the country town, its 'gut-wrenching tales'. His new Instagram profile is 'something of that'. He is launching farm stays and farm market lamb and he'll be pushing the publicity for those ventures. 'So unlike me to voluntarily step into the limelight,' he adds.

The stories are tediously familiar: is the fabulist holding on to his fictions?

I'M VERTICAL NOW. OTHER MESSAGES ARE coming in, via text, Facebook, email. Their volume and honesty, the trauma embedded within, are astounding. One woman writes to tell me about her former partner: 'My brain still can't fathom it, mostly because believing in "goodness and truth" are my default positions.' Says another of her experience: 'It was beyond any normal standards of behaviour: he was a white pointer shark in a pool full of children.'

Multiple women write to say they are smart and educated, they thought they weren't capable of being fooled. One man says my story reminded him of a psychopath with whom he had business dealings; he had learnt as a result that 'skilled manipulators are able to juggle an extraordinarily complex farrago of lies – all instinct and no empathy'.

I make an espresso as I read an email from another man: 'The relationship you describe is so frighteningly similar to an experience of my own. It took me years to understand that the woman I was dealing with was either a toxic narcissist or a sociopath and the emotional impact was devastating.' I think of my conversation with Professor Grenyer about human personality as I continue reading. 'She is not evil, she is a disordered personality who is acting out her true and only nature. We don't think a crocodile is evil because of the brutal way it catches and consumes its prey. It is just being a crocodile. So it is with the psychopath and narcissist. Their actions and impacts are horrific but they are just being themselves.'

As I sit down in my courtyard with coffee and laptop, another message lands: 'My name is Tessa. I think I went out with the same guy. I just read the story and am positively shaking. I would be keen to hear from you! So weirded out right now. It is the EXACT same story!!!'

Joe talked about Tessa all the time.

•

Kirstie looks around the bar until she finds me. Her face is set, the Arctic chill moves with her towards me. She's wearing jeans, boots, a leather jacket over a low-cut shirt, her auburn hair loose around her shoulders, strong eyeliner. She's gorgeous. It's a week since our phone call. She slips on to the stool beside me. 'I need a drink,' she says. I discovered the nature and extent of Joe's deceptions over months; she's had only days. She hasn't been sleeping. 'I'm wild with anger.' She must be in shock, too, I think.

She tells me that for a few minutes after she'd answered my call, she'd thought I was some mad woman trolling her. She'd nearly hung up. Then she realised she knew my name, had seen my byline. She remembers thinking, *oh, please don't tell me that wonderful man is not wonderful.*

Their relationship ended in the middle of 2016. Joe told her that his ex-wife had abandoned their custody arrangements, he would now have his children almost full-time, and he couldn't juggle them and a relationship. Kirstie had parted with him, still in love, thinking he was noble, self-sacrificing. She'd had no idea about his bankruptcy, his criminal record, his infidelity. Our mutual acquaintance, Susan, had not told her about me. Kirstie offers a grim laugh. 'You know, when we first started going out, he said, "I expect complete loyalty from you."'

FOR A WHILE AFTER THEY MET, Kirstie was only half-interested in Joe. She was preoccupied – moving apartments, planning a trip overseas – and she found him controlling. He wanted her to go to Tasmania with him. 'When I got home he'd emailed me air tickets from his travel agent,' she tells me. 'I hadn't even agreed to go.' But her thoughts soon shifted. He took her to lunch and afterwards they walked through a park with his kelpie. 'I fell asleep in the sun and the dog was cuddled in against me and he said that was the moment he realised he felt very serious about me. It's the way he hooks you in . . . "My dog and you," and you go *whoa*; you don't even realise that's what's happening to you subconsciously.'

She was ensnared. And then the barrage of excuses, cancellations, crises, alibis and absences started: his father was close to death; he had to go and meet his father's illegitimate daughter, who wanted to be at the bedside; his father was better and was returning to China, where he lived; his mother was in a car accident; his mother was staying with him because she was getting migraines from the repolished floorboards of her harbourside apartment; his son had concussion.

'Oh yes, I got the floorboard migraines and the son's concussion, too,' I say. 'But did you get the ear issues?'

'Oh my god, I had four hundred ear infections with that man, I can't tell you.'

'What about the vintage wooden cruiser?'

'Oh my *god*,' she says. One day Joe offered to take her and a group of her friends out on the harbour for sunset cocktails. His three-act play started with a set-up – he drew a map for her to show the location of the jetty from which he would collect them. Through the morning he texted about the canapés he'd bought. Mid-afternoon, he introduced the play's turning point: he'd come upon a couple in a speedboat that had hit rocks. Over the next few hours he built the tension, introducing complications and higher stakes: he'd thrown them a lifeline from his big boat; there were hairy moments – his vessel was gashed in the rescue attempt. Then he outlined the aftermath: he'd towed their boat back to the marina and now the couple wanted to take everyone out to dinner as an apology for ruining their night. He texted Kirstie a photograph of the damage to his cruiser. But of course, given there was no boat, there could be no rescue attempt, no apologetic couple. The story couldn't end that way. Finally Joe messaged her to say he needed to go home and collapse; his heroics had exhausted him.

I thought the stories I had to share were devastatingly good, but Kirstie's are threatening to eclipse them. I relate another: on the phone the morning after a mighty storm, he told me he'd worked into the early hours with his chainsaw to clear fallen trees from roads in his neighbourhood; fire brigade officers were so grateful for his assistance they invited him to pop into the local station for a cup of tea and a look-around. I tell Kirstie that I thought at the time it was a bit odd. 'But then I thought, *well, maybe that's what men do* – boy's own adventures and all that. Now I can see he wanted to be seen as a hero, a benefactor.' The rescue at sea, the chainsawing effort – they can be filed alongside all the other likely fictional deeds: the cakes he made for his children's lunchboxes, the mini bottles of champagne he handed out when he was out trick or treating with his children, the money he put on the bar at the country pub after winning the Melbourne Cup sweep.

We move on to the subject of Joe's house. He gave Kirstie the same excuse for why she couldn't visit him there – he was protecting his children from further trauma. 'It's just appalling how he used Mary and James and Charlotte to prop up his lies,' I say. Kirstie has another story: one day she drove out of the city to meet Joe at a rental house by the beach, which he'd booked for her birthday. Before she got there, a message arrived to say that his ex-wife had kidnapped the children and he wouldn't make it to the beach because he needed to deal with the situation. Kirstie spent her birthday crying in a cheap motel, halfway to a beach house likely never booked, halfway to nowhere. 'The most disgusting thing is the way his stories would play out bit by bit until you felt demented and tortured . . . drip-feeding his victims like addicts,' she says, turning her head away.

Another time, at the last minute Joe cancelled a holiday on which he and Kirstie were to bring their children together. He turned up on her doorstep, sweating, upset, 'agitated beyond belief'. He had, he told her, made a terrible mistake. Charlotte was just not comfortable with the shared holiday. He pulled a wad of cash out of his pocket – $3500, as Kirstie recalls – and told her to take her daughters away for a luxury break. Around the same time he gave her an expensive antique gold bracelet.

But something is weird here – and it's not just that neither of us have a clue where Joe's money comes from. It seems impossible that he could have contrived such emotion, just as it seems impossible he could have contrived the jelly man whom Peter saw after the collapse of their business partnership, and the pale and shaky creature who arrived at my door weeks after my friends'

Townsville wedding. It's as though a behemoth of complication, agony, terror lies beneath.

OVER PIZZA AND CALAMARI, KIRSTIE AND I analyse how Joe moved between us. I squirm and slam back my drink through a conversation about dates and times that illuminate an uncomfortable one degree of separation between us. We look at messages and photos from around the last weekend of August 2014. Joe told Kirstie that on the Saturday morning they'd go to his ski lodge for the weekend (I can't ski so don't feel in the least offended he didn't tell me about his fantasy ski lodge). On the evening of Friday 29 August, they had drinks and talked about the powder cover. They slept together that night. The next morning he manufactured a crisis – she thinks it might have been something about the Family Court – to explain why he had to race off to be with his children.

He raced off instead to spend his second weekend with me – at the little house on the river. We slept together. I whispered to him that I thought I might be falling in love. On the afternoon of Sunday 31 August we took the tinnie out to explore the river. Around the same time, back in the city, Kirstie was taking a melancholy walk by the harbour. On Monday 1 September, soon after I kissed him goodbye and slipped a chocolate bar into his pocket – nourishment for the long drive out west to collect some well-hung rams – he texted Kirstie to thank her for her patience and to tell her that he now had his children for a week. 'The ex has missed her deadline to file anything in court, so from what I understand, that is that for her case.'

239

It's endless: the weekend he cancelled on me saying he'd poisoned himself with sheep drench, he had a pleasant, uneventful couple of days with Kirstie. The day I should have dumped him – the day he failed to turn up for a pre-Christmas barbecue to meet my family – they went to the beach. She remembers the days they spent together in January 2015 on the Central Coast and in the Hunter Valley while I fretted about his snake-bitten dog: one night, they played the board game Mouse Trap, one lunch they ate at a well-known local restaurant.

The morning a few months later when Joe bolted out my door conjuring up a *Walden*-esque image to explain that he needed to be alone, sweetening the desertion with a line designed to mislead – 'I want to ask you a question soon' – they took a drive into the country. While I fell apart, he took Kirstie to Happy Valley for the first time. He introduced her to the owner, they toured the grand house then wandered over to the fishing shack and planned where they would build a sunset drinks bar. Later she put together some name and packaging ideas for the wine and oil – turns out they were the ideas he showed me and on which he wanted my honest opinion, the ideas he said had been done by some 'branding chaps' he knew.

I tell Kirstie about the day he said we'd go and stay at the property's fishing shack; how we were packed up and about to walk out my front door when he took a call to say that his son was being rushed to hospital after slipping and hitting his head. 'I can't tell you how many times things like that happened,' Kirstie says.

Oh, she'd often been suspicious, yes. She too had wondered how a farmer's hands could be so soft and pale and clean. But he'd gone on about the danger of sheep parasites. 'I thought he must scrub the shit out of them.' He took her to the country town, and to a property and shack he said were his. I pull up the photograph he sent me of a shack – the shack I saw when he took me there, the shack I found when I returned to the country on my own. 'It's not the same one,' she says. 'The one he showed me was like a container and didn't have a chimney.' She asked him to send her a photograph of the inside of the shack. He never did. He'd arrive at her place stinking of campfire smoke; now she thinks he must have been camping rough.

'Did he take you to the motel?'

'Oh my god,' she says. 'He told me I was the only woman he'd ever taken there!' We look at each other, shake our heads. Kirstie looks into her glass for a moment, then up at me with a small smile. 'Do you reckon they knew which room to put which woman in?'

THE NEGRONIS, EXHAUSTION, SHOCK . . . they're all contributing to an edge of hysteria in our conversation. 'Do you think he had a whiteboard?' Kirstie asks. It takes me a minute to see what she's suggesting; when I do, I laugh so much I wobble on my stool. I'm getting the picture now: Joe standing at his whiteboard pondering plotlines and excuses, switching between multi-coloured marker pens, biting his lip in concentration. Two columns – one for Kirstie, one for me – to help him keep his stories straight. No, three columns: the third for the stories he bestowed upon both relationships.

He told us both he needed to 'break the bubble' that separated his life from ours. He took us both to Tasmania's MONA. He took us both to Mackerel Beach, to the country town's motel and cafe. But my man was an architect who raved about the quality of the cafe's coffee. Kirstie's bloke worked in private equity and went on about how he loved its chops. Joe never mentioned his architectural background to her. When he talked with Kirstie about his ex-wife, he always called her Colleen, never Mary. He told me he'd made an offer on a block of Mackerel Beach land where he wanted to build a modest low-slung house; he told Kirstie he'd just bought a house on the Mackerel Beach hill with stunning views. 'I can't tell you how many times I nearly got to that house,' she says. For her birthday one year, he told her they'd go across to stay at the house after a meal at a Palm Beach restaurant. He said he'd booked a water taxi, but after dinner as they stood on the wharf waiting for it, he got a text announcing the taxis had finished for the night. Another time, they got the ferry across to the beach, but before they had walked halfway to the house another phone call came in, this time about his children, to give him an excuse as to why they had to turn around and go back.

His was a high-wire act with his wits the only safety net; an exhausting, ad-libbed theatre sports of sorts as he wildly grasped for ideas to keep his fantasies afloat. There were so many occasions when things could have gone wrong and his performance could have collapsed. What if Kirstie had ignored him on any of those occasions and insisted they go to the Mackerel Beach house? What if there'd been accidental encounters with one of us when he was out with the other? What if either one of us had decided to pay him a surprise visit at his harbourside home? On a couple of occasions Kirstie threatened to do just that. 'Within minutes he'd be at my place – that should have been a red flag,' she says.

I tell Kirstie about the night my brother organised complimentary champagne and dumplings for them at the city restaurant. She is aghast. 'That was your brother?!' She says she was the one to suggest they go there. 'He could easily have said, "I've already been, let's try Glass at the Hilton," or any other diversion – it's not that he wasn't good at them.' She muses for a moment. 'I reckon he knew what would happen and he loved the adrenalin rush.'

AS WE WAIT TO PAY THE BILL, Kirstie shows me a photograph on her phone. She's in a swimsuit and sarong and Joe is behind her in a striped shirt, one arm hooking her close to him. They were out for a day on one of her friend's boats. 'He had breakfast with you that morning,' she says. 'Look, the same shirt.' It was the day I posted a shot on Instagram showing a section of his arm in the striped shirt and his hand holding a lead running to the kelpie's neck; we'd had breakfast at a sidewalk table at the butterfly cafe. I was so happy that morning. I look at them together on the boat, how happy they look, how protectively he seems to hold her, and a bolt of jealousy strikes. I curse myself for harbouring still so illogical an emotion.

But I'm silly with relief. For months I've dreaded this encounter, the potential confrontation, and now it is done. Kirstie and I have formed, it feels, an alliance. It is founded in anger and pain, but there is more to it than that: we are bound by a story bigger than us, a story so unlikely, a story with a villain of such crazy extent that our shared knowledge is a subliminal hum – no one else but us will ever know what it is to have been in the eye of this storm.

On the footpath now, I restrain myself from throwing my arms around her out of sheer gratitude. Instead, I remember something else I wanted to mention. 'Did he talk all the time about his past girlfriends?'

'Oh yes, drove me nuts,' she replies.

'I told him to stop it . . . I couldn't stand it.' I check them off: the doctor he took to Tasmania who paid for nothing; a younger woman who was a bit of a hippy and wanted to have his baby; Tessa, who, he told me, was the only woman he'd ever loved aside from me. 'He didn't mention a divorcee with two daughters,' I say, and I'm trying to be funny.

Kirstie is at a much earlier stage in her recovery and is wrestling with her own incongruous emotions. 'What am I, chopped liver?!'

•

Towards the end of her excellent book *The Confidence Game*, Russian-American writer Maria Konnikova explores the matter of reputation. It is, she says, the most important thing we have. For the victim of a con, money, the ruinous loss of it, can be a lesser concern than loss of reputation. Konnikova writes: 'That is precisely what the confidence artist is counting on, even after, despite our best efforts at self-delusion, it becomes apparent that we've been taken for a ride: that our reputational motivation will be strong enough to keep us quiet.' The con artist wants to 'go on to play the same game he's just played with some new mark' and 'the last thing [he wants] is for someone to complain and thus draw attention to the whole enterprise'.

I gave much thought to the reputational wound I might sustain if I wrote my story. And so, it seems, did Joe. I hear on the grapevine now that he is scoffing – what an idiot she was to write that story, what man would ever go out with her now? Has he spent the months between the day he received my email revealing I knew about his lies, and the day of my article's publication, hoping he would be immune from exposure because reputational motivation would mute me?

In any case, he's been hauled from the shadows now. I hear not just from a torrent of people who have fallen for similar characters but from people who know *this* character. They have recognised Joe, his dog and his ute, his predilections, his deals. They put flesh on bones, colour in the contours, add lightbulb moments of detail – *aha*, so now I see the secret to the magician's trick, and, *boom*, that's where the rabbit came from!

And with each new, astonishing message, a surreal, otherworldly sense builds in me: this is too much, this cannot all be real, this is some bizarre conspiracy and I am being manipulated by multitudes. I am Truman Burbank trapped 'in the largest studio ever constructed'; everyone is performing a role for my benefit, my every move is plotted, my every emotion observed. 'A lot of strange things have been happening,' Burbank says in *The Truman Show*. 'Everybody seems to be in on it.' A spotlight falls from the sky. A tunnel of rain falls only on him. Someone passes by wearing a badge; it says, 'How's it going to end?'

I RECEIVE A PRIVATE MESSAGE ON Facebook from a woman who knows Joe's ex-wife Mary. She tells me that he put Mary through so much embarrassment over ten years, and that he is 'wicked' and 'vengeful'. After reading my article, she says Mary felt empathy for me. It was a 'watershed' moment, the woman writes. And, she says, Mary wants to meet me.

About ten days after publication, I drive out to a pub in the suburbs. I wait nervously in the bar, clutching a lemonade, still feeling as though I'm in Seahaven, in Truman Burbank's arcological dome, and the cameras are following me. I watch the faces of every woman who walks in the door. *Is that her?* I think, *or perhaps it's her?* Soon, two women arrive and it's clear they are Mary and her friend. We find a table where we stay for the next two hours. I cannot write about what was said; I have given an undertaking to Mary that I will not. But by the end of the night, my solipsistic sense that I am performing a role for others' entertainment has lifted. I am in the real world. What happened to both of us was real and devastating. And Mary is lovely, warm, level-headed and completely rational.

A WOMAN WHO LIVES NEAR JOE'S former harbourside home emails to say that she often saw Joe around with his kelpie – and things 'never quite added up' about him. She overheard phone conversations about Happy Valley, and others in which Joe talked about 'the Yanks' he was doing business with. The woman's email sheds light on a question neither Kirstie nor I had an answer to – where Joe actually lives. 'I'm pretty sure he lives in a boat off the marina. He certainly showers in the toilet block there and the derelict Defender had an abandoned vehicle sticker put on it and has since been towed,' she writes.

I think back and remember Joe's scruffiness, how he used the washing machine at the properties we stayed in when we had our weekends away. Now I can explain to my mother why he didn't iron his shirt when he took her out for dinner.

In another email, someone who once had a professional relationship with Joe adds weight to that theory. 'Last I heard, he now lives on a boat.' This person was also fed a series of lies. 'He tells a good story, especially anything business-related, but it's 99.9 per cent fantasy. He can be very convincing unless you thoroughly investigate what he is telling you or you really trust your gut instinct. In my decades of work I have never met anyone like him.' Another bloke writes to say that his business dealings with Joe wasted years of his life and he was out of pocket to the tune of a couple of hundred thousand dollars. Joe's 'deals' were all 'smoke and mirrors'; furthermore, he did not disclose the fact he was an undischarged bankrupt at the time of their dealings.

In the office one day, an editor stops by my desk to say she'll forward me an interesting letter that has been submitted for the Letters page – a response to my article. When it lands in my inbox, I absorb it in a glance. In that moment, another mystery is solved – how Joe could have had such an intimate connection to, and detailed knowledge of, Happy Valley.

'Like Stephanie Wood, I also suffered at the hand of Joe X and his delusional "purchase" of Happy Valley.' The writer is the real estate agent Joe often talked about in relation to the property. It is, I think to myself, an example of 'hindsight bias'. It may seem obvious from another vantage point that Joe had been fooling the real estate agent as well, but it was only after my article's publication, as trickles of information kept on coming in to gradually illuminate his capacity to spin believable but fictitious tales, that I could see things clearly. Until the agent's email, my scrambled brain was still puzzling over the Happy Valley connection, how it was that he'd wrangled the visit to the property and my guided tour of it.

Within twenty-four hours, another email has arrived on the same matter; someone is offering to give me further information about 'the strange dealings encountered with the man you wrote about'. I ring him. And now I'm talking to Liam, the investor with whom Joe pretended to compete for the property.

At the time, Liam thought Joe was credible. Again, hindsight offers a different perspective. 'He just spoke so much shit . . . I should have been aware.' For months as Liam negotiated with Happy Valley's owner, Joe meddled. The owner kept referring to Joe's 'offer'. The process dragged on and the price edged up. Throughout, Joe had a lawyer acting on his behalf. At some point before he eventually secured the property, Liam did some searches and started to realise things weren't right: he found the same article I had, reporting that Joe's co-director Peter had been struck off the architect's register. Now Liam realises that Joe never had the funds to buy Happy Valley – that it was all an act. And he knows something else: beyond the vast amount of time he lost in the process, he lost money too. Joe's involvement led him to pay several million dollars more for the property than he might otherwise have had to.

I HAVE BEEN STUDYING JOE'S INSTAGRAM account. Well, of course I have. And the more I've learnt, the more intriguing a specimen he has become. In his profile he describes himself as a 'grazier', although nothing he posts suggests he actually owns or works a property. I am quite sure his hands are still clean and white. He shares rural vistas and takes a jocular tone: general country scenes, his dog, a boat on the harbour at dawn, his daughter, his daughter with two horses ('three fillies'), his son, a flock of sheep, his dog, more country scenes, more boats, his dog, a coffee, a pastry, Mackerel Beach scenes, his dog. I still feel a little pang when I see pictures of his lovely kelpie. But only days after the publication of my article he posts a picture of the dog's distinctive collar and a caption that makes it clear the dog has died. The Defender deceased, and now the kelpie.

MORE EMAILS ARRIVE IN MY INBOX. And these ones throw me, injecting me with a rush of inarticulate emotion, slapping me with a renewed sense of the surreal nature of this story. Several members of Joe's family have reached out to me. They are clearly dismayed by my article, but they don't sound surprised by it; they've heard 'startlingly similar' ones from others who've known Joe over the years. They apologise for his behaviour, for not having managed 'to steer him away from this way of being'. And here is further confirmation that Joe lives on a boat: they tell me that staff at the marina can show me his real 'yacht'. They say he seems to have no visible means of support. In fact, they suspect he gets food and petrol 'by nefarious means'.

The more I consider the words on the screen in front of me, the heavier they seem; ballast of emotion, exhaustion and anger. The family members thank me for speaking out; I wonder what it has taken to write such a note to a journalist about their kin. And now they come to the point of their email. They ask me whether I know if Joe has any remaining money or assets. They realise it's unlikely, but they want to know because if he has they hope to claim it for their mother. She had her home repossessed because of Joe.

I thought there could be nothing left that could surprise me about Joe. I was wrong. This information is appalling. I return to my investigation. A new search reveals that Joe's bankruptcy trustee has decided to withdraw the objection to his discharge; the trustee is not aware of any other assets that could be realised for the benefit of creditors. The family clearly knows this. They will know too that within weeks Joe will be free to engage in business again, free of any obligation to repay many of the debts that put him in bankruptcy.

And now, for the first time, I get access to the list of creditors' claims: Joe owes more to his elderly mother than any other creditor – about $450,000. He evidently defaulted on a loan secured by her home. It is not clear where she lives now, but she does not live in her old family home in the suburb where she spent most of her life and in which Joe built his house; nor does she live in an apartment with a view of the Opera House and newly repolished floorboards.

•

Kirstie and I are in regular contact. I want to know she is managing. She wants to vent. She is thinking back over nearly three years of her relationship with Joe, all the moments that jarred, all the odd things, all the distress. 'You've handed me my freedom; you're an angel sent from the universe,' she tells me in a message. She can now lay to rest the image she held of him as a devoted father, lay to rest the love. But thought processes and emotions do not follow orders; hers drag her on a wild ride that I cannot help but join, bumping along behind her, snared and shaken and reliving my own trauma of discovery from the year before.

Her texts pepper my days:

'My friends want to kill him.'

'I notice we both have big boobs – he used to hang onto mine like a motherless squirrel.'

'He is a bankrupt homeless hobo sponging off women to live.'

'He paid for everything, and in cash. He told me he bought gold bullion and hid it. I saw some he pulled out of his pocket.'

'A young local Landcare ranger supposedly came to check his erosion etc. He told me she was hitting on him.'

'I am starting a spreadsheet.'

'Slept like a log – enjoyed *Masterchef*, pizzas and wine with three 18-year-olds uplifting me, this morning though I am sobbing with it all.'

'THIS IS JUST ALL SO ROCKINGLY weird, isn't it?' I'm on the phone to Tessa, Joe's former girlfriend, the woman he talked about with such enthusiam. Her voice makes it clear that she's strong, independent, irreverent. She's astonished at the turn of events that has led to our conversation.

This is what Joe told me about Tessa. She was the smartest woman he'd ever met; he fell in love with her one day when she jumped into the water to swim with his children; one day she found him in the shower sobbing and she said to him, 'You poor bastard,' and got in fully clothed to embrace him; he bought tickets for them to go on an Antarctic cruise but she left him before they could go; he was in the middle of buying a Mackerel Beach property to be their home but then she left him.

This is what I found out about Tessa. One day while Joe and I were still dating, I googled her. Past the LinkedIn page, past an inactive Twitter account, and on to a tacky discovery: Liars CheatersRUs, where people can 'report a liar or a cheater' (the site has since been taken down). Tessa, according to an anonymous listing on the site, was a madwoman, married, but she always had a string of other men who thought she was faithful to them. Underneath the post were a dozen or more nasty comments written by different people. She was a bitch who had always been like this, said one, adding that she needed to have a guy on the go before she got rid of the current one. Another called her a 'skank'. One described a porn-ish photograph he'd seen in which Tessie was being bent over by another guy.

'You won't believe what I found,' I said to Joe next time I saw him.

'Oh yes,' he said, 'I knew that was there. It's terrible. I posted a comment defending her.' I pulled up the page on my computer and Joe pointed out what he said he'd written: a message describing the other commenters as cowards who hid behind their computers. Now, two years on, I look at the vicious comments again and notice something else: two of them, purportedly written by two different men, have each used the same old-fashioned word – 'whomever'.

This is what Tessa tells me about Joe. She met him through the same dating site as Kirstie and I had, she thinks around 2011, after she'd separated from her husband. Her interest was piqued because he wrote well. 'And most guys don't write very well.' He told her he was separated. When she met him, straight off she thought he was a bit odd. 'He was too keen, but then trying to act aloof as well.' But she knows she can be too harsh on people so she saw him a few more times, to give him a chance. She wasn't taking the relationship very seriously. Joe was. He gave her gifts and something about the way he did it bothered her: it wasn't done lightly. 'It always felt like it was, *right, so see, this is an expression of my ownership.*' Within weeks, he took her to meet his mother (at the home she would later lose); he took her to meet a friend with a property in the country; he had her to stay at his harbourside home. She could see there were women's clothes in the closet and children's things everywhere; he told her that he and his ex-wife were sharing the house for the children's sake and she'd taken them away for a while.

When they went out, Tessa always did the driving. Joe told her he'd rolled his car; he talked about buying a Defender. One day he told her he hadn't been able to sleep, and walking the streets in the early hours, some guys had beaten him up.

'I thought, *well, that's the most stupid thing I ever heard, that's bullshit.*' She asked him what the police had said. He told her he hadn't reported it. He told her another story, something about eating kangaroo meat, something about getting a worm in his head.

'I heard that one too,' I say.

'I was like, "Dude, I don't know . . ."' Tessa tells me. 'Even the delivery of the stories, I didn't believe them. I just thought, *nothing is adding up about you.* The best way I can describe him is he's a person who struggled for relevance.'

'Did you hop into the shower one day fully clothed to comfort him?'

'No, I did not!'

Joe told Tessa he was going to buy a house for her at Mackerel Beach. She thought, *like, are you serious? I've known you for a couple of months.* Huge 'weird vibes'. She started to back away. It was, she says, 'Two to three months of sort of vaguely being interested in him, and then three months trying to get the hell away from him; he was actually starting to freak me out.' Afterwards he sent her texts that made her uncomfortable. He made a comment about how he could break in through her window. She told him to leave her alone. He sent her a present in the mail. She told him to stop contacting her. Her ex-husband, with whom she had maintained a friendship, started to get some unusual online correspondence. 'I was genuinely scared,' Tessa says.

Some time later, she discovered the existence of the Liars CheatersRUs post about her. 'I read it and I laughed my head off; anyone who knows me knows I am not even remotely like that,' she says. 'Obviously the person who wrote that has felt completely powerless and that was the only way they could retaliate.'

This is what Joe told Kirstie about his relationship with Tessa: the moment they saw each other they would have *urgent* sex. Sometimes, he said, they would have urgent sex on a disused ferry in the harbour.

This is what Tessa tells me about urgent sex: 'I don't think so. Unless there was something I don't know about.' She pauses for a moment. 'Urgent sex on a disused ferry – that almost sounds like the start of a joke.'

WHEN I GET OFF THE PHONE after my conversation with Tessa, I think about Joe's stories. They are all that he has. They are primal. It is clear he has transformed his desperate hunger – to be a re-incarnation of his grandfather, to have a big life, to be a grazier (not a farmer), to be affluent and urbane and well connected and have his house on the harbour – into something solid, something he can touch, the real thing. The stories have overtaken his reality and enslaved him. They are all that hold an amoral man with a diffuse sense of self upright. I read a line in an email from one of his family members over and over. He speculates that Joe's delusions are so dense and intricate that they are completely real to him. And, with that line before me, I can finally see just why he was so convincing – some part of him *believes* every fiction he utters.

•

I'm wondering now about the relationship between personality disorders and delusions. Can they coexist? Or are delusions a characteristic or symptom of personality disorders? I remember something the writer Matt Taibbi explored in an article he wrote for *Rolling Stone*, 'The Madness of Donald Trump'. 'Everyone with half a brain and a recent copy of the DSM . . . knew the diagnosis on Trump the instant he joined the race,' Taibbi wrote. 'Trump fits the clinical definition of a narcissistic personality so completely that it will be a shock if future psychiatrists don't rename the disorder after him.' In his archetypal, magnificent style, Taibbi talked about the countless little fairytales Trump tells himself 'about his power and infallibility to which he clings like a dope fiend to a $10 bill'. I think of Joe's farms and sheep and boats and deals. 'I'm really rich,' Trump tells a crowd in a stadium. 'I have a disgusting amount of money,' Joe tells me, and it's an irrelevant detail that he doesn't.

For the *Rolling Stone* piece, Taibbi turned to John Gartner, a psychologist who led a Change.org petition that gathered more than 70,000 signatures from mental health professionals declaring Trump showed a serious mental illness and must be removed as president. Gartner told Taibbi that Trump's 'increasing tendency to obsess over persecution theories – and not just parrot meaningless stupidities like the inaugural crowd story but seemingly believe them – shows that he's crossing a meaningful diagnostic line into psychotic delusions, common among malignant narcissists. "We're not talking about a gross psychotic disorder," Gartner says. "We're talking about a way in which people with severe personality disorders can regress to what they call transient psychotic states . . . It's a more subtle kind of psychosis, but it goes over the boundary into psychosis."'

A study published in 2018 in the journal *Applied Cognitive Psychology* throws a slightly different light on how it's possible for someone to come to believe things that are patently false, a theory in which it's less a pathology and more a learnt behavior. Led by Danielle Polage, an associate professor of psychology at Central Washington University, the study concluded that a person can come to believe an autobiographical event took place, even if it didn't, if he or she tells enough lies to support the idea of the existence of the event. In her paper, Polage cited other research suggesting that 'rehearsing the lie and inhibiting the truth causes liars to forget what the truth actually is'.

Polage's study makes it clear that the very act of lying can alter the liar's perception of truth. Participants tried to convince an interviewer that the events they were discussing in the interview were true. Some of the events discussed had happened to the participants and some had not. 'Some of the events required participants to create false stories about events that had not happened to them (false assents), and some true events were falsely denied (false denials) . . . Results showed that consistent false assents increased belief in those false events and that consistent false denials decreased belief in those true events,' Polage wrote. The more you lie, the more likely you are to believe your lies.

Meanwhile, an article on the Radio New Zealand website, 'A World of Their Own', refers to a paper written by Eli Somer, a professor of clinical psychology at the University of Haifa in Israel. Somer developed the term 'Maladaptive Daydreaming' after he treated a number of patients who told him of their 'secretive, internal fantasy life'. As he spent more time with these patients, the doctor came to understand that their imaginary lives were 'hyper-real, minutely detailed scripts that played on the walls of their minds for great chunks of their waking hours. They dreamt of idealised versions of themselves. Of close friendships, fame, romance, rescue and escape.'

And now I cannot help but think of Joe on his country drives – him telling me 'I could do this all day' once when we were on the road. Sometimes, he said, he talked to himself, and I thought nothing of that then because who hasn't at one time or another. I picture red dust kicking up around his ute as he drives and dreams and lies to himself and sinks deeper into the worlds of his mind, until he has altogether transported himself – levitating from a dusty country road into an imaginarium where he is rich and powerful and celebrated, where his words are variously witty or commanding, where the characters he has created look to him with adoration or fear on cue. I think of Gatsby, 'the colossal vitality of his illusion' about Daisy, the 'fantastic conceits' that haunted him. 'A universe of ineffable gaudiness spun itself out in his brain while the clock ticked on the wash-stand and the moon soaked with wet light his tangled clothes upon the floor. Each night he added to the pattern of his fancies until drowsiness closed down upon some vivid scene . . .'

I come upon an article published in *New York* magazine's 'The Cut' in January 2017, a few days after Donald Trump's inauguration. Its headline: 'A Therapist Attempts to Explain Donald Trump's Rocky First Few Days in Office'. Therapist and author of *Disarming the Narcissist* Wendy Behary told the article's author, Jesse Singal, that it wasn't surprising Trump had broadcast false claims about the size of the crowd that watched his swearing-in. 'He has to believe it,' said Behary. 'He consciously overrides the "truth" because the "truth" would be fraught with shame – the narcissist's kryptonite.'

One day when we were still together, Joe told me about one of his neighbours, a man whose life was crumbling, a broken relationship, debt. Joe said that the man had built a fire in his backyard and sat beside it, with a bottle of alcohol, wailing. Did he say he went to try to calm the man, or extinguish the blaze? I can't recall. I wonder now, though – was Joe telling me his own story?

•

I invite Kirstie to my apartment for dinner. We have new information to discuss. After we've eaten, I share with Kirstie what I've learnt in the past weeks. I tell her about my conversation with Tessa and the messages from Joe's family. I tell her that one of his family members said that in this whole story Joe's lost house on the harbour was the biggest character of all, such was his attachment to it.

That nugget has illuminated what someone I'll call Daniel has told me. I have learnt that Mary has sold the house Joe built and moved out of the neighbourhood with their children. Daniel is the man who bought the house. He contacted me because, he said, he had some information he thought I might be interested in. We met for coffee and he told me that his car and his girlfriend's car were both vandalised while parked outside his house – substantial dents and on more than one occasion broken windscreen wipers.

Daniel was livid. He reported it to police and, after a discussion with a detective, installed a security system. One day he kayaked out to the boat he knew Joe was on – so small a boat that 'you'd almost call it a large rowing boat'. After he called out and Joe emerged, Daniel introduced himself, then accused him of the vandalism. And, in 'the sweetest, softest voice', Joe told him that it had been done to his vehicles in the past and it was kids in the neighbourhood. Joe changed the subject; he wanted, he said, to buy his house back. Furthermore, he said, his ex-wife was a terrible person and had once broken his arm. And then: oh, Joe said, his mother had known Daniel's mother.

'I'll give him this, he had a technique to, for a nanosecond, make me doubt what I firmly believed he had done,' Daniel told me. 'He had such a soft, sweet, butter-wouldn't-melt-in-his-mouth attitude, but that, maybe, is the key to the act, to appear so innocent that you start to doubt – maybe he's not that kind of person.' As Daniel dipped his paddle back in the water to return to shore, he said one last thing to Joe: 'If you've got an offer to make on my house, make it by Monday and it's yours.' Daniel invented a large ballpark figure. He hasn't heard from Joe since.

But Daniel has heard from other people. One day he came home to discover that the police had slipped a card under his front door asking him to contact them. When he called, an officer told him that Joe had dined at a restaurant in a neighbouring suburb and on being presented with the bill told staff he'd left his credit card in his car. He showed them his driver's licence, which still carried his old address – now Daniel's address – and said he'd go and get the credit card from his car and be back in a moment. He didn't return. On two or three other occasions Daniel has opened the door to people with official documents for Joe.

'I wonder if he got the love letter I sent to Joe before I heard from you,' Kirstie says after I've finished relating the story. I tell her that next time I talk to Daniel I'll ask him if he has received any unsolicited declarations of affection.

Kirstie has things to tell me, too. She's met the new woman in Joe's life – even in a big city, one connection can lead to another. We have touched down now in the Land of Soap Opera. She tells me that the woman, let's call her Ruth, is heartbroken about what she has learnt about her counterfeit lover. And Kirstie is shell-shocked all over again: now she knows that even after I dumped Joe in late 2015, he continued his romantic treachery. Some time early in 2016, he met Ruth online and they started a relationship. One day recently, Kirstie and Ruth spent hours on the phone, comparing diaries, going through the same awful process Kirstie and I endured to discover the depth and breadth of Joe's lies. A few days later, they bumped into each other at a pub; as the cover band played INXS's 'Never Tear Us Apart', they cried together.

Kirstie now has grisly insight into Joe's behaviour during a weekend she spent with him at a country house hotel in 2016. Over the course of the weekend, Joe sent Ruth dozens of text messages – including a photograph he'd taken earlier that day of Kirstie wandering in the hotel garden. He told Ruth that the woman in the photograph was a marriage celebrant he'd met who might be able to help them with the farm-stay/wedding-venue business they were planning.

'I feel like I've been emotionally raped,' Kirstie says. It's after midnight now and we're in my courtyard, shivering, smoking and drinking single malt whisky. I'm cadging Kirstie's ciga-rettes – since my first phone call she's taken up smoking again.

For more than two years I have paid no attention whatsoever to my own health. 'The bullshit I went through, the agony. I'm exhausted even thinking about it. I really wish I could sue him; either one of us could have been driven to suicide.' She exhales a long 'aggghhh' at the end of her sentence; it is the sound of utter devastation.

I tell her about the depression I fell into in the weeks after Joe failed to turn up for the flight to my friends' wedding. How he triggered my anxiety.

As we move back inside, Kirstie looks again at photos in her phone taken through the weeks he refused to talk with me. 'Oh, that's right,' she says. 'We went shopping at David Jones; he wanted my help to kit out the Mackerel Beach house . . . I never did get to see all that stuff we bought actually in the house.'

'But, remember, he didn't have a house at Mackerel!'

Kirstie pauses for a minute. 'Oh my god,' she says. 'Of course . . .'

She tells me the story. One day when I was likely in a foetal position on my mother's couch, she and Joe spent hours picking out items for the beach house he said he'd bought – towels, napkins, bed linen, kitchen appliances, crockery, cutlery. A staff member followed them around; gradually a pile of items grew near the service desk. She shows me a photograph of cushions and packs of linen piled on a bed in the department store. 'We chose a different colour for each room, for each child. I chose a pale-green KitchenAid mixer and he decided he wanted the full range. He said he and the kids wanted to wake up and smell pancakes.'

Then Joe said he wanted a break. 'We went to a cafe and he said, "You know what, I've always loved the styling of India

Hicks – everything white against dark wood."' Kirstie had a fit. 'I said, "That girl will drop dead if you do that to her!" She and I had just spent two hours getting the right pillows to go with a set for Charlotte's room. But Joe was adamant. What they'd chosen wasn't what he wanted. So we had to put everything back and start again.'

'What happened when you finished?'

Kirstie thinks. And then she remembers. Her eyes are wide as she speaks, and she starts to shake her head. 'He looked in his wallet and said to the assistant that he'd left his credit card at home; he said that he'd ring in the number later.'

'Did you take any of the items home with you?'

She shakes her head harder. They were all to be delivered. 'Oh my god,' she says.

I flick through my phone to see what I have to contribute to this nutty show-and-tell. 'Look,' I say. 'Do you like the shirt I gave him?' I show Kirstie a photograph of Joe wearing the blue-green-check shirt.

'Good grief,' she says. 'He told me that he'd had a tailor make it for him.'

IF JOE HAD ASKED ME FOR MONEY, I would have seen him immediately. But that wasn't what he wanted to take from me, or from Kirstie. He needed something else from us: he needed us to play supporting roles to his magnificent lead character in the boundless, exuberant pantomime of his life. And he needed us to fill the role of audience members, too: he needed us to clap.

'For a con artist, no matter the chosen racket – Ponzi schemes, à la Madoff; feats of imposturing, as from *Catch Me If You Can*; romance scams; psychic scams; old-fashioned street grift – the end goal is the same: personal profit,' wrote Maria Konnikova in a *New Yorker* article, 'Donald Trump, Con Artist?', published eight months before the 2016 presidential election. 'But the profit need not be financial. Often, it isn't. Underlying almost any con is the desire for power – for control over other people's lives. That power can take the form of reputation, adulation, or the thrill of knowing oneself to be the orchestrator of others' fates – of being a sort of mini-god.'

Adulation, that's what Joe's ugly appetite craved. And I was complicit, a handmaiden to his ego. I allowed myself to be controlled and manipulated; I subsumed my own character, my own story, my own needs. I let him drain my well to fill his hollow soul.

10

HOW COULD THAT HAVE HAPPENED TO ME?

I have returned to my childhood home. For years we have been clearing it out, sporadically, as time and emotion will allow. My mother, who now lives by the sea, does not like to come here to the house without me and so it sits, from one visit to the next, full but empty, haunted. Sometimes I come into the kitchen to find her sitting at the table, staring into space and memory. 'It seems so long since I've seen your father,' she says one day. Her face is a dark cloud. The stiff sleeve of his dinner-suit jacket . . . she says she can still feel it brushing her bare arm as they walked down the aisle of the church all those years ago. I struggle to find responses to memories like these.

Once, it was a little house, but it grew. My parents added an extension, then another when my ailing maternal grand-parents came to live with us. Almost by accident it became a five-bedroom, three-bathroom museum with a billiard room and library. It is inconceivably cluttered, a dusty crypt for a delirium of things: thousands of books, toby jugs, teddy bears, screwdrivers, clocks, chandeliers, cassette tapes, candles, records, frocks, figurines, porcelain, knitting needles, dolls, sheet music, saddles. My father once counted the number of places in the house there were to put a bottom: eighty-two, he announced with mirth – sofas, antique settees, lounge suites, bentwood chairs, stools, armchairs, stiff-backed dining chairs. Nothing was ever thrown out. And there was a lot to be kept: in the 1930s, my grandmother's sister, Amy, married a Danish-American sea captain and they moved to San Francisco, where she became an enthusiastic hostess with a collection of fancy household items, including a gothic-Spanish-revival dining setting, a waffle iron, smoky-green parfait glasses for St Patrick's Day and matching ones in red for Christmas. She and the sea captain did not have children. The sea captain died too soon. Eventually Amy returned to Australia with all her things, and when she died my grandmother inherited her estate. When my grandparents moved in with us, they were accompanied by their own and Amy's possessions. A truck blocked the street for hours. You could hear the seams of our house stretching and groaning to accommodate the new arrivals.

Now, as I exhume the past, as I jump at the bony remains of a rat in the shed and run from scampering huntsmen in the garage, as I pack boxes and trot up and down stairs, something is becoming clear. This house is a shrine to love. Here are Amy and her sea captain's love relics: I lift the lid on a white box to find her 1930s silk wedding dress, the elbow-length white-kid gloves, a spray of faux flowers. The dress and veil are yellowed and spotted with age marks. Elsewhere, I find a card from Amy to my grandmother. She finishes it with a PS: 'I wish you would write more often . . . widows and old maids fly their flag alone, you know.'

Here's a sepia-washed photograph of Nana, my father's mother, snuggling close to Les, the grandfather I never met. They are young and beautiful. How they loved each other, is what I've been told. But Les suffered a catastrophic heart attack aged only fifty-one, while he was Labor leader of the Opposition during the ugly politics of late-1950s Queensland. Nana's distress was such that she was at home and sedated during his state funeral. She never really recovered from the loss of her serene, decent husband.

My mother's love affair is, though, the noisiest ghost in this house. Here's her wedding dress, and the shoes – 1960s cream stilettos with lace insets, the leather insoles lifting and curling in on themselves with age. And here's a newspaper clipping, from the *Darling Downs Gazette*, dated 13 December 1965: 'Of interest to people of Southern Queensland, particularly those of the Downs, and in Southern States, is the Wood–Hadorn wedding, which will be solemnised in Sydney at 6 o'clock this evening. The prospective bridegroom, Mr Peter Wood, is the endorsed Australian Labor Party candidate for Toowoomba East in next year's state election. The bride has chosen a lovely gown of chiffon and French ribbon lace which will be a charming foil for her blonde colouring.'

Other ageing objects seared in my consciousness emerge: my mother's pink honeymoon negligee shimmies out of a wardrobe. I remember this, it has always been here, a provocative hint at things beyond a little girl's understanding. Dad's blue-and-white-striped seersucker shirt. My mother sewed it for him in the 1970s; he wore it when we went to the beach, when he mowed the lawn. He hated mowing the lawn. His terry-towelling bathrobe with a jaunty pattern of yellow-and-blue boats. 'I loved making clothes for your father,' she says. Dad's handwriting, on old shopping lists ('milk, bread, arborial [*sic*] rice'), on the backs of envelopes, in notebooks scrawled with electioneering notes.

One day my mother and I dig through old music. I sit on the floor surrounded by LPs, EPs, singles, and souvenir a few with sleeve designs I like – *La Bohème*'s glorious '*Che gelida manina*', the first encounter between impoverished bohemians Rodolfo and Mimi in early nineteenth-century Paris. 'What a frozen little hand, let me warm it for you . . . the moon is near us here.' Did my parents listen to the aria together? My mother, sorting sheet music at the table, starts to sing; she's found 'Moon River', those damn two drifters. It was played at my father's funeral. On cue, the single emerges from the pile in front of me: Side 1, 'Moon River' and 'Latin Golightly'; Side 2, 'Breakfast at Tiffany's' and 'Mr Yunioshi'. On the sleeve, a photograph of Audrey Hepburn/ Holly Golightly/Lulamae: black satin Givenchy gown, black satin gloves to above her elbow, chunky Tiffany strands of pearls, diamante ornament in her sleek beehive, long cigarette holder. A bewitching character in the film, less so in the Truman Capote novella. 'A *real* phony' are the words Capote put in the mouth of Hollywood talent agent O. J. Berman to describe her. 'You can beat your brains out for her, and she'll hand you horseshit on a platter.'

I pick up an LP, *The Keys to Her Apartment: An Intimate Album for Young Lovers*; cocktail-hour music, songs such as 'Love Walked

In' and 'There Will Never Be Another You', from American piano players Ferrante & Teicher. The album was frequently on my mind while Joe and I were together. *I'll give him my keys when I've seen his house*, I thought over and over, and each time the record cover (a breasty blonde in part-shadow, leaning on a pile of books, head tilted, eyes closed, seemingly on the brink of rapture) flashed through my mind. I never trusted him enough to give him the keys to my apartment. I put Ferrante & Teicher on the discard pile. A requiem for love.

At night here in this haunted house, I jot notes in a fever. I must not forget the countless details of this process. They throw light on multiple and intersecting elements of life and loss and grief; the recording of the details will help me to let go – of my father, of old sadnesses, of the foolish mythology of love that embedded itself in my being under this roof, and grew and grew until I came to see it as a predestined, immutable reality.

•

I'm in the butterfly cafe when I find Joe's second email in my inbox. It *could* be an apology for his behaviour – he says he's sorry that he hurt me, sorry that he deceived me. But then again maybe I'm meant to take an entirely different message from it. Perhaps, I think, he wants me to know of the pain I've caused *him*: he says that as a result of his 'deception and lies' he's had a difficult few weeks. I suspect this might be a reference to Ruth and the stress the discovery of his deceit has put on their relationship. But in a sign of the behaviour I have now come to expect from him, he adds that 'the truth has set me free', that he's gone back to being who he once was – 'Mr Straighty-One-Eighty' no less, that he has now moved into the life he wants. And he says, he's stopped 'hating the world for injustice' – the injustice he feels he has suffered time and again.

I did not respond to his first email; I conclude that this second missive is more attention-seeking. I file it, order another coffee, move on to other messages in my inbox.

I'VE BEEN TRYING TO SETTLE, to drag some routine and stability back into my life, but again I'm in the midst of a storm. My company is offering voluntary redundancies and, along with dozens of colleagues, I'm considering whether I should apply for one. The mood at work is grim – there are stop-work meetings, huddles in corridors and corners, worried faces everywhere. There is some chance that if too few people apply, the company might tap staff to leave.

For me there is one overriding reason to stay: I have the job of my dreams, a rare and precious role as a features writer, which gives me time to explore substantial subject matter in long articles. But I am, I think sometimes, the twenty-first-century equivalent of a lace-maker, a glove-maker, a stay-maker: soon, there will be no need for me – my craft is dying; the media industry, especially the print media industry, is struggling. I know that if I take a redundancy now, it's unlikely I'll ever get such a brilliant job again; these days, this type of work is mainly done by freelancers who eke out a living writing for an ever-depleting pool of publications. And I worry that if I go, I will spend ever more time in silence and solitude – working from home alone. Still, there are compelling reasons to jump: Amelia, whose editing sensibilities I admire, is moving overseas and it's not clear who her successor will be. Meanwhile, the union-negotiated terms of our redundancy provisions are generous; if I go, the money will buy me time and freedom to explore other projects.

Yes, no, yes, no, yes. Indecision torments me. On a Friday morning in June 2017, an hour before the deadline to apply for a redundancy, I throw my application in. Within a week I learn it has been accepted. I'm filled with excitement, with relief. But excitement and anxiety are fellow travellers; the old feelings rush back, the catch in my breath, the skin tingle, the fear. Redundant. Where will I belong now?

AND NOW JOE HAS SOMETHING TO PLAY WITH. Desperate for answers and understanding, soon after the publication of my article, Kirstie had hurled a barrage of questions at him via text and email. Sporadically, Joe responded. Now, knowing I have chosen to take a redundancy, she gets in touch. She feels I should know what he's saying about me. Joe has told her that I was sacked from my job but that I'd tried to make it look like I'd volunteered for a redundancy. (I wrote a note about my decision to leave *Good Weekend* on Facebook; perhaps he saw it.)

Still, it seems that there was at least some contrition. 'He said he was horrified at the level he had sunk to and had spent a lot of time bawling about the misery he'd made for people,' Kirstie tells me. In an attempt to explain his behaviour, he told her that his lies had given him a purpose when everything seemed bleak.

Now, though, in an echo of his email comment to me, he said he was done with lies. He told Kirstie that he had his old self back and the life he wanted and nothing was going to change that. 'And how's this,' Kirstie texts me. 'He warned me that in the future I should stay away from *formally damaged fuckers* like him.' (Presumably he meant 'formerly'.)

Joe shared other information with Kirstie. As the exchange between them unfolded, he talked about the fact that he had funds in trust accounts, sheep in his super fund, options all over the place that could be settled, that he had paid back millions in debt over the years, and now was trading in oil. He talked about top-level meetings about to take place in Astana in Kazakhstan. With the president's family, in fact. 'He said that he wasn't going to be a *wage slave*,' Kirstie tells me.

He also told Kirstie a number of other things about me: I am obsessed with money, I am blackmailing him, I have been threatening him, I stole money from my mother to fund the purchase of my apartment, there is some question about my sexuality and how I schooled myself in certain techniques on YouTube, and I abandoned my Cambodian foster child to a 'horrendous existence' after I felt slighted by an email from her. It takes a while to absorb this new information about myself about which I had not previously been aware, and to absorb something I didn't know about my redundancy – apparently my bosses were ready to get rid of me anyway because of my drug connections and my unhinged, drugged-up behaviour.

'Are you alright?' Kirstie asks me in a text. I tell her I'm fine, that I can't stop laughing. She has one more thing she feels I should know: Joe had sent her a message to say that I was 'an outright criminal'. His message included a screen-grab of a document. A court listing – a 'Stephanie Ann Wood' was listed to appear in Mount Druitt court in western Sydney on 15 June 2017. My middle name is Anne with an 'e', but just to be sure I haven't sleep-walked into a criminal act, I make inquiries with the courts. The offending Stephanie Wood, who apparently was found to be in possession of stolen goods, has a date of birth that makes her young enough to be my daughter.

I RETURN TO THE SEA BATHS. It is spring now and there is a crisp breeze but I plunge in and swim hard. I try to empty my brain and let it fill with the underwater burble, to focus on my stroke, on the reach forward, then the pull back, to propel myself through the pool. I think as I swim that I have never seen anything as beautiful as the explosions of bubbles that spring from my hands as they cleave the water – champagne, diamonds, sequins. Under here are ribbons of wriggling light, drifting seaweeds, turban snails gleaming like pearls, a small brown fish with a white spot, a gathering of fussing, flitting fingerlings, the yellow-bellied shell of a dead crab lifting and jerking along the bottom with the water's movement . . .

The dead crab breaks my trance state. My mind pauses on an anecdote I've heard Kate McClymont tell. On the eve of the 1995 Golden Slipper, she broke a story in the *Sydney Morning Herald* about organised crime groups and jockeys fixing races. As a result of her work, two-time Melbourne Cup winning jockey Jim Cassidy was disqualified from racing for a period. When they passed each other outside the stewards inquiry at

Royal Randwick Racecourse, Cassidy turned to her, spat on her back, and said, 'You fucking bitch! You've ruined my life!' She has, Kate says, often thought about that day. 'Even if you just write the truth, in the mind of the person you're writing about, it's always your fault.'

•

In Melbourne for a weekend, I catch up for coffee with one of the dozens of women who have emailed me since my article was published. I have now received hundreds of responses to my story – mostly from women, some from men, some from the LGBT community – telling me of toppling into similar physical (as opposed to online only) relationships with similar serial fabulists.

The women who have written to me are rational, insightful, highly literate, highly intelligent. And they share not only similar experiences but similar lingering reactions; an ongoing effort of self-analysis, a profound sense of bewilderment. 'What the fuck was that?'; 'I'm not stupid. *How could that have happened to me?*'

Leah, an executive with serious university qualifications, is petite, auburn-haired and strikingly pretty. There is about her a gentleness, a wariness, which taken together could be read as vulnerability, or sensitivity. Her email documented the story of her 'sociopathic ex-husband' with whom she has two small daughters. The details are, again, shocking: the man constructed a breathtaking industrial complex of fabrication and deceit.

But I am less interested in the specifics of Leah's monster than I am in her insights about herself. 'I always had a nagging doubt about him which was extinguished so often by the force of my need to believe, to block out the alternative, to hope, to be positive, to allow the dream to continue to have air,' she said in her email. I cried as I read it; she told me my own story. 'I am different to many of my friends. They wouldn't have tolerated my guy after one date, certainly not after his first indiscretion. But I was blinkered, pointing at the meagre crumbs he threw to me to justify me continuing to toe the line with him, to obey him, to adapt to a pattern in our relationship that was so completely unacceptable.'

Leah's story throws a spotlight on the factor that, for some women, might offer an answer to the question 'How could that have happened to me?' There is no academic research yet to support the theory I have, no statistics I have found, but abundant pop psychology and the anecdotes women have shared with me suggest that some of us might be more vulnerable than others to predatory and personality-disordered men.

Now, as we sit in a busy cafe surrounded by suits and small talk, Leah shares some of her emotional history. 'I've had to do much soul-searching to understand how I, an intelligent, successful and attractive woman, managed to come under his spell,' she tells me. 'Now I believe it is a deep-down lack of self-love and self-worth.'

Since she was a child, Leah has known that her mother dislikes her. She does not say this lightly, or with any sense of self-pity or intent to apportion blame. It is merely something she realises now has had a profound effect on her relationship choices. 'My mother's dislike has been there since I can remember. She was jealous of my father's attention toward his first-born daughter. And that jealousy followed me through my life, really.'

Leah has a vivid memory of a blistering row between her parents; she thinks she might have been three or four. 'I remember my mother sticking her tongue out at me and saying, "It's all your fault."' As Leah grew older, if her father defended her, her mother's standard, angry retort would be, 'You're always on her side.' She was strict; she criticised what Leah wore, how she looked. 'The way I see it is she felt that because I was quite good at things, or got a lot of attention for things, she always felt like she had to keep me in my place.'

Her mother's behaviour completely eroded Leah's confidence. She came to believe that she was 'essentially unloveable'; she came to be someone who was desperate to please and eager to be accommodating. 'I seemed to look for relationships that confirmed my low self-esteem; I accepted that I should expect to be treated badly. That's what I felt I deserved. Instead of expecting, as a lot of my friends do, to be treated like a princess, subconsciously I think I expected that someone would probably be unfaithful to me, lie to me.'

'TELL ME ABOUT YOUR CHILDHOOD.' A cliché, yes, but one of the most important questions of all. 'We cannot understand [someone's] love . . . without knowing a great deal about the history of patterns of attachment that extend back into [their] childhood,' says the great American philosopher Martha Nussbaum in *Upheavals of Thought: The Intelligence of Emotions*. 'Past loves shadow present attachments, and take up residence within them.'

I explore this matter further with someone who has been recommended to me as an expert in the areas of attachment, communication and intimate relationships – Dr Zoe Hazelwood, a senior lecturer in the school of psychology and counselling at QUT in Brisbane. 'Our early caregiving experiences provide us with a tremendous amount of information about our own worth as a person and our own capacity to have and to participate in loving relationships,' Hazelwood tells me during a phone interview. 'When it comes to looking at a person's adult relationship behaviour, the very first place to look is: where was it all modelled? Where did you experience your first loving relationship? What sort of needs were you having met or not having met? What did you learn was acceptable and unacceptable in relationships?' She goes on to say that the influence of how a person navigates early adolescent relationships when they start to move away from primary caregivers, as well as past adult relationships, also contributes in the shaping of future ones. But I'm barely listening now. My eyes have filled. I have been waylaid by my own childhood.

It was complex. My mother, who temperamentally is ruthlessly honest, ruthlessly self-critical, has given me permission for this reflection. She believes she suffered postnatal depression, and in the late 1960s it went undiagnosed. I don't recall her being affectionate – physically or emotionally – to me as a child, and perhaps this was the reason. I remember her anger, not her affection. Meanwhile, politics consumed my father: during parliamentary sitting weeks he was away in Brisbane; when he was home his time was filled with meetings, constituents' needs, campaigning. Things got tougher after he lost his seat: he sank into a grave depression that went untreated for nearly a decade. Then my grandparents came to live with us and the family dynamic became even more fraught as my mother tried to manage her full-time job as a teacher and to care for all of us.

My mother remembers something else. At some point, in a context she can't recall, my father said to her, 'I can't give the children affection because you get jealous.' I think of the little-girl me. My mother was unable to give that person what she needed. My father pulled away from giving it. And I am stunned by the irony: I was collateral damage in my mother's relentless narrative of her holy love affair, a narrative that would ultimately shape my own search for love.

Now she says, 'How could I have been so bloody stupid?'

I AM IN MY PSYCHOLOGIST'S OFFICE. She is leading me towards an understanding of 'How could that have happened to me?' On her whiteboard she draws a central circle with radiating spikes. At the end of each spike she scribbles a different element of my behaviour in the world. In the circle, she writes words to describe my central operating system, my fallacious, self-sabotaging beliefs. 'I'm not loveable. I'm not enough.'

I am seeing things that it has taken a lifetime to see.

In my relationship with Joe, with every letdown, with every cancellation, the feeling registered, not even a thought, but a feeling: 'This is all I deserve.' And there was something else: every time the idea crept in that perhaps he was vanishing to another woman, the feeling came to me that no one else would be interested in such an odd man. He couldn't be with someone else. But me? He was all I deserved.

EACH OF THE MANY WOMEN I have spoken with has become a detective investigating their own life. We pick over our pasts, looking for evidence, for smoking guns, for clues. Was it our mother in the study with her criticism, or our father in the conservatory with his indifference? Because what else can we do? How else can we understand the monstrous deceptions that have been visited upon us?

Benita Alexander, who had four glamorous dresses made for her grand wedding to the fraudulent surgeon Paolo Macchiarini, tells me that when she was in high school her parents went through a bitter divorce. Without warning, her mother left. Her father soon remarried. 'He asked me to move out when I was seventeen,' she told me during our Skype conversation. She's convinced abandonment issues that originated in that period are the reason she has struggled in relationships. No matter how triumphant she has been in work, underneath it all is a little girl who wants someone to wrap their arms around her, tell her they love her, that they're going to take care of her and everything is going to be just fine. 'I was very vulnerable in that aspect, and that's what Paolo did. These men have a radar detector of sorts . . . they know who's vulnerable, they know who they can play with, and they're very good at it.'

In an underground Sydney bar, I have drinks with another woman, Sophia, a high-achieving Melbourne-based gallerist who has lived in New York, Tokyo and London. She has velvety brown eyes, wavy brown hair, and is voluptuously beautiful. She fell in love with Lucas, a man who looked as though he'd just walked off a catwalk. She met him over dumplings with a bunch of friends, he set his unwavering focus on her, and by the end of the night the two of them were in a spa tub together.

He lived interstate. He went home. She thought that was the end of it. Then, a few days later, he called to say he couldn't stop thinking about her. He told her that meeting her had been like seeing a zebra when before there had only been horses. He told her he was in the process of separating from his wife. A relationship started. She flew back and forth, back and forth. She spent time with him at a house he'd rented. Eventually she moved interstate to be with him. 'I was on cloud nine.' Flowers, weekends away, romance. She tips her head back a little and I think that she looks like some exotic Polynesian beauty, a muse for a Gauguin painting.

They bought a farm together. The collapse over the next year was complex and slow and devastating. Sophia realised she had to finish with him, fast, when with her at the wheel one night, driving at 100 kilometres an hour on the highway, he punched her. 'He forced me off the road and then tried to strangle me.' She would come to learn that he hadn't separated from his wife until months into their relationship, that he'd been visiting prostitutes, and that his erratic behaviour included leaving a hotel without paying the bill and driving a luxury car on to a beach and abandoning it. Eventually he had several admissions to psychiatric facilities. From the start, Lucas had told her he had bipolar disorder, but now, knowing the lies he told – the grandiose stories that turned out to be fictions – she believes he has elements of narcissistic personality disorder. The police told her they thought he was a psychopath. Sophia thinks he has the capacity to kill someone.

A waiter tosses around a cocktail shaker as Sophia starts to tell me about her childhood. She was an only child until she was eight, trapped in the middle of her parents' dysfunctional marriage. 'They were so busy fighting they forgot to pay attention to me.' Sophia immersed herself in books, in stories of princes and princesses, in Enid Blyton adventures with their happily-ever-after endings; she took their messages to heart despite the calamity of her parents' relationship.

Her childhood was a fever dream: her father got a job in Europe and took her and her mother with him. They came home, her parents separated, her mother fell in love with another man, disappeared, had a child with him, returned to her father, they moved houses constantly, they moved between city and country, Sophia moved between schools. One day, in the middle of an argument with her mother, in a moment of venomous insanity, her father turned to her and told her he wasn't her father (he *was* her father). Now Sophia can barely talk, such is the impact of the recollection. She is choking, her eyes are shining with moisture. The fever dream continued: her father talked about leaving the country again, then didn't, her mother focused all her attention on Sophia's younger half-sister, the stock-market crash left her parents with untenable debt and stress, her mother left her father again, left the city, taking her sister with her. 'Incredibly traumatic,' Sophia says of her mother's departures. She was sixteen. Her father fell into a deep depression. She became a de facto housekeeper for him. She didn't talk to her mother for a year.

She desperately wanted to feel needed and special. She had never felt needed and special. And she can see now how her childhood belief that one day a man would come along who was everything she had been waiting for, coupled with this longing to be needed, led her to let men into her life too quickly, and to let them mistreat her. She dated the guy she first had sex with a few times, but once they slept together he disappeared. 'It sort of started a bad pattern of choices in men.' The guy she shared a flat with briefly, whom she fell crazy in love with, never spent a full night with her. They never went out for dinner or to the movies. At a party one day, someone gave her acid. She didn't realise what it was. That night, the guy had anal sex with her without consent. She knew he was in relationships with other women. 'I convinced myself I didn't care because I was in love with him,' Sophia says, starting to cry again. She wanted it to work out with him so very much. She gave him (or did he take?) a decade or more of her emotional and physical life. The man is now a major CEO, married, children, an alpha male; hear him pound his chest.

'He's another one in the line of charming, narcissistic men in my life,' Sophia says. 'And I allowed him to prime me for a relationship with someone like Lucas. I should have seen Lucas coming. Everyone else around me saw elements of Lucas's character that should have given rise to some concerns, but I romanticised his demands of me. So when we were living in different cities and he asked me to call him every single night after I got home, I didn't realise that might not be the sign of someone who really loves you, that could be someone who wants to control you.'

When I think of Sophia, a picture comes to me of a pretty little dark-haired girl, her head buried in a book, her parents hurling verbal grenades around her. And I think of Jeanette Winterson, who buried herself in books in a library in a small Lancashire town. I think of Winterson's stunning *Why Be Happy When You Could Be Normal?*, in which she writes of the tragedy of her childhood, her devastating relationship with her adoptive mother, her lifelong hunger for love and belonging, the patterns of rejection, the 'calcifications' around her heart. 'When love is unreliable and you are a child, you assume that it is the nature of love – its quality – to be unreliable,' Winterson writes. 'In the beginning the love you get is the love that sets.'

KIRSTIE AND I HAVE ANOTHER CONVERSATION. She has, she tells me, always had a solid sense of self and strong self-esteem. She always considered that she'd had a nurturing and happy upbringing. But since the breakdown of her relationship with Joe, she has started to interrogate her childhood. Now she can see she blocked out anything unpleasant.

One of her brothers was mentally ill – she thinks he would be diagnosed today as having schizophrenia. From around the time she was ten, the household was disrupted and her mother was distracted and anxious. In her teenage years, Kirstie's relationship with her mother deteriorated. She remembers often having to mind her little sister; she remembers one day they were left in the car outside a hospital for some hours and she started to use the car cigarette lighter to burn pieces of paper. Someone came out of a nearby house and told her to cut it out.

She just wanted to be normal like all the other kids. She just wanted to play netball and get a hot boyfriend. 'I shoved everything under the carpet.' Now she's seeing how the land-scape of her childhood might have played some role in why she stayed with Joe for so long. 'I have this amazing ability to push things under the carpet,' she says. Her daughters didn't like Joe. Her friends tried to tell her that he was bad news. 'Everyone was trying to tell me, everybody.'

KIRSTIE AND I BOTH GET THE same email from Joe. He's had enough, he says. If we continue to state that he is bankrupt, he will definitely 'launch into a court action'. He's not a bankrupt, he says, and he has no debts. Neither Kirstie nor I have been talking about his bankruptcy, or his release from it. We exchange text message shrugs.

Some time later he emails me again. Now he is upset that on the website I've had built in preparation for life as a free-lancer, I've included a link to the *Good Weekend* story about my experience with him. He writes in quasi-legalese; he thinks he's been treated unfairly because of what he terms my 'false claims'. He has, he says, 'suffered discrimination in my business dealings' and he will commence Supreme Court proceedings if I do not remove the article, and those proceedings might include 'an affi-davit and subpoena of every interaction between' us. He doesn't state what the false claims are. There were no false claims in my article. There is nothing in our recorded interactions, nothing in emails, photographs or text messages about which I should be concerned. I leave my website as it is.

But I keep an eye on his Instagram account. A few days after the threatening email, Joe posts a picture of a sign, presumably taken in the country. 'Fox poison laid on this property . . . caution' is the red-lettered wording. He adds his own caption: 'Careful' it says. He posts another photograph the next day, a photograph of the butterfly cafe, the cafe just around the corner from my apartment.

11

THE GETTING OF WISDOM

Insanity visits me in my sleep; I tumble through baroque night-mares. *He* stalks me. I'm in a courtroom, testifying against him in some criminal matter, and I'm frozen with fear. I'm at a bar and he's at a table in the distance. A woman is with him but she is barely there, an apparition. He strips, he wraps himself in a news-paper, he dances, he is adjusting decanters on a drinks trolley and seems about to lift it and throw it at me. It's chaos. I'm terrified. I wake rigid, exhausted, my heart pounding.

He is not the only one to cast shadows across my sleep. I still have dreams about Ben, the journalist who took up my twenties. In a story about truth and deceit, how can I not declare this information. I was an accomplice in deceit. For the first years of our relationship, Ben was married. I was a thief in the night. He left his wife for me. I cannot ignore that fact. I can make excuses: I was nineteen when it started – silly, selfish, vulner-able, naive. He was twelve years older. Initially, I was flattered and overwhelmed by his attention – I was in my first year of work at a local newspaper, he was an attractive senior member of staff. I became convinced he was *the one* and that *it had to be*. It was passionate and dramatic. But excuses won't make it go away. And excuses won't make him leave my dreams, my nightmares, where he appears just often enough, always in hazy, pitiful form, to guarantee I won't forget my mistake and its contribution to damage done.

It exhausts me to think about it: the stolen moments, the anguish, the time wasted, his wife, the shame, the guilt. Something that begins so poorly cannot hope to have a happy ending, or even a happy middle. After Ben left his wife, he became depressed. And there were signs even then that he'd be unlikely to maintain his fidelity to me – at a party I stumbled upon him kissing another woman – but I was so foolish, so determined.

I moved to London to work for a period, following my mother's Kodachrome-coloured footsteps. Ben could not get the work visa required to join me but we declared we'd be true to each other. I could not see how muddied our truth already was. I maintained a vigil of long-distance, lonely devotion. I did not cast a glance at another man. I worked as a casual sub-editor at national newspapers and studied for a Cordon Bleu diploma that led to cooking jobs on a Scottish sporting estate and for a Belgian countess. Ben wrote three, four letters to me a week. I've not been able to throw away those letters, great stacks of them.

Now, years later, I take from a shelf the box that holds them, make myself lift its lid. I pull out the letter on the top of the pile and see again for the first time in years Ben's lovely spiky handwriting on onion-skin airmail paper. The letter is undated but it's clear he wrote it towards the end of my time away – he refers to the flight I have booked to come home to Brisbane. Had I told him by then that I was uncertain about returning for good, that finally I was utterly immersed in my new life away? I don't recall. I have, though, a visceral recollection of reading this letter, the sad-sick-worried awareness that descended as I did. I had changed and he had not. And I had absolutely no idea what to do. His letter made it clear he had similar concerns; in it he asked me if I'd be able to settle happily back into my old life. Had I changed too much? But he also told me how much I meant to him. 'Come home, darling,' he said.

I CAME HOME. I GOT A JOB in Brisbane, immersed myself in the relationship again, then discovered he had – possibly for most of the time I'd been away, and despite his hundreds of letters and earnest declaration that we'd come too far and made too many promises to each other to 'wreck what we have with personal gratification' – been seriously involved with another woman. He had also developed a gambling problem.

We broke up, he begged me to return to him, we got back together, he continued the affair. One Sunday morning: coffee and croissants together at my place, the phone rings, it's *her*, she says he doesn't love me, he loves her. And there he is, sitting on my couch, a mouthful of pastry. A week of unhinged drama follows: my grief and rage, his breakdown, an ambulance called in the night.

A month or two later I was offered a job at *The Age*. I moved to Melbourne. In phone calls, Ben harassed me, begged me to be with him, threatened to harm himself. Eventually I told him to stop calling me. We never spoke again. I was not yet thirty.

Some years later I went to his funeral in a little church in a country town. A heart attack, everyone said. I sat at the back of the church. I watched from a distance as he was buried in a tiny cemetery. I had absolutely no idea what to feel. Once, I had thought he was a good, gentle man who was in love with me. Later I decided he was a good, gentle man who was in love with me but deeply troubled. Now all I know for sure is that he was a man who was deeply troubled. And in dark moments I ask myself if I deserved the suffering our relationship gave me, whether my failure in love is a karmic consequence of my complicity in deceit?

In the lists I wrote when I was with Joe, one of the items was 'That Joe is like Ben and cannot be with just one woman', and then my reply to myself: 'Hardly any men behave as Ben did.'

The loves that turned into ugly things have all left their marks, little pockets of pain stitched into my consciousness, remnants of awareness about cruelty and deceit and betrayal. And I wonder now if these scraps of experience have embedded themselves within my neurochemistry, and sound an alarm in certain situations to leave my body stricken with the symptoms of anxiety and my soul aching for the loss of truth.

YOU DO NOT, WHEN YOU ARE NINETEEN, or twenty-one, or even twenty-five, see the limits of life. You do not pause to consider consequences. You are greedy for experience and pleasure and attention. I have a phone chat with an older friend who wanted very much to have a family, children, that life, but who remains alone. 'It's not a happy story,' she says of the dalliances of her twenties and thirties, and the place to which they have led her. Irresolute relationships can, she muses, 'knock the edges off you for the rest of your life'. She makes a fragmentary comment then that haunts me: 'the hand reaching from the grave', and I think I understand what she is referring to. I think of all the things we might change if we could pull ourselves back from the edge, back into the past and try again.

•

Resilience is a human being's default position. That's what Professor Jane Shakespeare-Finch tells me when we talk on the phone about the bitter legacy of the emotional abuse inflicted by a narcissistic partner. 'We're wired to survive,' she says. 'It doesn't mean we're wired to survive without some residual damage.'

Shakespeare-Finch is a professor in the School of Psychology and Counselling at QUT and president of the Australasian Society for Traumatic Stress Studies. We talk about the complexity of emotions in the aftermath of relationships that turn out to have been shot through with treachery. She explains how most people have default assumptions: the world is a benevolent place; relationships should look a certain way. In my case, I formed assumptions about Joe and my future with him.

'You had your assumptions breached,' Shakespeare-Finch tells me. 'It was a traumatic experience because the schemas you had in your mind about people and your place in [the world] were shattered by something unexpected and overwhelming. And that forces you into a situation of initially intrusive rumination.' She says it's common for people in such situations to become hyper-aroused, with heightened anxiety levels and startle reflexes. 'And those responses are completely normal responses for normal people who experienced something in their lives that's far from normal.'

People continue to contact me to tell me of the damage that has been done in their lives. Says one woman in an email: 'It's like I lived seven years in a cult. By the time he left, I'd lost my ability to cook. I love food. I've cooked all my life.' Another: 'I know the long, slow recovery, a special kind of grief, as you put yourself back together and try not to be so wary of future hope that a word of interest from a man sends you home to the dog and the Netflix binges.' And: 'I don't trust anyone anymore, least of all my own judgement. So it is self-imposed exile, a choice to follow the safe route for the rest of my days, alone and celibate.'

But the damage a partner with narcissistic tendencies inflicts is rarely singular, rarely merely emotional. Too frequently the emotional distress and erosion of self are accompanied by a complex mash-up of mental and physical health issues, or financial catastrophe, or criminal repercussion, or vexatious legal action, or complicated and ongoing unpleasantness of one description or another. One woman told me about the suspicious death of a beloved family pet. Rarely does that most vital thing, a woman's work, not suffer in one way or another. More than one person who wrote to me after the publication of my article talked about the huge upheavals in their lives – of having lost homes, or given up high-paying jobs; moving interstate or overseas for lovers, away from friends and family, before discovering awful truths. More than one wrote to say their relationship with their children had been compromised or lost because they had decided, in the best interests of the children, to be the one to move out of the family home to still the conflict with their manipulative partner. Others talked of the trauma of forced connection: 'Once your lives are inextricably linked through children it never ends.'

I RIDE MY BIKE TO A CAFE in my neighbourhood to meet Andrea. She emailed me about her relationship with a man who was frequently absent because, he said, he needed to visit his terminally ill father in the country, then needed to be alone to mourn his death. He was actually leaving her to go home to his live-in girlfriend. She tells me of her slow collapse when, after months of what he'd led her to believe was a committed relationship, he ghosted her. 'My work was suffering,' Andrea says. She works in a fascinating job in a creative field. She loves her work. 'I got pulled into my boss's office regarding a piece of research I'd done and he just ripped it to shreds because it was horrendous. My head wasn't in the game.'

The man she thought was her boyfriend returned to her briefly, declared his love for her, then ghosted her again. 'I started to get really bad anxiety, it was all I could think about.' On social media she found a photograph of her boyfriend with his girlfriend – together with his very-much-alive father. 'I was a bloody mess.' She flew home to her parents, she took medication for anxiety and panic attacks, she sat on her parents' couch for hour upon hour and applied pencils to a mindfulness colouring-in book. She spent thousands on therapy. 'I have all but given up on being in a relationship again,' Andrea tells me. She's in her thirties.

Benita Alexander, the New York journalist who fell for the mendacious surgeon Paolo Macchiarini, also sustained multiple, devastating blows. Ahead of their illusory Italian wedding and new life together in Spain, having left her job at NBC, she took her daughter out of school – a private school she had attended since kindergarten and at which it was difficult to get a place. Then the fairytale fell apart. 'I was broke, I was out of work and I was struggling. Here I am, a single mom, and I have a mortgage to pay and I have a daughter to take care of, and that's when the fallout really hit – the financial reality of what he'd done to me; that he had allowed me to quit my job.' Additionally, she'd spent about $50,000 on wedding expenses. Macchiarini said he would cover those costs. Of course, he never did.

Perhaps too soon for her mental health, Benita directed her anger and journalism skills towards investigating Macchiarini. 'I was concerned about his patients,' she says. 'I thought I could use my story to expose him.' She cooperated with the *Vanity Fair* reporter Adam Ciralsky, but was ill-prepared for the consequences. 'It would have been much easier for me just to walk away from it and try to go on with my life, but I felt a responsibility. I didn't know it was going to cost me as much as it did.'

The mocking, the abuse, the trolling that followed the article's publication were vile enough, but then the Murdoch tabloid the *New York Post* picked up the story. The paper didn't contact Benita for comment and ran a photograph of her that must have been found online. It was taken at a costume party: she wore a bright red wig and her cheeks were heavily rouged. 'I'm like, why would you do that? . . . Probably because they thought I looked like some kind of porn star.'

There were repercussions, too, in her professional life: she'd started her relationship with Macchiarini while she was working on a story about him, an ethically uncomfortable position, and now that fact was public. She struggled to find work. 'I was basically blackballed from my own industry. That's when I hit my low-low-low. It was terrifying. I didn't know what I was going to do, and it felt so unfair. I'm trying to expose him, how am I the bad guy here? There was one night somewhere in the middle of it all that some friends tried to take me out salsa dancing, and I ran out of the club just crying; like I literally collapsed in the street in a ball of tears.'

I have a phone conversation with another woman, Cheryl. She emailed me after my article was published. 'He brought me to a suicide attempt in my late twenties and destroyed my life,' she wrote. Now, as she relays her story over the phone, I feel again a sense of horror; I will never cease to be appalled by the ruinous capacity of those with these malignant characteristics.

Cheryl tells me she met this man in the mid-1980s when she was twenty-four. She worked in head office, he worked for the company in another town. 'I've been hearing about a cute secretary,' he said on the phone one day. Each time he called he flirted with her. When finally she met him she thought he was 'drop-dead gorgeous, charming, well-spoken, charismatic'. For nearly a decade he visited her at home, perhaps a couple of times a week, and they made love. He would have seen her more often, he told her, but he was always travelling for work, trying to build his career. 'But you're the only one for me,' he said. 'We'll get married when things settle down.' The explanations he gave as to why she could not visit his home or meet his friends and family were plausible.

'I was so young and naive,' Cheryl says. Eventually, she discovered he was engaged to another woman and didn't live where he'd said; that nothing he'd said was true. 'It was just like the elevator had dropped from beneath me.' She tried to kill herself. Afterwards, her mental health was such that doctors told her she would never be able to work again. She was forced to go on a disability pension, financially ruined. 'Now I won't be with anyone and my mental health is gone,' Cheryl says. 'It ruined my life.'

I TALK ON THE PHONE WITH GARY. He's the man who contacted me about his former long-term, live-in girlfriend, the man who compared those with personality disorders to crocodiles acting out their 'true and only nature'. His girlfriend was beautiful and exotic, and he was intoxicated. 'She seemed to just know the things about me that I liked to hear . . . and then there was the sex,' Gary says. He pauses meaningfully.

Early on, he worked out that his girlfriend frequently lied to him; later he realised she must have been having affairs. He still can't understand why he stayed with her and accepted things he would never normally have tolerated. 'Anybody who hasn't been through it just simply doesn't understand,' he says, 'and it can be a very lonely place to be, exiting that.' It took him a decade to get himself out of the relationship. By then his digestive system was a mess, he'd taken his eye off the stock market on which he relied for income and had lost a fortune, and his reputation was in tatters. He says his former partner fabricated stories about him in the small community in which they both still live. 'Some people just look at me with daggers, with hate.'

But he pushed through; he did what psychologists like to describe as 'the work' to understand what had happened to him, and now he can see the things that have brought him back to life. He came to see his former partner as she really was – incapable of changing. Second, he cut off all contact. 'The importance of this is too easy to underestimate,' he says. 'Any contact will be used by them to continue the abuse. Knowing what she was was not enough of a defence against her manipulative ways.' Finally, he says, he saw a professional therapist. He realises now that until then, many people around him with whom he had shared his story had unknowingly or thoughtlessly trivialised it. 'What mattered was the validation of my experience; that it had been sustained, covert abuse and my suffering was intense and real and I was not dramatising it.'

I think of something Professor Shakespeare-Finch said during our conversation: that we are, in these situations, negotiating with ourselves. 'What is life for me now and who am I in the world now in light of this experience I've had?' In many cases, she says, people who've been through such things have what she describes as post-traumatic growth – 'positive personal transformative changes'.

The post-traumatic growth model doesn't mean that difficult emotions can't be triggered by certain events, but it has a forward momentum. 'Negotiating these experiences can create a sense in ourselves of an increased wisdom, or a changed narrative of our life, one that's more adaptive moving forward. I guess my take-home message is, yeah, horrible things happen to good people, but that doesn't have to define who we are. And I think that you develop trust again when you get a clear sense in your own mind that this was about this person, that this is not about all people, that there are wonderful people in the world. It's about creating a new narrative, with that as part of the story of your life, but not defining your life and your future.'

•

In summer I visit my mother again. One afternoon I take the path down through the dunes to the beach below her house, through groves of pandanus palms and scraggy she-oaks. I watch for snakes. A week earlier, watering her herbs, my mother was startled by a brown snake of generous proportion, languid between the basil and a clumping patch of ginger. She called the snake catcher; by the time he got there, it had slithered away.

I've been swimming at this beach since I was a little girl. We're never sure what we'll find here; it's unpredictable, a beach of mean rips and deep channels and wild, dumping waves. Sometimes it's wiser to walk away from it. It's the sort of surf where you need to make calculations: what is the intent of this approaching swell? How wicked is that darker area of water?

A few years ago my mother and I nearly drowned here. She was seventy-seven. She'd body-surfed all her life, taken self-esteem and joy from the waves. And then, this day, swimming together, she shouted 'Grab my hand!' – and suddenly she was grey-white, panicked. We'd not noticed ourselves drift and now we were some metres outside the flags. My mother was in a rip.

My hand clutched hers. Somehow, I raised my other hand to catch attention. I shouted over and over, 'Help!' As the water sucked at us, thoughts surged. Is this how I will lose her? Will she drag me under? A wave washed over her, I kept hold of her hand and then, somehow, we were in the shallows and lifesavers were holding my mother up and escorting her out of the water. Someone brought a chair and soon she was sitting, her ample bottom on white plastic. She looked, in the words she had so often used to describe herself emerging from the surf and which made me laugh, like 'the wreck of the Hesperus'. The lifesavers and I stood around her. My legs were feeble under me, I thought I might collapse. The colour returned to my mother's face. With an audience now, she was off: 'Oh yes, I love the surf, I've bodysurfed my entire life.'

MY MOTHER'S LEGS ARE NOT WHAT THEY WERE, and these days I come to the beach alone. Today, the surf is so loud it nearly drowns out the shrieks of children playing at the edge. 'Caution' the lifesavers' sign reads. 'Strong side sweep, flash rips forming, waist-deep swimming only.' And there's another peril: as I walk towards the water, something pops under my foot. A bluebottle. When we were kids, my brother and I used to hit their jelly bodies with our heels; the explosion was fabulous. These days I'm more cautious – I know the sting of those pretty blue tentacles. I look at the bluebottles scattered on the sand and decide they've come in on an earlier tide. I look at the water and decide I will not be deterred.

It's messy: dumpers at the shoreline, more benign waves just beyond. Some lift me gently; others I dive under as I've been doing since I was a child. Beneath their powerful sweep it's cloudy, a swirl of sand and foam. Nothing is clear. But as I slip back up towards the surface, there it is again, the stunning, miraculous moment, the gradation of blue-greens flowing into the glassy edge between curling wave and sky, shards of refracted light, an infinite aqua colour-wheel. I dive again as another wave looms over me; resurface, held in the water's silken embrace. And I see there are swimmers further out, past the break. That's where I want to be. Tomorrow I will return and perhaps the water will be calmer and I will be braver and will swim out further, out into the sea.

•

My friend Simone and I have dinner at a new Korean restaurant. Simone is smart, beautiful, compassionate, funny and, like so many other smart, beautiful, compassionate, funny women, she is single. From time to time, when she can bear it, she activates her online dating profile. Now she tells me about a new man with whom she has been exchanging messages, a father of two young daughters. He seems nice enough, although she's frustrated he won't commit to a time to meet. She can't see the point in endless texting; she thinks they should just catch up to see if there's a spark. 'And there's something else that worries me,' she says. 'I don't know whether I want to be a stepmother.' Simone pauses, bibimbap poised on her chopsticks. She looks at me. I look at her. We fall about laughing.

'Noooooooooo!' I wail. Other diners turn to stare. Simone has offered wise and warm counsel to me. Now it's my turn.

'We've got to stop thinking like this,' I say, and by *we* I mean any woman prone to premature, relationship-related thought patterns. 'We just have to! You haven't even met him; he might have bad breath or body odour; he might secretly speak in tongues or be a Trump supporter! Don't even start to think about your relationship with his daughters!'

I tell Simone about a *New Yorker* cartoon I love, by the artist Ariel Molvig, a little sketch of a man and a woman. The man is offering flowers to the woman. Both man and woman have a thought bubble over their head. The woman's thought bubble reads: 'Flowers dates romance propose marriage honeymoon sex snuggle kiss pregnancy baby kids school grandkids.' The man's thought bubble overlaps the woman's, as a Venn diagram. One word is common: 'sex'. There's nothing else in the man's bubble.

I tell Simone about the New York-based illustrator and writer Mari Andrew, who has a million followers on Instagram, where, in pocket-sized pieces of art and prose, she shares her sorrows, joys and dating reflections. In a recent post, headed 'Things I've Mistaken for Signs of True Love', her list started with 'Some element of tragedy' and 'Aloofness à la Austen' and went on to include 'The fact that he likes sardines too; the fact that he follows Roxane Gay'.

I tell Simone about the weekend I spent in a cottage in a valley with a man I barely knew – 'You could be an axe murderer,' I joked with him. But then he told me he loved a book I loved about a Greek island and from that, and in the grip of pumping neurotransmitters and hormones, I drew multiple conclusions about his character and took a ridiculous leap forward in my thinking. It should have been the start of a trial period; rather than clutching at worthless omens, I should have been steady and clear-eyed, examining him for likeability, reliability, honesty and integrity. I should have rejected the whirlwind. Perhaps then I might have escaped unscathed.

What is it with this embedded, maladaptive behaviour; this tendency to sketch fairytales, to place weight in ideas and dreams rather than reason and facts gathered over time; this tendency to take little things, mere specks of dust, and polish them, and invest them with meaning, and mistake them for the future?

Science will have something to say about the biological imperatives behind such behaviour, but I blame the whole relentless, overwhelming narrative about what a woman's life should look like. And I blame the fairytales, the fucking fairytales: *Cinderella* and *Sleeping Beauty*; Doris Day and Audrey Hepburn; Bogart and Bacall, the fairytales told by my mother, as well as those of the media, advertising and marketing industries; *When Harry Met Sally*, *Pretty Woman*, *Sleepless in Seattle*, Bridget Jones, *Eat Pray Love* and even, for god's sake, the 2018 film *Book Club*, in which four actors who should have known better – Jane Fonda, Diane Keaton, Candice Bergen and Mary Steenburgen – deliver a toe-curling piece of princess mythology for senior citizens.

Sometimes I think we have moved barely a step forward from what Dorothy Parker described a century or so ago: in her short story 'A Telephone Call', the female protagonist sat and waited for a man to ring, and while she waited she scraped together some specks of dust to convince herself that he would call, that he would love her because, she reminded herself, he 'called me "darling" twice'.

WE MUST STOP SEEING OMENS. And there's something else: we must stop confusing terms of endearment, flattery, kisses or sex for signs of love. I was confused, and you know how that worked out for me. The lesson: apply Kondo-esque principles to your daydreams – declutter them, discard every last word of flattery. Whatever you do, do not dwell on the flattery he has ladled out until he has dished up multiple deeds to match.

If you find yourself clinging to his flattery, if you can't bring yourself to accept the possibility that it might be flimsy or false, try this: in your search box, start typing the word 'compliment for wom . . .' or 'compliment for gir . . .'. Just look at what comes up: '10 compliments women can't resist'; 'The five compliments every girl wants to hear from a guy'; 'Dirty compliments that end in sex every time'; 'What to say to a woman after sex'; 'How to break up with a woman the classy way'. That flattery you're clinging on to . . . well, it might not even be original.

And sex. We should never ever misunderstand sex. Most of us know this, but in the heat of the moment some of us forget. I forgot. Sex is not emotional connection. Sex is not love. A hot, sweaty night during or after which he says you're very special, or he's exclusively yours, or he's had a fond vision of you with grey hair baking for him, does not mean you've found *the one*. If you think you might be at risk of mistaking sex for love, go home immediately – to Anaïs Nin, or to your favourite joyful device, or to watch Doris Day and Rock Hudson make eyes at each other (and we know how that worked out for all the women who wanted to throw their underwear at him).

'You kissed me and I was thrilled!' says Day's Carol Templeton to Hudson's sleazy, double-dealing, role-playing, ad-man character Jerry Webster in *Lover Come Back*.

'A kiss? What does that prove?' replies Webster. 'It's like finding out you can light a stove. It doesn't make you a cook.'

YEARS AGO, A MALE COLLEAGUE TOLD me it would be a brave man who ever took me on. He meant in a romantic sense. I worried over his words for years. Could it be that the combination of my single-mindedness, my bluntness, my firm view of what needed to be done to create the high-quality publication we produced, were negatives? Was I letting those qualities bleed into my private life? Should I be softer? Did I have too many opinions and was I harsh in their delivery? Was all that an unattractive combination? *Was I too much?*

When I was with Joe, I brooded over similar thoughts. I laboured not to be that too-much woman, and, with an injection of anxiety, my spine dissolved and I took on the demure feminine attributes celebrated in nineteenth-century marriage manuals. I might as well have been wearing petticoats and a laced corset. I was polite, I was patient, I was calm, I was loving, I was gentle and understanding. I did not push, I did not impose or hassle. I did not complain. I mean, what sort of woman would I have been if I'd complained when he said he had to rush off to attend to one child's catastrophe or another? I didn't want to be intense. I didn't want to be hysterical. Women are always accused of being hysterical. I did not, under any circumstance, want to get angry.

In September 2018, *New York* magazine columnist Heather Havrilesky described Supreme Court nominee Brett Kavanaugh's testimony to the Senate Judiciary Committee defending himself against Christine Blasey Ford's allegations of sexual assault: 'He was sweaty and flushed and overwhelmed and pissed off, the way no woman gets to be ever.'

In an opinion piece in the *New York Times* the following day, Rebecca Traister wrote of Blasey Ford's precise, calm and deferential testimony. 'She described a past sexual assault and the more recent media assault on her in excruciating and vulnerable detail, but did not yell, did not betray a hint of the fury she had every reason to feel as she was forced to put her pain on display for the nation. That is how women have been told to behave when they are angry: to not let anyone know, and to joke and to be sweet and rational and vulnerable.'

I was sweet and rational and vulnerable. Others have been so, too. One woman emailed to tell me about her relationship experience: 'There are so many times I should have called my ex out but I didn't want to be impolite. More fool me. He's now in prison where he belongs.' Politeness has not helped any of us.

A couple of months after the Kavanaugh testimony, in a column for *Daily Life*, Clementine Ford discussed women's personalities. 'If you're a woman with even the vaguest outline of a personality, you've probably been called "intimidating" at some point in your life,' Ford says. The author of *Fight Like a Girl* and *Boys Will Be Boys* notes that women have so often been advised to downplay their personalities and mute their intelligence to protect men's fragile egos. I read to the end of her column, past her thoughts that 'women aren't mirrors held up to reflect the brilliance of men' and that it's important girls and boys not grow up believing they should slot into these roles. And then, with her closing line, I want to stand up in the bleachers and cheer: 'Besides, maybe it isn't that women are "too much" at all,' she says. 'Maybe it's just that the men who care about that are too damn little.'

DON'T EVER PUT YOUR CHARACTER ON MUTE. Don't ever hold back your anger when your anger is warranted. Determine your boundaries and protect them as though your life depends on it. Because it might. This is what Sophia, the woman who reminds me of a Gauguin painting, told me: 'I don't know how to say no to men. If I'm attracted to them and they seem like a decent man, I think they push my boundaries and I don't know how to say "No, actually you've crossed the line now." It took for Lucas to hit me for that to happen.'

I like the approach proposed by Martha Stout, the author of *The Sociopath Next Door*: 'When considering a new relationship of any kind, practice the Rule of Threes regarding the claims and promises a person makes, and the responsibilities he or she has . . . One lie, one broken promise, or a single neglected responsibility may be a misunderstanding instead. Two may involve a serious mistake. But *three* lies say you're dealing with a liar, and deceit is the linchpin of conscienceless behavior. Cut your losses and get out as soon as you can.'

I remember now something that Tessa, the woman who briefly dated Joe, said after I told her I had always analysed whether men I went out with could conceivably be *the one*. 'I've got the opposite thinking, which is none of them are *the one*,' she replied. 'My girlfriends and I, we're all more of the opinion that what you really need is multiple blokes: you need one who's like the electrician-slash-plumber-slash-tradie, one who's a chef, one who's a good masseur, one who likes travelling . . .'

'Is there a mechanic among them for car repairs?'

'Yeah, yeah . . . and you pull them in and out as needs be.' Tessa's tone turned serious: 'My mum died when she was fifty-three, so I just keep thinking that's not very far off, life's short. And it was the same with the whole Joe thing; the minute I was like, *oh my god, you're weird,* I thought, *I'm not wasting one more second with you.'*

'GO WITH YOUR GUT,' PEOPLE SAY. 'Listen to your instinct.' As though that's going to be enough to stop you one day discovering you've been pashing a snake disguised as a man in moleskins. I'll let others lean on those notional faculties; mine are clearly faulty. Was it my instinct sending me signals about Joe, or was I just anxious? I'm not sure I ever could have told the difference. As a guide, we need something more concrete than instinct – perhaps a taxonomic catalogue of the characteristics and behaviours of a little-known but dangerous species. As one woman said to me, 'How can you watch out for something when you don't know it exists; when it's beyond your worst imagination?'

I'd suggest the inclusion of a few key points in any such catalogue. First, beware of Drama Man or Drama Woman: beware of the one whose life seems an unfolding catastrophe of accident-prone children, veterinary calamities, business debacles and emergency visits to the dentist. *Always* beware of vanishing acts and the unlikely, ridiculous and implausible excuses for them. Unless you actually see it with your own eyes, beware the man who says he's been poisoned by sheep drench. Like, *really*, no one gets poisoned by sheep drench.

Lord, all the other things I'd add. Beware the man (or woman) who contradicts himself, whose stories shift from one day to the next. And beware the man who has nothing nice to say about his ex, especially the man who says she's a psycho or any variation on the theme: most likely she will turn out to be a sane and reasonable human being who's been put through a special form of hell.

Oh yes, this is important: beware the man who always makes his problems someone else's fault; the man who plays the wounded victim, who offloads blame, smearing someone else's reputation and in the process painting himself as a hero. Beware the man who tells you everything and shows you nothing; who, for example, after a decent period of time has elapsed – and let's declare two months the deadline – is still coming up with excuses as to why he can't show you where he lives or introduce you to his family and friends. And, of course, beware the man who asks for a loan, or who says he's just waiting for payment to come through for X or Y or Z, or who knows a fabulous scheme you'd be mad not to invest in, or who quickly wants to pool income, bank accounts, property. Keep your financial independence. *Always* keep your financial independence.

And here's something else for the catalogue: do your due diligence. *Look.* It's not snooping. It's smart. I get it, it's tough to look, you don't want to look, you want to keep your hands over your eyes, and you're not the only one. On Skype one day

I chat to a former *Wall Street Journal* colleague – Phil Segal, a Canadian finance journalist who is now an investigative attorney in Manhattan. His firm conducts a range of due diligence searches, including for clients whose soon-to-be-ex-husbands might be hiding assets. Not so long ago Phil advertised on the dating site eharmony, pitching his services at people who might want to investigate the background of someone they'd met on the site. 'The click rate was so low,' Phil says. 'There was just no interest. Nobody wants it to go bad and so nobody wants to check the other person out; they just want it to work out so much.'

Look. Take your hands away from your eyes. Check the other person out. Resist wilful blindness and be wise to the information you might be choosing to filter out because it makes you uncomfortable. *Look.* For small fees, you can do title deed, bankruptcy and company searches online. *Look.* And, when you've done the online searches, do the physical ones. Visit your sweetheart; visit him where he says he lives, where he says he works. If he's a decent sort, he'll be happy to see you and the champagne and flowers you've taken as a prop. And, well, if he's not who he says he is, then you will know.

I do my best to avoid clichés, but please can I throw in a few: past behaviour is the best guide to future behaviour; if they cheated with you, they have the capacity to cheat on you; you can't fix people, you can't change people; the treatment you accept as the relationship begins is the treatment you will continue to get.

And think about that other cliché – 'doing the work'. Do the work to build your self-confidence. Tessa did not hesitate for a minute in walking away from Joe because she placed no value in his opinion of her. 'Self-esteem is so important,' she told me. 'It won't stop you meeting those people. You're going to meet them, and you might even go out with them, but I didn't once think that any of his behaviour was to do with me. I just thought it was him.'

Doing the work, according to Tessa, is learning how to praise yourself. 'It's about setting yourself a challenge, and then tackling it – and then appreciate yourself for it: *you know what, that was hard for me!* And even if it's something small, like deciding you're going to knit something when you don't know how to knit, it doesn't really matter. I think women, culturally, are not taught to praise themselves – they think they'll be seen as arrogant – but praise yourself.'

Something else keeps jumping into my head: British comedian Dawn French has said that her father gave her 'armour'. 'I was full of confidence and I didn't settle for creeps,' French told a *Daily Life* journalist.

If no one else has given us a suit of armour, we simply must assemble one for ourselves.

•

I don't go to the butterfly cafe very often these days. I think the owners have changed and for me it seems to have lost some of its soul, although the vintage dolls with horror-movie eyes still line the shelves. I suspect the photo Joe posted on Instagram was an old one he took when we were together. I doubt he's been back.

Word is he's still living with Ruth, and certainly her picture was popping up every so often on his Instagram feed. But who knows. One day he posted a photograph of a one-man tent pitched on a harbour beach, a tinnie pulled up alongside it. A couple of days later he shared a close-up shot of his eye, black and bruised. 'Colourful argument,' he captioned it.

A friend saw him not so long ago in the city: in the upmarket food court of a city office tower where busy lawyers and bankers have their offices and gentlemen's outfitters their shopfronts, he walked slowly, his head down. Her description threw into my mind a vision of him in the country pub: sitting on his own, the flicker of his gaze, intricate stories unfurling in his head, his soft white hands. I thought of a photograph Kirstie took of him during their relationship: in trousers and a sweater on a winter beach, a small figure in the distance with sloping shoulders and an air of defeat. It was the beach where he'd claimed to have sold a vast volume of land and kept a little parcel for himself on which he would build a house with a view of the sea.

Kirstie and I keep trying to catch up but life is busy and we haven't yet managed to get into each other's diaries. For a while she was seeing another man but it's over now; she says he felt she wanted too much of him and he couldn't manage the demands of a relationship. 'I can't live on my own, I find it hard to live with anyone else.' But she's keeping herself busy and trying to hold on to how she felt when she completed a section of the Camino de Santiago pilgrim's trail in Spain not so long ago. 'They call the Camino a "mobile therapist's couch" – getting to the end of it strips all the other stuff away.'

She doesn't think of Joe at all these days. To me he's an abstraction now. If his face comes to mind, it's that of the wild-eyed creature who arrived one day at my door without shoes. He's just a little eccentric, I told myself that day. Now I wonder how he was ever able to act the part of a normal man.

•

I can't help myself: despite everything, I find myself frequently returning to the question of love. Damn, I don't ever want to let go of the idea of it. I ruminate on Dorothy Parker's reflection 'There was nothing more fun than a man' and Patti Smith's imperative, 'Never let go of that fiery sadness called desire.' But love and desire rarely come through natural selection anymore. You don't need me to dig up research to prove that, these days, romantic encounter is more often than not initiated via algorithm. And the research of one academic I interviewed has found that men high in 'dark triad' traits (narcissism, psychopathy and Machiavellianism) are more likely to use dating apps than men without such traits. Can I bear to return to that awkward, pitiless dance?

When I get to thinking about the horrors of it, I turn to Gloria Steinem's position on the matter, expressed on t-shirts and totes from Copenhagen to Portland to Melbourne – 'A woman without a man is like a fish without a bicycle'. One suffragette's advice, recorded in a 1918 pamphlet, foreshadows Steinem's sentiments: 'Do not marry at all,' the suffragette advises. 'But if you must, avoid the Beauty Men, Flirts, and the Bounders, Tailor's Dummies, and the Football Enthusiasts. Look for a strong, tame man, a fire-lighter, coal-getter, window cleaner, and yard swiller. Don't expect too much.' And I think of something my smart, independent (and single) godmother Clare said to me in an email after the breakup: 'I often quote, probably incorrectly – "Fortunate is the woman who has the man she needs; more fortunate is the woman who doesn't have the man she does not need." Better to be with yourself than losing yourself in a relationship with someone who turns your life into a nightmare. It's about managing the hand you're dealt.'

When she was sixty-two, on her own, speaking no Mandarin, Clare moved to the teeming Chinese city of Ningbo to teach small children English. I visited her there while I lived in Hong Kong. One night we went to a concert. Coming out on to the street late at night in pouring rain, we tried to find a cab. One after the other swooshed past. Finally, Clare, petite, gentle, sodden, persuaded one to stop. As she opened the back door, a couple of young men pushed past her into the back seat. Clare engaged the competition with all the ferocity and skill of a UFC fighter. We got the cab.

I STILL WANT THE DREAM. I want the brave man who will take me on, as I will be brave to take him on. 'My god, the cauliflowers are good this year,' I want to say, standing arm in arm with him at dusk, the sexiest time of day, surveying the vegetable beds we've dug together, feeling his warmth, his flesh. My skin is still hungry. I still want the rush. Something a lusty gay friend once said to me niggles. With the carelessness of one who was deeply and frequently sexually fulfilled, he threw a bit of Auden at me:

When you see a fair form, chase it
And if possible embrace it,
Be it a girl or a boy.
Don't be bashful: be brash, be fresh
Life is short, so enjoy
Whatever contact your flesh
May at the moment crave:
There's no sex-life in the grave

I am keeping watch for fair forms. I am rehearsing brashness and freshness. I am assembling my armour: it will have over-lapping plates of learnt wisdom and a certain but not hardened cynicism; with a little polishing, it will acquire a sheen of quiet, calm confidence. I am continuing the work that needs to be done to exorcise the deeply embedded conviction that without another I am nothing; that without the fleshy touch, without someone's enfolding arms, my world is cold and meaningless. I am practising pragmatism, too: perhaps the man with whom I tend brassicas should not be the one I admit to my bed. Perhaps in our pursuit of 'the one', we end up asking more of one than one could ever deliver.

IT'S DUSK AS I WRITE THIS in my Sydney study by lamplight. I have a glass of good riesling beside me. The window is wide open to my lush courtyard. I could not be happier. This morning I swam out into the ocean. Now, after a steamy day, storms are sweeping across the city. The sky flickers with light, the thunder is incredible, hail is expected. I love a good storm.

One wall in my study is a sepia-hued ancestral gallery, and when I turn towards it I am overcome by a sense of love, comfort and belonging, surrounded by my people. Here is that joyful photograph of Nana and her adored Les, the grandfather I never met; a 1930s wedding portrait of Great-Aunt Amy, a Juliet-style cap veil over bobbed hair, the tulle tumbling over her shoulders; my father, looking like a teenager, in one of his first campaign posters ('for capable, active, full-time representation'); my mother and father on the day they married, glowing. My brother and his wife on a beach on the day a celebrant declared them man and wife as their three children watched; my nieces and nephew, who have given me more joy than any of them know.

I put on a playlist of arias. Is it just a coincidence that the first one that comes up is Puccini's '*O mio babbino caro*', from the opera *Gianni Schicchi*? My parents played this as I grew up, and before he died my father chose it for his funeral. Lauretta entreats her father to allow her to marry Rinuccio – 'Oh my dear papa/I love him, he is handsome, handsome.' She threatens to throw herself into the River Arno if he won't let her have her way. 'I am anguished and tormented,' she sings, and her voice soars with the exquisite agony of her situation. Next on the playlist is *Ah fors'è lui/Sempre Libera*, from Verdi's *La Traviata* – my mother's favourite, the opera that brought Julia Roberts to tears in *Pretty Woman*. At the end of Act I, the courtesan Violetta sings about the attractive bourgeois Alfredo – 'Ah, perhaps he is the one.' And then, with some reflection on the matter: 'Madness! This is a futile delirium! . . . I must stay always free, cavorting from joy to joy.'

Now, listening to the storm, to this glorious music, I realise something. Everything has been leading towards this: I could not have done anything else but write a book about love.

EPILOGUE

DIVE

One afternoon I return to the ladies baths, my thinking place. It is grey and drizzly. But for one other woman in a red bathing suit doing slow laps, it is all mine – a rare, delirious joy – and I run down the stairs with the excitement of a child about to swim for the first time since last summer. The stillness is infinite, the water dark and velvety, more jade than turquoise, the sea beyond the pool wall a platinum swathe that blurs into the palest periwinkle blue where it meets the sky.

I could not explain blue before, all the blues, the blue-greens and blue-greys, how they made me feel, the catch in my breath, the multi-tonal thrill of them, but then I found American writer Rebecca Solnit's words on blue – the 'color of horizons . . . of anything far away . . . the color of an emotion, the color of solitude and of desire, the color of there seen from here, the color of where you are not'. And I found the exquisite *Werner's Nomenclature of Colours: Adapted to Zoology, Botany, Chemistry,*

Mineralogy, Anatomy, and the Arts, a book first published in 1814 and carried by Charles Darwin on the HMS *Beagle*. German geologist Abraham Gottlob Werner developed a system to describe colours based on the colours of minerals. The Scottish botanical painter Patrick Syme created charts based on Werner's work and included examples of each colour from the animal and plant kingdoms. In his divine hand-coloured work, ultramarine blue, for example, takes glorious, poetic flight: it is described as the 'upper side of the wings of a small blue heath butterfly', it is the flower borage, it is azure stone or lapis lazuli. Greens, too, become poetry – the 'egg of a thrush', or the 'beauty spot on the wing of a teal drake' or the 'leaves of leeks in winter' – the colour of the dark water that surrounds me now.

I take some idle strokes, float on my back, porpoise-dive to the bottom, again and again, pursuing glimpses of a tiny fish with electric-blue markings that flits and ducks and hides under rocks. The tide is going out but a rogue wave crashes over the pool wall and over me, and I gasp as the colder water foams like seltzer on my skin. I pause, rest my elbows on the wall, kick my legs behind me, and look out towards Wedding Cake Island.

For millennia Indigenous people swam here in a natural rock pool hugged by a sandstone cliff face. Colonists followed their example, and by the 1870s the local council had excavated the rock to deepen the pool, defined it with concrete walls on two sides and segregated it for ladies. (In 1995 the pool was exempted from the state's Anti-Discrimination Act.) I think about how many women before me are likely to have rested their elbows where mine are, laughed as waves crashed over them, and looked out to that low, rocky island with its sea-foam icing. I think, too, about all the women who have found friendships here, or passed on words of kindness or encouragement, as today a group of older women did to me as we crossed paths at the entrance. 'The water is beautiful,' said one, and her friends nodded enthusiastically. So beautiful they just had to share the good news with a stranger. There is here a sense of gentle continuity. I feel I am one of an unbroken chain of women who have, over generations, come to the pool seeking inspiration or motivation or answers; who have brought fears and worries, about love or health or money or who knows what else; who have come to cleanse themselves of anger or pain or trauma, or to expel their demons. And I wonder how many women have felt their troubles soften, even dissolve, in this water, and have returned to the world feeling lighter.

I look across to Wedding Cake Island and think about the concept of human damage. I have sometimes been susceptible to the mythology, to the idea that I am damaged. I have thought that my wounds must be as evident as if I had just yesterday been punched hard in the eye. But I know now that this thinking is absurd. If I turn my back on the iconic little island, beaten and battered by the sea for aeons, I come to face the sandstone cliff face that forms two walls of the pool. The sandstone is layered with colour – tan, pink, cream, ochre – and over centuries has been contoured by the wind and sand. We do not think of it as damaged, we look at it and we think it is lovely.

So, too, is a life, a character, shaped and variegated and enriched in the wild moments and the storms, by difficulties and mistakes, misfortunes, humiliations, tragedies and traumas. I am not the person I was before. I do not want to be the person

I was before. I like myself now better than I ever did. I like my bruises, the sore sad spots and the scars. I treasure them as precious spoils of war, evidence that I fell over, then got back up again, that I fought wild beasts – including the beast that is my brain – and won. That I am strong, that I can roar.

I'M TRAINING FOR MY FIRST OCEAN SWIMMING RACE. And I have found my muse. As I gasp and flail up and down the pool building my fitness, I summon up a vision of the Sydney-born million-dollar mermaid Annette Kellerman, the finest figure of radical womanhood you could imagine. She is too little remarked upon, this indomitable 'lady swimmer', who was born with a weakness in her legs that required her to wear steel braces through the early years of her childhood. Her father put her in a pool, and by 1902, while still a teenager, she had achieved two world records, including for the 100-yard swim. Three years later, Miss Kellerman became the first woman to try to conquer the English Channel. She didn't make it all the way on her first attempt, nor on two subsequent attempts, but with a neck-to-knee bathing suit that chafed, her goggles glued on and her pores rubbed with porpoise oil, I think you'll agree that whether she came ashore at Calais or not is beside the point. In Paris, she competed against seventeen men in a seven-mile race down the Seine. In Massachusetts in 1907 at the beach she wore a close-fitting one-piece swimsuit of her own design, which showed her knees, and was arrested for indecency. She was an incredible athlete who could hold her breath for three minutes and twenty seconds, who in multiple silent movies, her 'fairytale films', wore silvery mermaid tails and fabulous, filmy, pearly, wafting costumes; who laughed with joy underwater as bubbles danced around her. She was eighty-nine when she died on the Gold Coast in 1975. Her husband had died some years earlier. She did not have children. She was still doing high kicks well into her old age.

In school sport, I always came last, I was always the last picked for the team. I'm scared of being laughed at in a sporting arena; I'm scared of not having enough breath in me for the ocean swim, of coming last – again. But I feel sure that Miss Kellerman would counsel me to drop my fearful thoughts. I think she would tell me to get in and to breathe and to keep going.

I like to think, too, that she might once have swum at the ladies baths; that some elemental part of her remains there for me to absorb. 'You see, the water always teaches me a new story,' she wrote in her wonderful, wise book *How to Swim*, published in 1918. 'Swimming cultivates imagination; the man with the most is he who can swim his solitary course night or day and forget a black earth full of people that push.'

I CAN SEE NOW THAT I AM ENOUGH AS ME, I am good as me, I am whole without another, without others, and therefore better for another should that possibility come to pass. 'Thank god we have done away with spinsterhood,' Clare said in an email the other day. 'Now I must get back to the dye potting projects on my patio; it is a gorgeous sunny day and I am making the most of it.'

A solitary course is not to be feared; it is not a compromise position but merely an alternative. Not an impediment to anything but an opening to opportunity, a chance for a forward charge. Not a cause for unhappiness but for joy. You get to choose which path to take, where you will invest your energy, what contribution you will make to the world, who you will give your time to, and how you will become the biggest, boldest, most brilliant version of you. There will be bad bits, of course there will be bad bits – everyone's life has bad bits. They're just not posted on Instagram.

I think I'm lucky: I understand now that I am an introvert and I imagine it's easier for an introvert to embrace a solitary course than it is for an extrovert. But for all of us, it is the best gift we can give ourselves, to train ourselves in the art of solitude, because none of us can ever know when it might come to visit and decide to stay like some annoying relative you don't know how to evict. And if we know how to deal with solitude we will better know how to deal with loneliness, and there are few among us who will not one day have to look that beast in the eye.

I know now how lucky I am to be able to return to myself with pleasure. My head is a cool place to hang out. Often, I find it a better place to be than with others. And I remember something that another extraordinary woman, the comedian Hannah Gadsby, said during an interview with the *Guardian*: 'If a documentary crew were to follow me around, they'd probably think they were making a film about the saddest person in the world . . . but I'm throwing the best thought orgies.' Without question, Gadsby's are better than mine but, my god, I love my thought orgies. We all need to learn to throw the best thought orgies.

Ideas for life I believe have merit: never stop exploring – thoughts, people, places, your abilities, your strength, nature.

Follow a life of adventure and exhilaration and extreme sport. Or be idle and gentle and thoughtful. Lie on the floor of a forest and look at the sky, knit tea-cosies, write a small, perfect entry in a diary every day. Embrace the people you love. Be curious; keep learning, keep asking questions. Listen, really listen, when other people talk. Find humour everywhere. Collect something that makes you laugh (but please note – shopping is not a hobby). Ignore Marie Kondo, everyone needs a big collection of books. Whatever you do, make art of one sort or another, no matter how average you feel it might be; stick with it, try again, don't give up. Focus, focus, focus on something you love doing until you have reached such a state of flow that you've forgotten your name and what day it is. Listen to a new piece of music every day. Listen to country and western music. Don't look with green eyes at other people's lives; look at where you are and what you're doing and at all the little wonderful things in your every day. Lots of little wonderful things add up to a life a little more wonderful. Forget the life you wanted or expected, grab the life you have. Learn to say 'sorry' graciously and mean it. Be kind. Roll with the punches, they'll keep coming, as will change. Nothing ever stays the same. Eliminate self-pity, bitterness, judgement, regret and any grievance more than a month old. You are the architect of your own life. Take responsibility for it, don't blame anyone else. Smile at strangers. Stop belting yourself up. Get the right medication from your doctor. Find a good psychologist who comes to know you better than you know yourself. Look for joy everywhere.

THE SEA IS BIG. THE WATER IS ICY, breath-taking. The dumpers punch me back. A vicious, curling wave approaches, and as I dive under it I'm surrounded by flying arms and legs. A body tumbles past. 'Dive!' someone yells, and as I sweep low through the next looming wave and try to grab at the sand and pull myself through, I feel the surging power of the water above me. I resurface, swim on, breathless and exhausted already and I've only just started. 'Dive!' roars the voice, and again I'm in a turbulent underworld, a dark swirling mess of sand and spume. I come up to the light again, and for a moment the sea settles and I swim and sight as we've been taught – lift your head to the front, check your direction, turn your head to the side, breathe, repeat.

I see my first destination: beyond the breaking water, a man straddling a surfboard and holding aloft a yellow marker. I must swim to him and then around him before returning to the shore. But he is still 30 metres or more away and the water is glacial, stealing my breath. I am frozen from the inside. Keep swimming, don't stop, relax into your stroke, breathe. The water settles into a gentler swell, my breath slows, and finally the man on the board is at my right shoulder. But then I'm fighting with two dozen others, trying to loop around him for the return trip. Legs, arms, bodies collide. Someone's leg strikes my shoulder; my foot slaps someone's hand. I arc wider to find clear space, strike out for the shore, a yellow building in my sights, but I'm short-sighted and it disappears on me, blurs, moves. As I reach the breakers I glance backwards under my arm while I breathe, looking for waves to catch or to fear. 'The waves are your friend,' the coach has told us, 'they'll take you to shore.' Not this one coming from behind now – it's a mean, mountainous grey mouth with teeth. Gasping for breath, I turn back and dive under it. My chest is heaving as I resurface; when I look towards the shore the yellow building seems barely closer. My goggles have misted up. Keep swimming, don't stop, relax into your stroke, breathe. I look behind again and see a wave that might be friendlier, offer me a ride; I swim harder and it picks me up, and for a moment seems to hold me suspended in the air. Then it drops me and hurls me forward in a rush of churning water. I feel sand underfoot. I pull myself to my feet, my legs are wobbly. Around me, others are doing the same. We stumble to the shore. We stand in the cold air, hugging ourselves for warmth. Our faces are pale.

WE KNOW NOW HOW UGLY SOME DAYS CAN GET. We also know how to deal with those days, the big surfs, the frightful waves, the frigid water. That day was the worst – we haven't had another like it, and as the weeks pass, when we gather for our training sessions, each of us seems a little taller, a little more confident, a little faster to dash into the surf with high-kneed ungainly urgency. We are all sorts: athletic young women in their twenties; an Asian-born Australian girl who is terrified of the water but each week returns and swims out bravely; a cluster of older, rounder women; a couple of young men; a few people who, like me, are drawn to the sea but have never been able to swim much further than the length of a backyard pool. Some days now I'm swimming a kilometre or more beyond the break.

One day, one stunning, gleaming blue day, we look for the rip, the darker water untroubled by breaking waves, and we enter there, stroke with the current, letting it pull us out through all the blues and greens. And as the shoreline recedes, so too everything else – thought, ancient sadness, anxiety, fear – fades into blurred distance. This is all there is – my body, weightless, and the sea, holding me in its copper-green verdigris embrace, the colour of the tail of a small long-tailed green parrot. I take a breath, sink into the water, lower and lower, expelling bubbles, trying to catch and keep this moment of blue-green bliss, trying to snatch an image I can hold until I am here again.

RACE DAY IS CLOSING IN. When I'm tired and flat and want to hide, I think I must have been mad to have considered I could do such a thing. Other days, though, when I have sailed through a training session, or smashed my way out through the surf to the open water beyond and kept swimming, I think it might be possible.

I'm still scared of sharks, of the unknown underwater beyond my vision, the things that might brush up against me. I have concerns about bluebottles: I've endured three vicious stings this year and carry tiny red scar trails on an arm and knee. I'm still worried I might come last. My ambitions are modest: I just want to finish, not last. I am picturing how race day will look as volleys of people rush into the sea at the start, the crush of bodies in the shallows. I imagine it might be easy to stumble and fall, or be knocked to my knees by a wave, so I'm rehearsing in my head what I will do; how, if I fall, I will get up, and if I stumble again, I will get up again, and I will start swimming and diving under waves as they loom, and then surface to swim and swim, because I want to get out there, beyond the break, to the blue-green depths I love.

NOTES

Chapter 1: An Introduction to Romance

Gornick, Vivian, *Fierce Attachments*, Daunt Books, 2015, p. 130

Chapter 2: The Other Woman

Pavia, Will, 'Esther Perel: The World's Most Wanted Sex Therapist', *The Times*, 16 December 2017

Perel, Esther, 'Rethinking Infidelity . . . A Talk for Anyone Who Has Ever Loved', TED2015; https://www.estherperel.com/my-story

Johnson, Sue, *Hold Me Tight: Seven Conversations for a Lifetime of Love*, Little, Brown, 2008, p. 12 (Kindle edition)

Hardwick, Elizabeth, *Seduction and Betrayal: Women and Literature*, New York Review of Books, 2001, p. 172 (Kindle edition)

Winterson, Jeanette, *Why Be Happy When You Could Be Normal?*, Vintage, 2011, p. 132 (Kindle edition)

Rosenwald, Michael S., '"My Dearest Ruth": The Remarkable Devotion of Ruth Bader Ginsburg's Husband', *Washington Post*, 25 October 2018

327

Bader Ginsburg, Ruth, 'Ruth Bader Ginsburg's Advice for Living', *New York Times*, 1 October 2016

Len Catron, Mandy, 'To Fall in Love With Anyone, Do This', *New York Times*, 9 January 2015

Len Catron, Mandy, *How to Fall in Love With Anyone*, Simon & Schuster, 2017

Jones, Daniel, 'The 36 Questions that Lead to Love', *New York Times*, 9 January 2015

Len Catron, Mandy, 'Falling in Love is the Easy Part', TEDxChapmanU, 2015

De Botton, Alain, *Essays in Love*, Picador, 1993, p. 108

Chapter 5: Two Weddings and a Funeral

De Botton, Alain, *Essays in Love*, Picador, 1993, p. 19

Wood, Stephanie, 'The Savage Descent of Mustang Sallie', *Good Weekend* magazine, 24 February 2016

Fisher, Helen, *Anatomy of Love: A Natural History of Mating, Marriage and Why We Stray*, W.W. Norton & Company, 2016, p. 154 (Kindle edition)

Chapter 6: A Cabinet of Curiosities

Verrender, Ian, 'Is This Australia's Greatest Con Man?', *Sydney Morning Herald*, 10 December 1994

Shand, Adam, 'Conned', Bluestone column, *The Bulletin* online, 2007

Vištica, Olinka, and Grubišić, Dražen, 'The Art of Broken Hearts: from a Smashed Mannequin to a Bottled Wedding Dress', *Observer*, 19 November 2017

De Botton, Alain, *Essays in Love*, Picador, 1993, pp. 11, 53

Tobin, Vera, 'The Science of the Plot Twist: How Writers Exploit our Brains', *The Conversation*, 11 May 2018

Tobin, Vera, *Elements of Surprise: Our Mental Limits and the Satisfaction of Plot*, Harvard University Press, 2018, pp. 14, 105 (Kindle edition)

Heffernan, Margaret, *Wilful Blindness: Why We Ignore the Obvious at our Peril*, Simon & Schuster, 2011, p. 96 (Kindle edition)

Schulman, Nev, *In Real Life: Love Lies & Identity in the Digital Age*, Hodder & Stoughton, 2014

ABC, *Four Corners*, 'Meet the Scammers', 11 February 2019

Chapter 7: Disordered

James, Henry, *The Portrait of a Lady*, Wordsworth Editions, 1996, pp. 431, 367

Thurber, James, 'The Secret Life of Walter Mitty', *New Yorker*, 18 March 1939

Fitzgerald, F. Scott, *The Great Gatsby*, Amazon Digital Services LLC, 2013, p. 48 (Kindle edition)

Wood, Patrick, 'Landmark Report Reveals a Woman Dies Every Week Due to Australia's Domestic Violence Crisis', ABC News, 28 February 2018

Australian Institute of Health and Welfare, 'Family Domestic and Sexual Violence in Australia, 2018' https://www.aihw.gov.au/reports/domestic-violence/family-domestic-sexual-violence-in-australia-2018/contents/table-of-contents

Australian Human Rights Commission, 'Everyone's Business: Fourth National Survey on Sexual Harassment in Australian Workplaces', 2018 https://www.humanrights.gov.au/sites/default/files/document/publication/AHRC_WORKPLACE_SH_2018.pdf

Sales, Leigh, McCutcheon, Peter, and Denness, Callum, 'I Didn't Sleep for a Week', ABC News, 19 September 2018 https://www.abc.net.au/news/2018-09-18/catherine-marriott-on-alleged-sexual-harassment-by-barnaby-joyce/10255518

Yaxley, Louise, 'Barnaby Joyce Resigns as Deputy Prime Minister', ABC News, 24 February 2018 https://www.abc.net.au/news/2018-02-23/barnaby-joyce-resigns/9477942

Kenny, Mark, 'A Grey Area', *Sydney Morning Herald*, 3 March 2018

Fahrenthold, David A., 'Trump Recorded Having Extremely Lewd Conversation about Women in 2005', *Washington Post*, 8 October 2016

Havrilesky, Heather, *Don't Call it "'Toxic Masculinity'". They're Sociopathic Baby Men'*, The Cut, *New York* magazine, 6 October 2017

Wood, Stephanie, 'How Social Media Has Changed Everything for Teenage Girls', *Good Weekend* magazine, 21 January 2017

Sales, Nancy Jo, 'Tinder and the Dawn of the "Dating Apocalypse"', *Vanity Fair*, September 2015

Menagh, Joanna, 'Tinder Revenge Porn Conman Leigh Abbot Jailed for Extortion', ABC News, 5 May 2017 https://www.abc.net.au/news/2017-05-05/tinder-fish-in-the-sea-revenge-porn-conman-leigh-abbot-jailed/8501816

Australian Competition & Consumer Commission (ACCC), Scamwatch, 2018 Dating and Romance Statistics https://www.scamwatch.gov.au/about-scamwatch/scam-statistics?scamid=13&date=2018

Federal Trade Commission, Romance Scams, https://www.ftc.gov/news-events/press-releases/2019/02/new-ftc-data-spotlight-details-big-jump-losses-complaints-about

Goffard, Christopher, 'Dirty John', *Los Angeles Times*, 1 October 2017

Goldberg Lesley, "Dirty John" Anthology, *Hollywood Reporter*, 28 January 2018

Dibdin, Emma, 'Here's the Full Transcript of Jimmy Kimmel's Extremely Good Oscars Opening Monologue', *Elle*, 5 March 2018

'Drone Stalking Several Women in Rural Port Lincoln Community Part of Growing UAV Concerns', ABC News, 3 November 2017 https://www.abc.net.au/news/2017-11-02/drone-stalking-several-women-in-port-lincoln-rural-community/9112926

May, Tiffany, and Lee, Su-Hyun, 'Is There a Spy Camera in That Bathroom? In Seoul, 8,000 Workers will Check', *New York Times*, 3 September 2018

Martin, Brittany, 'The Woman Behind "Bye Felipe" Has Written the Ultimate Guide to Modern Dating', *Los Angeles Magazine*, 21 August 2018

Penny, Laurie, 'The Queer Art of Failing Better', *The Baffler* magazine, 24 July 2018

American Psychiatric Association, *Diagnostic and Statistical Manual of Mental Disorders* (DSM), fifth edition

Project Air, A Personality Disorders Strategy, 'What Are Personality Disorders?' https://www.projectairstrategy.org/content/groups/public/@web/@project-air/documents/doc/uow243932.pdf

Australian Government, Department of Health, 'Diabetes: How Common Is Diabetes', 23 November 2016 http://www.health.gov.au/internet/main/publishing.nsf/Content/chronic-diabetes

American Psychiatric Association, *DSM-IV and DSM-5 Criteria for Personality Disorders*, 2012

Josie Charles: Website: http://narcissist-sociopath-awareness.com/
Instagram: @narcissist.sociopath.awarenes2
Twitter: @narcopathaware
Facebook: Narcissist Sociopath Awareness
Email: narcissist.sociopath.awareness@gmail.com

Chapter 8: Who the Hell Are You?

Wood, Stephanie, 'Childless: How Women Without Kids Are Treated in 2016', *Good Weekend* magazine, 19 July 2016

Monroe, Rachel, 'The Perfect Man Who Wasn't', *The Atlantic*, April 2018

Vander Hayden, Aly, 'Photos: Scammer Derek Alldred's Many Props and Personas Used in His Love Cons', Oxygen Crime Time, 4 February 2019

Saavedra, Marie, 'Con Man's Trail of Broken Hearts, Empty Bank Accounts Ends in North Texas', WFAA, 17 September 2018 https://www.wfaa.com/article/news/crime/con-mans-trail-of-broken-hearts-empty-bank-accounts-ends-in-north-texas/287-595642471

Nine Entertainment, *A Current Affair*, 'Brett Joseph – Conman and Fraud', 2012 and 2016 https://www.youtube.com/watch?v=oFGRZt4bWQo

Ramirez, Marc, 'Collin County Woman Calls off Southfork Wedding After Outing Fiance as "Tinder Love Rat" from Australia', *Dallas News*, March 2017

BBC News, 'M16 Conman Mark Acklom Arrested in Switzerland', BBC News, 3 July 2018

Woods, Lara, 'My Mother was Victim to one of Europe's Most-Wanted Men', *Telegraph*, 29 October 2016

Brunt, Martin, 'British Conman Wanted for £850,000 Fraud', Sky News, 19 October 2016 https://news.sky.com/story/british-conman-wanted-for-850-000-divorcee-fraud-10622971

Thrasher, John, '"Seduced by Evil" Premieres February 9 on Oxygen', Oxygen Crime Time, 24 January 2019 https://www.oxygen.com/seduced-by-evil/crime-time/seduced-by-evil-premieres-february-9-on-oxygen

Ciralsky, Adam, 'The Celebrity Surgeon Who Used Love, Money, and the Pope to Scam an NBC News Producer', *Vanity Fair*, February 2016

KI News, 'The Macchiarini Case: Timeline', Karolinska Institutet, 25 June 2018 https://ki.se/en/news/the-macchiarini-case-timeline

Rasko, John, and Power, Carl, 'Dr Con Man: the Rise and Fall of a Celebrity Scientist Who Fooled Almost Everyone', *Guardian*, 1 September 2017

'Investigation Reopened into Scandal-Hit Surgeon Paolo Macchiarini', *The Local Sweden*, 11 December 2018 https://www.thelocal.se/20181211/investigation-reopened-into-scandal-hit-surgeon-paolo-macchiarini

Personality Disorders and Related Traits, Prominent Personality Traits or Patterns, *ICD-11 International Classification of Diseases for Mortality and Morbidity Statistics*, World Health Organization, December 2018

Chapter 9: All the Similar Stories

Konnikova, Maria, *The Confidence Game*, Canongate Books, 2012, pp. 285–6 (Kindle edition)

Taibbi, Matt, 'The Madness of Donald Trump', *Rolling Stone*, 19 September 2017

Polage, Danielle C., 'Liar, Liar: Consistent Lying Decreases Belief in the Truth', *Applied Cognitive Psychology*, 2018;1–10 https://onlinelibrary.wiley.com/doi/abs/10.1002/acp.3489

Kamm, Rebecca, 'A World of Their Own', *The Wireless*, RNZ, 15 August 2016

Fitzgerald, F. Scott, *The Great Gatsby*, Amazon Digital Services LLC, 2013, p. 73 (Kindle edition)

Singal, Jesse, 'A Therapist Attempts to Explain Donald Trump's Rocky First Few Days in Office', The Cut, *New York* magazine, 25 January 2017

Konnikova, Maria, 'Donald Trump, Con Artist?', *New Yorker*, 19 March 2016

Chapter 10: How Could That Have Happened to Me?

Wood, Stephanie, 'Home Truths', *Good Weekend* magazine, 30 April 2015

Capote, Truman, *Breakfast at Tiffany's*, Hamish Hamilton, 2011, p. 27

Nussbaum, Martha C., *Upheavals of Thought: The Intelligence of Emotions*, Cambridge University Press, 2001, p. 2 (Kindle edition)

Winterson, *Why Be Happy When You Could Be Normal?*, Vintage, 2011, p. 76 and p. 185 (Kindle edition)

Chapter 11: The Getting of Wisdom

Havrilesky, Heather, 'Mediocre White Man Falls Apart and Is Promptly Put Back Together', The Cut, *New York* magazine, 28 September 2018

Traister, Rebecca, 'Fury Is a Political Weapon. And Women Need to Yield It', *New York Times*, 29 September 2018

Ford, Clementine, 'People Would Consider You Really Beautiful if You Didn't Talk So Much', *Daily Life*, 7 December 2018

Stout, Martha, *The Sociopath Next Door: The Ruthless Versus the Rest of Us*, Harmony Books, 2005, p. 156 (Kindle edition)

Jonason, P. K., and Bulyk, Rachel, Western Sydney University 'Who Uses Tinder (and Other Dating Apps)?: Sex-Specific Personality Effects', (paper under review; manuscript submitted 2018)

W. H. Auden, 'The Entertainment of the Senses', *Thank You, Fog: Last Poems*, Random House, New York, 1972, 1973

Epilogue: Dive

Solnit, Rebecca, *A Field Guide to Getting Lost*, Canongate, 2017, p. 29

Syme, Patrick, and Werner, Abraham Gottlob, *Werner's Nomenclature of Colours: Adapted to Zoology, Botany, Chemistry, Mineralogy, Anatomy, and the Arts*, Smithsonian Books, 2018

Popova, Maria, 'Eleven Kinds of Blue: Werner's Pioneering 19th-Century Nomenclature of the Colors, Beloved by Darwin', Brainpickings https://www.brainpickings.org/2018/02/06/werner-nomenclature-of-colours/

Kellerman, Annette, *How to Swim*, George H. Doran Company, 1918, p. 35 and p. 37

Valentish, Jenny, 'I Broke the Contract: How Hannah Gadsby's Trauma Transformed Comedy', *Guardian*, 16 July 2018

ACKNOWLEDGEMENTS

This was a tough project and I owe thanks to those who pushed me forward, held me up, or offered assistance in one form or another along the way to help me stumble over the finishing line.

This book could not have happened without the guidance and confidence of Amelia Lester, an astute and adventurous *Good Weekend* magazine editor. Amelia, thank you so much for seeing this story, giving it space, and shepherding it into the magazine with such care and tenderness. (And thank you too for all the other stories!)

I send much gratitude to my former Fairfax Media colleagues who encouraged me to have confidence in my writing ability – to Kirsten Galliott, Lauren Quaintance, Michelle Hurley, Garry Linnell, Ben Naparstek, Greg Callaghan, Tim Elliott and Michaela Whitbourn. To the wonderful Richard Coleman for your considered thoughts, and Kate McClymont and Anne Davies for tearing your attention away from matters of major corruption to offer your advice on my story.

To my support team, Adrienne and Valerie, for the wisdom, the encouragement and care. To the James Street garden community, the people and the plants (especially the sweetpeas and the purple beans and the lettuce). To the CanToo Foundation and its coaches and mentors, who convinced me I could swim the distance and stare down big fat mean waves.

So many others thanks are due: to the remarkable Rev. Graham Long, a good man, the best man I know, for your counsel and compassion. To Julie Gibbs and Foong Ling Kong for your thoughts and insight. To Wendy Tuohy for the injection of confidence at a critical moment. To a bunch of other brilliant women: Caitlin Shea, Kylie Munnich and Dr Alecia Simmonds, whose research into the history of romantic suffering and deceit in Australia is fascinating and extraordinary and deserves great attention.

So much love and thanks to other precious friends: to Robin Cowcher and Melissa Reynolds for always picking up, for tolerating my tears; to Joel Meares, Dinah Jane and Mossy, Mere and Rich, Catherine Martin, Megan Fletcher, Jane and Deirdre and Kate. To dear Ros and Phillippa – thanks for the finger sandwiches! To Slattery – thanks for the advice and the chats.

I send much gratitude to Clare Forster, my agent at Curtis Brown Australia; to my publisher Meredith Curnow and to Catherine Hill, the brilliant editor of this book. Without their grace, wisdom and support I doubt I would have made it.

And to my family: To dear Uncle Billie and Auntie Bev – your support has been everything and with you in the world I can almost bear the fact that Dad isn't. To my darling brother David: I love you so much. To Jo: I couldn't love you more if you were my sister. To Marni, Finn and Matilda: I love you guys to the moon and back. To Mummy: Thank you, Mummy . . . for reading endlessly to me when I was little, for giving me a love of words, for cooking and caring for me when I couldn't for myself, for your love, and for your honesty. It has helped me understand where I have come from and why I am me.

Finally, I want to thank the many people who have shared their stories for this book: Peter and Tessa, thank you for your candour. And thank you to all the brave women who have revealed their histories and their wounds to me with generosity and frankness – Josie and Benita, Leah, Sophia, Andrea and Cheryl.

And above all, Kirstie, thank you. Your determination, your courage, and your strength are an inspiration.

Stephanie Wood is an award-winning long-form features writer, known for her rare ability to tell substantial, compelling stories across a range of subjects. She is a former senior staff writer at Fairfax Media's *Good Weekend* magazine.